# 2021 SUNDAY MISSAL (USA EDITION) LARGE PRINT

## SPIRITUAL GROWTH PLANNER

*EUCHARISTIC PRAYERS*

AND

## EASTER TRIDIUM LITURGY

D1304025

# CATHOLIC LITURGICAL WORLD

## THIS MISSAL BELONGS TO:

NAME:

PHONE NUMBER:

ADDRESS:

# DEDICATION

*This book is dedicated to the Most Holy Trinity through the intercession of Our Lady of Perpetual HELP.*

# CONTENTS

Acknowledgments     i

1   THE NEW ORDER OF MASS IN ENGLISH AND LATIN LANGUAGES   8

2   EUCHARISTIC PRAYERS I IN ENGLISH AND LATIN LANGUAGES   14

3   EUCHARISTIC PRAYERS II IN ENGLISH AND LATIN LANGUAGES   20

4   EUCHARISTIC PRAYERS III IN ENGLISH LANGUAGE   23

5   EUCHARISTIC PRAYERS IV IN ENGLISH AND LATIN LANGUAGES   26

6   JANUARY   33

7   FEBRUARY   51

8   MARCH   66

9   APRIL   92
    9.1 EASTER TRIDIUM LITURGY   92
    9.2 HOLY THURSDAY   92
    9.3 RENEWAL OF PRIESTLY PROMISES   93
    9.4 GOOD FRIDAY   99
    9.5 EASTER SATURDAY   110
    9.6 BAPTISMAL LITURGY   129

10   MAY   148

11   JUNE   172

12   JULY   199

13   AUGUST   210

14   SEPTEMBER   227

15   OCTOBER   238

16   NOVEMBER   253

17   DECEMBER   267

# ACKNOWLEDGMENTS

This is to acknowledge the unquantifiable contributions made by every member of the Catholic Liturgical World Team coordinated by Rev Fr. Martins and Rev. Sr. Lucia. May the Most Holy Trinity meet all those who will use this book at their respective points of needs and uplift them spiritually and materially, so that at the end of our earthly sojourn we all will be crowned with the supreme Crown of Heaven.

We also wish to acknowledge the turbulence the world is plunged into in 2020. We pray that the remaining part of 2020 and 2021 will be a year of healing and restoration for all those who have been negatively affected.

**Our Lady of Perpetual Help, please intercede for the world and especially the family and friends that will make use of this missal.**

## CHEERS TO A GLORIOUS 2021!

## 1.0 THE ORDER OF MASS IN ENGLISH AND LATIN LANGUAGES

| INTRODUCTORY RITES | |
|---|---|
| **Greeting** | |
| **P.** In the name of the Father, and of the Son, and of the Holy Spirit. | **P.** In nómine Patris, et Fílii, et Spíritus Sancti. |
| **C.** Amen. | **C.** Amen. |
| **(Form A)** | **(Form A)** |
| **P:** The grace of our Lord Jesus Christ and the love of God and the fellowship of the Holy Spirit be with you all. | **P:** Gràtia Dòmini nostri Jesu Christi, et càritas Dei, et communicàtio Sancti Spìritus sit cum omnibus vobis. |
| **C:** And with your spirit. | **C:** Et cum spiritu tuo. |
| **(Form B)** | **(Form B)** |
| **P:** The grace and peace of God our Father and the Lord Jesus Christ be with you. | **P:** Gratia vobis et pax a Deo Patre nostro et Dominio Jesu Christo. |
| **C:** And with your spirit. | **C:** Et cum spiritu tuo. |
| **(or)** | **(vel)** |
| **C:** Blessed be God, the Father of our Lord Jesus Chirst. | **C:** Benedictus Deus et Pater Domini nostri Jesu Christi. |
| **(Form C)** | **(FormC)** |
| **P:** The Lord be with you. (or a bishop says "Peace be with you") | **P:** Dòminus vobìscum. (B: Pax vobis) |
| **C:** and with our spirit. | **C:** Et cum spiritu tuo. |
| | |
| **PENITENTIAL RITE** | **ACTUS PAENITENTIALIS** |
| **(Form A)** | **(Form A)** |
| **P:** Brethren (brothers and sisters), to prepare ourselves to celebrate the sacred mysteries, let us call to mind our sins. | **P:** Fratres, agnoscàmus peccàta nostra, ut apti simus ad sacra mystèria celebrànda. |
| **A: I Confess to Almighty God** and to | **A: Confíteor Deo omnipoténti** et |

you, my brothers and sisters, that I have greatly sinned, in my thoughts and in my words, in what I have done and in what I have failed to do, through my fault, through my fault, through my most grievous fault; therefore I ask Blessed Mary ever-Virgin, all the Angels and Saints, and you, my brothers and sisters, to pray for me to the Lord our God.

P: Lord have mercy.
C: Lord have mercy.
P: Christ have mercy.
C: Christ have mercy
P: Lord have mercy.
C: Lord have mercy
P: May Almighty God have mercy on us, forgive us our sins, and bring us to everlasting life

C: Amen.

**(Form B)**
P: Lord, we have sinned against you.
C: Lord, have mercy.
P: Lord, show us your mercy and love.
C: And grant us your salvation.
P: May almighty God have mercy on us, forgive us our sins, and bring us to everlasting life.
C: Amen.

**(Form C)**
P: You were sent to heal the contrite: Lord have mercy.

C: Lord have mercy.

vobis, fratres, quia peccavi nimis cogitatione, verbo, opere et omissione: mea culpa, mea culpa, mea maxima culpa. Ideo precor Beatam Mariam semper Virginem, omnes Angelos et Sanctos, et vos, fratres, orare pro me ad Dominum Deum nostrum.

P: Kyrie elèison.
C: Kyrie elèison.
P: Christe elèison.
C: Christe elèison.
P: Kyrie elèison.
C: Kyrie elèison.
P: Misereàtur nostril omnìpotens Deus et, dimìssis peccàtis nostris, perdùcat nos ad vitam aetèrnam.
C: Amen.

**(Form B)**
P: Miserere nostri, Domine.
C: Quia peccavimus tibi.
P: Ostende nobis, Domine, misericordiam tuam.
C: Et salutare tuum da nobis.
P: Misereàtur nostril omnìpotens Deus et, dimìssis peccàtis nostris, perdùcat nos ad vitam aetèrnam.
C: Amen.

**(Form C)**
P: Qui missus es sanare contritos corde: Kyrie elèison.

C: Kyrie elèison.

| | |
|---|---|
| **P:** You came to call sinners: Christ have mercy. | **P:** Qui peccatores vocare venisti: Christe, elèison. |
| **C:** Christ have mercy. | **C:** Christe, elèison. |
| **P:** You plead for us at the right hand of the Father: Lord have mercy. | **P:** Qui ad dexteram Patris sedes, ad interpellandum pro nobis: Kyrie elèison. |
| **C:** Lord have mercy. | **C:** Kyrie elèison. |
| **P:** May almighty God have mercy on us, forgive us our sins, and bring us to everlasting life. | **P:** Misereàtur nostril omnìpotens Deus et, dimìssis peccàtis nostris, perdùcat nos ad vitam aetèrnam. |
| **C:** Amen | **C:** Amen. . |
| *(please omit the Gloria during Advent and Lent)* | *(please omit the Gloria during Advent and Lent)* |

| | |
|---|---|
| **GLORY TO GOD IN THE HIGHEST.** And on earth peace to people of good will. We praise You. We bless You. We adore You. We glorify You. We give You thanks for Your great glory, Lord God, heavenly King, O God Almighty Father. Lord Jesus Christ, Only-begotten Son. Lord God, Lamb of God, Son of the Father, You take away the sins of the world, have mercy on us. You take away the sins of the world, receive our prayer. You are seated at the right hand of the Father, have mercy on us. For You alone are the Holy; You alone are Lord; You alone are the Most High, Jesus Christ, with the Holy Spirit, in the Glory of God the Father. *Amen.* | **GLORIA IN EXCELSIS DEO.** Et in terra pax hominibus bonae voluntatis. Laudamus te. Benedicimus te. Adoramus te. Glorificamus te. Gratias agimus tibi propter magnam gloriam tuam. Domine Deus, rex coelestis, Deus pater omnipotens. Domine Fili unigenite, Jesu Christe. Domine Deus, Agnus Dei, Filius patris. Qui tollis peccata mundi, miserere nobis. Qui tollis peccata mundi, suscipe deprecationem nostram. Qui sedes ad dexteram patris, miserere nobis. Quoniam tu solus sanctus. Tu solus Dominus. Tu solus Altissimus, Jesu Christe, cum sancto spiritu in gloria Dei patris. *Amen.* |

| | |
|---|---|
| **OPENING PRAYER** **P:** Let us pray. (prayer) **C:** Amen. | **COLLECTA** **P:** Oremus. (prayer) **C:** Amen. |

| LITURGY OF THE WORD | LECTIO PRIMA |
|---|---|
| (after the reading) | (after the reading) |
| **L:** The word of the Lord. | **L:** Verbum Dòmini. |
| **C.** Thanks be to God. | **C:** Deo gratias. |
| **RESPONSORIAL PSALM** | **PSALMUS** |
| **Second Reading** | **Lectio Secunda** |
| (after the reading) | (after the reading) |
| **L:** The word of the Lord. | **L:** Verbum Dòmini. |
| **C.** Thanks be to God. | **C:** Deo gratias. |
| | |
| Alleluia | Alleluia |
| | |
| **GOSPEL** | **EVANGELIUM** |
| **P:** The Lord be with you | **P:** Dòminus vobìscum. |
| **C:** and with your spirit | **C:** Et cum spiritu tuo. |
| **P:** A reading from the holy gospel according to **N.** | **P:** Lèctio sancti Evangèlii secùndum **N.** |
| **C:** glory to you O, Lord. | **C:** Glòria tibi, Domine. |
| (after the reading) | (after the reading) |
| **P:** the gospel of the Lord. | **P:** Verbum Dòmini. |
| **C:** praise to you Lord Jesus Christ. | **C:** Laus tibi, Christe. |
| | |
| **HOMILY** | **HOMILIA** |
| | |
| **The Creed** | **Credo** |
| I believe in one God, the Father Almighty, maker of heaven and earth, of all things visible and invisible. I believe in one Lord Jesus Christ, the Only Begotten Son of God, born of the Father before all ages. | Credo in unum Deum, Patrem omnipotentem, factorem caeli et terrae, visibilium omnium et invisibilium, Et in unum Dominum Iesum Christum, Filium Dei unigenitum, et ex Patre natum, ante Omnia saecula. |
| God from God, Light from Light, true God from true God, begotten, not made, consubstantial with the Father; through him all things were made. For us men and for our | Deum de Deo, lumen de Lumine, Deum verum de Deo vero, genitum, non factum, consubstantialem Patri: per quem omnia facta sunt. Qui propter nos homines et propter |

| | |
|---|---|
| salvation. He came down from heaven, and by the Holy Spirit was incarnate of the Virgin Mary, and became man. | nostram salute descendit de caelis. Et incarnatus est de Spiritu Sancto ex Maria Virgine, et homo factus est. |
| For our sake he was crucified under Pontius Pilate, he suffered death and was buried, and rose again on the third day in accordance with the Scriptures. He ascended into heaven and is seated at the right hand of the Father. | Crucifixus etiam pro nobis sub Pontio Pilato; passus et sepultus est, et resurrexit tertia die, secundem Scripturas, et ascendit in caelum, sedet ad dexteram Patris. |
| He will come again in glory to judge the living and the dead and his kingdom will have no end. | Et iterum venturus est cum gloria, iudicare vivos et mortuos, cuius regni non erit finis. |
| I believe in the Holy Spirit, the Lord, the giver of life, who proceeds from the Father and the Son. | Et in Spiritum Sanctum, Dominum et vivificantem: qui ex Patre Filioque procedit. |
| Who with the Father and the Son is adored and glorified, who has spoken through the prophets. | Qui cum Patre et Filio simul adoratur et conglorificatur: qui locutus est per prophetas. |
| I believe in one, holy, catholic and apostolic Church. | Et nuam, sanctam, catholicam et apostolicam Ecclesiam. |
| I confess one Baptism for the forgiveness of sins and I look forward to the resurrection of the dead and the life of the world to come. Amen. | Confiteor unum baptisma in remissionem peccatorum. Et exspecto resurrectionem mortuorum, et vitam venturi saeculi. Amen. |
| **PREPARATION OF THE ALTAR AND THE GIFTS** | |
| **P.** Blessed are you, Lord God of all creation, for through your goodness we have received the bread we offer you: fruit of the earth and work of human hands, it will become for us the bread of life. **C:** Blessed be God forever. | **P.** Benedictus es, Dómine, Deus univérsi, quia de tua largitáte accépimus panem, quem tibi offérimus, fructum terræ et óperis mánuum hóminum: ex quo nobis fiet panis vitæ. **C:** Benedìctus Deus in Sàecula. |
| | |

| | |
|---|---|
| **P.** By the mystery of this water and wine may we come to share in the divinity of Christ who humbled himself to share our humanity. | **P.** Per huiuis aquae et vini mystérium eius efficiámur divinitátis consórtes, qui humanitátis nostrae fíeri dignátus est párticeps. |
| **P.** Blessed are you, Lord God of all creation, for through your goodness we have received the wine we offer you: fruit of the vine and work of human hands, it will become our spiritual drink.<br>**C:** Blessed be God forever. | **P.** Benedictus es, Dómine, Deus univérsi, quia de tua largitáte accépimus vinum, quod tibi offérimus, fructum vitis et óperis mánuum hóminum, ex quo nobis fiet panis potus spiritális.<br>**C:** Benedìctus Deus in Sàecula. |
| **P.** With humble spirit and contrite heart may we be accepted by you, O Lord, and may our sacrifice in your sight this day be pleasing to you, Lord God. | **P.** In spíritu humilitátis et in ánimo contrite suscipiámur a te, Dómine; et sic fiat sacrifícium nostrum in conspéctu tuo hódie, ut pláceat tibi, Dómine Deus. |
| **P.** Wash me, O Lord, from my iniquity and cleanse me from my sin | **P.** Lava me, Dómine, ab iniquitáte mea, et a peccáto meo munda me |
| **P.** Pray, brethren (brothers and sisters), that my sacrifice and yours may be acceptable to God, the almighty Father.<br>**C.** May the Lord accept the sacrifice at your hands for the praise and glory of his name, for our good and the good of all his holy Church. | **P.** Oráte, fratres: ut meum acvestrum sacrifícium acceptàbile fiat apud Deum Patrem omnipoténtem.<br>**C.** Suscípiat Dóminus sacrifícium de mánibus tuis praiad laudem et glóriam nóminis sui, ad utilitátem quoque nostram totiúsque Ecclésiæ suæ sanctæ. |
| **PRAYER OVER THE GIFTS**<br>**P:** (prayer)<br>**C:** Amen. | **ORATIO SUPER OBLATA**<br>**P:** (prayer)<br>**C:** Amen. |
| | |
| **EUCHARISTIC PRAYER** | **PREX EUCHARISTICA** |
| **P.** The Lord be with you.<br>**C.** And with your spirit.<br>**P.** Lift up your hearts. | **P:** Dòminus vobìscum<br>**C:** Et cum spiritu tuo.<br>**P:** Sursum Corda. |

| | |
|---|---|
| **C.** We lift them up to the Lord. | **C:** Habèmus ad Dòminum. |
| **P.** Let us give thanks to the Lord our God. | **P:** Gràtias agàmus Dòmino Deo nostro |
| **C.** It is right and just. | **C:** Dignum et iustum est. |

## 2.0 EUCHARISTIC PRAYER I WITH COMMON PREFACE I

*Please note that this Eucharistic Prayer does not have its own proper preface. Therefore, the **Common Preface I** that is selected here is subject to change depending on the salvific mystery that is being celebrated and what the rubrics indicate, alongside the initiative of the officiating priest.*

| | |
|---|---|
| **P.** It is truly right and just, our duty and our salvation, always and everywhere to give you thanks, Lord, Holy Father, Almighty and Eternal God, through Christ our Lord. | **P:** Vere dignum et iustum est aequum et salutàre, nos tibi semper et ubìque gràtias àgere: Domine, sancte Pater, omnipotens aeterne Deus: per Christum Dominum nostrum. |
| In Him you have been pleased to renew all things, giving us all a share in His fullness. For though He was in the form of God, He emptied Himself and by the blood of His cross brought peace to all creation. Therefore He has been exalted above all things, and to all who obey Him, has become the source of eternal salvation. And so, with Angels and Archangels, with Thrones and Dominions, and with all the hosts and Power of heaven, we sing the hymn of Your glory, as without end we acclaim: | In quo Omnia instaurare tibi complacuit, et de plenitudine eius nos omnes accipere trubuisti. Cum enim in forma Dei esset, exinanivit semetipsum, ac per sanguinem cruces suae pacificavit universa; unde exaltatus est super omnia et omnibus obtemperantibus sibi factus est causa salutis aeternae. Et ideo cum Angelis et Archangelis, cum Thronis et Dominationibus, cumque omni militia caelestis exercitus, hymnum gloriae tuae canimus, sine fine dicentes: |
| **C.** Holy, Holy, Holy Lord God of hosts. Heaven and earth are full of your glory. Hosanna in the highest. Blessed is He who comes in the name of the Lord. Hosanna in the | **C.** Sanctus, Sanctus, Sanctus, Dóminus Deus Sábaoth. Pleni sunt caeli et terra glória tua. Hosánna in excélsis. Benedíctus qui venit in nómine Domini. Hosánna in |

| | |
|---|---|
| highest. | excélsis. |
| | |
| **P.** To you, therefore, Most Merciful Father, we make humble prayer and petition through Jesus Christ, Your Son, our Lord: that You accept and bless + these gifts, these offerings, these holy and unblemished sacrifices, which we offer You firstly for Your holy catholic church. Be pleased to grant her peace, to guard, unite and govern her throughout the whole world, together with Your servant **N.** our Pope and **N.** our Bishop, and all those who, holding to the truth hand on the catholic and apostolic faith. | **P.** Te ígitur, clementíssime Pater, per Iesum Christum, Fílium tuum, Dóminum nostrum, súpplices rogámus ac pétimus, uti accépta habeas et benedícas + haec dona, haec múnera, haec sancta sacrificial illibáta, in primis, quae tibi offérimus pro Ecclésia tua sancta cathólica: quam pacificáre, custodíre, adunáre et régere dignéris toto orbe terrárum: una cum fámulo tuo Papa nostro **N.** et Antístite nostro **N.** et omnibus orthodóxis atque cathólicae et apostólicae fídei cultóribus. |
| Remember, Lord, Your servants **(N. and N.)** and all gathered here, whose faith and devotion are known to You. For them, we offer You this sacrifice of praise or they offer it for themselves and all who are dear to them: for the redemption of their souls, in hope of health and well-being, and paying their homage to You, the eternal God, living and true. | Meménto, Dómine, famulórum famularúmque tuárum **N.** et **N.** et ómnium circumstántium, quorum tibi fides cógnita est et nota devótio, pro quibus tibi offérimus: vel qui tibi ófferunt hoc sacrifícium laudis, pro se suísque ómnibus: pro redemptióne animárum suárum, pro spe salútis et incolumitátis suae: tibíque reddunt vota sua aetérno Deo, vivo et vero. |
| **P.** In communion with those whose memory we venerate, especially the glorious ever-Virgin Mary, Mother of our God and Lord, Jesus Christ, † and blessed Joseph, her Spouse, your blessed Apostles and Martyrs, Peter and Paul, Andrew, | **P.** Communicántes, et memóriam venerántes, in primis gloriósae semper Vírginis Maríae, Genetrícis Dei et Dómini nostri Iesu Christi: † sed et beáti Ioseph, eiúsdem Vírginis Sponsi, et beatórum Apostolórum ac Mártyrum tuórum, |

| | |
|---|---|
| (James, John, Philip, Bartholomew, Matthew, Simon and Jude; Linus, Cletus, Clement, Sixtus, Cornelius, Cyprian, Lawrence, Chrysogonus, John and Paul, Cosmos and Damian) and all your saints; we ask that through their merits and prayers, in all things we may be defended by your protecting help. (Through Christ our Lord. Amen.) | Petri et Pauli, Andréae, (Iacóbi, Ioánnis, Thomae, Iacóbi, Philíppi, Bartholomaei, Matthaei, Simónis et Thaddaei: Lini, Cleti, Cleméntis, Xysti, Cornélii, Cypriáni, Lauréntii, Chrysógoni, Ioánnis et Pauli, Cosmae et Damiáni) et ómnium Sanctórum tuórum; quorum méritis precibúsque oncédas, ut in ómnibus protectiónis tuae muniámur auxílio. (Per Christum Dóminum nostrum. Amen.) |
| Therefore, Lord, we pray: graciously accept this oblation of our service, that of your whole family; order our days in your peace, and command that we be delivered from eternal damnation and counted among the flock of those you have chosen. (Through Christ our Lord. Amen.) | Hanc ígitur oblatiónem servitútis nostrae, sed et cunctae famíliae tuae, quaesumus, Dómine, ut placates accípias: diésque nostros in tua pace dispónas, atque ab aetérna damnatióne nos éripi et in electórum tuórum iúbeas grege numerári. (Per Christum Dóminum nostrum. Amen.) |
| Be pleased, O God, we pray, to bless, acknowledge, and approve this offering in every respect; make it spiritual and acceptable, so that it may become for us the Body and Blood of your most beloved Son, our Lord Jesus Christ. | Quam oblatiónem tu, Deus, in ómnibus, quaesumus, benedíctam, adscríptam, ratam, rationábilem, acceptabilémque fácere dignéris: ut nobis Corpus et Sanguis fiat dilectíssimi Fílii tui, Dómini nostri Iesu Christi. |
| On the day before he was to suffer, he took bread in his holy and venerable hands, and with eyes raised to heaven to you, O God, his almighty Father, giving you thanks, he said the blessing, broke the bread and gave it to his disciples, saying: | Qui, prídie quam paterétur, accépit panem in sanctas ac venerábiles manus suas, et elevátis óculis in caelum ad te Deum Patrem suum omnipoténtem, tibi grátias agens benedíxit, fregit, dedítque discípulis suis, dicens: |
| **TAKE THIS, ALL OF YOU, AND EAT** | **ACCÍPITE ET MANDUCÁTE EX HOC** |

| | |
|---|---|
| OF IT, FOR THIS IS MY BODY WHICH WILL BE GIVEN UP FOR YOU. | OMNES: HOC EST ENIM CORPUS MEUM, QUOD PRO VOBIS TRADÉTUR. |
| In a similar way when supper was ended, he took this precious chalice in his holy and venerable hands, and once more giving you thanks, he said the blessing and gave the chalice to his disciples, saying: | Símili modo, postquam cenátum est, accípiens et hunc praeclárum cálicem in sanctas ac venerábiles manus suas, item tibi grátias agens benedíxit, dedítque discípulis suis, dicens: |
| TAKE THIS ALL OF YOU AND DRINK FROM IT, FOR THIS IS THE CHALICE OF MY BLOOD, THE BLOOD OF THE NEW AND ETERNAL COVENANT, WHICH WILL BE POURED OUT FOR YOU AND FOR MANY FOR THE FORGIVENESS OF SINS. DO THIS IN MEMORY OF ME. | ACCÍPITE ET BÍBITE EX EO OMNES: HIC EST ENIM CALIX SÁNGUINIS MEI NOVI ET AETÉRNI TESTAMÉNTI, QUI PRO VOBIS ET PRO MULTIS EFFUNDÉTUR IN REMISSIÓNEM PECCATÓRUM. HOC FÁCITE IN MEAM COMMEMORATIÓNEM |
| | |
| P: The mystery of faith: | P: Mystérium fídei. |
| A. we proclaim your Death, O Lord, and profess your resurrection until you come again. | A. Mortem tuam annuntiamus, Domine, et tuam resurrectionem confitemur, donec venias. |
| Or:<br>B. When we eat this bread and drink this cup, we proclaim your death, Lord Jesus, until you come in glory. | Vel:<br>B. Quotiescumque manducamus panem hunc et calicem bibimus, mortem tuam annuntiamus, Domine, donec venias. |
| Or:<br>C. Save us Saviour of the world, for by Your by your cross and resurrection you have set us free. | Vel:<br>C. Salvator mundi, salva nos, qui per crucem et resurrectionem tuam liberasti nos. |
| | |
| P. Therefore, O Lord, as we celebrate the memorial of the blessed Passion, the Resurrection | P. Unde et mémores, Dómine, nos servi tui, sed et plebs tua sancta, eiúsdem Christi, Fílii tui, Dómini |

| | |
|---|---|
| from the dead, and the glorious Ascension into heaven of Christ, your Son, our Lord, we, your servants and your holy people, offer to your glorious majesty from the gifts that you have given us, this pure victim, this holy victim, this spotless victim, the holy Bread of eternal life and the Chalice of everlasting salvation. | nostri, tam beátae passiónis, necnon et ab ínferis resurrectiónis, sed et in caelos gloriósae ascensiónis: offérimus praeclárae maiestáti tuae de tuis donis ac datis hóstiam puram, hóstiam sanctam, hóstiam immaculátam, Panem sanctum vitae aetérnae et Cálicem salútis perpétuae. |
| Be pleased to look upon these offerings with a serene and kindly countenance, and to accept them, as once you were pleased to accept the gifts of your servant Abel the just, the sacrifice of Abraham, our father in faith, and the offering of your high priest Melchizedek, a holy sacrifice, a spotless victim. | Supra quae propítio ac seréno vultu respícere dignéris: et accépta habére, sícuti accépta habére dignátus es múnera púeri tui iusti Abel, et sacrifícium Patriárchae nostril Abrahae, et quod tibi óbtulit summus sacérdos tuus Melchísedech, sanctum sacrifícium, Immaculátam hóstiam. |
| In humble prayer we ask you, almighty God: command that these gifts be borne by the hands of your holy Angel to your altar on high in the sight of your diving majesty, so that all of us, who through this participation at the altar receive the most holy Body and Blood of your Son, may be filled with every grace and heavenly blessing. (Through Christ our Lord. Amen.) | Súpplices te rogámus, omnípotens Deus: iube haec perférri per manus sancti Angeli tui in sublíme altáre tuum, in conspectus divínae maiestátis tuae; ut, quotquot ex hac altáris participation sacrosánctum Fílii tui Corpus et Sánguinem sumpsérimus, omni benedictióne caelésti et grátia repleámur. (Per Christum Dóminum nostrum. Amen.) |
| | |
| *****Commemoration of the Dead***** | *****Commemoratio pro Defunctis*** |
| Remember also, Lord, your servants **N.** and **N.,** who have gone | Meménto étiam, Dómine, famulórum famularúmque |

| | |
|---|---|
| before us with the sign of faith and rest in the sleep of peace. Grant them, O Lord, we pray, and all who sleep in Christ, a place of refreshment, light and peace. (Through Christ our Lord. Amen ) | tuárum **N.** et **N.,** qui nos praecessérunt cum signo fídei, et dórmiunt in somno pacis. Ipsis, Dómine, et ómnibus in Christo quiescéntibus, locum refrigérii, lucis et pacis, ut indúlgeas, deprecámur. (Per Christum Dóminum nostrum. Amen.) |
| To us, also, your servants, who, though sinners, hope in your abundant mercies, graciously grant some share and fellowship with your holy Apostles and Martyrs: with John the Baptist, Stephen, Matthias, Barnabas, (Ignatius, Alexander, Marcellinus, Peter, Felicity, Perpetua, Agatha, Lucy, Agnes, Cecilia, Anastasia) and all your Saints; admit us we beseech you, into their company, not weighing our merits, but granting us your pardon, through Christ our Lord. Through whom you continue to make all these good things O Lord; you sanctify them, fill them with life, bless them, and bestow them upon us. | Nobis quoque peccatóribus fámulis tuis, de multitúdine miseratiónum tuárum sperántibus, partem áliquam et societátem donáre dignéris cum tuis sanctis Apóstolis et Martyribus: cum Ioánne, Stéphano, Matthía, Bárnaba, (Ignátio, Alexándro, Marcellíno, Petro, Felicitáte, Perpétua, Agatha, Lúcia, Agnéte, Caecília, Anastásia) et omnibus Sanctis tuis: intra quorum nos consórtium, non aestimátor mériti, sed véniae, quaesumus, largítor admítte. Per Christum Dóminum nostrum. Per quem haec ómnia, Dómine, semper bona creas, sanctíficas, vivíficas, benedícis, et praestas nobis. |
| **CONCLUDING DOXOLGY** | |
| **P.** Through him, and with him, and in him, O God, Almighty Father, in the unity of the Holy Spirit, all glory and honor is yours, for ever and ever. **C.** Amen. | **P.** Per ipsum, et cum ipso, et in ipso, est tibi Deo Patri omnipoténti, in unitáte Spíritus Sancti, omnis honor et glória per ómnia saecula saeculórum. **C.** Amen. |
| | |

## 3.0 EUCHARISTIC PRAYER II WITH ITS PROPER PREFACE

| | |
|---|---|
| **P:** It is truly right and just, our duty and our salvation, always and everywhere to give you thanks Father most holy through your beloved Son, Jesus Christ, your word through whom you made all things, whom you sent as our Savior and Redeemer, incarnate by the Holy Spirit and born of the Virgin. | **P:** Vere dignum et iustum est aequum et salutàre, nos tibi sancte Pater, semper et ubìque gràtias àgere per Filium dilectiònis tuae Jesum Christum. Verbum tuum, per quod cuncta fecìsti: quem misìsti nobis Salvatòrem et Redemptòrem, incarnàtum de Spìritu Sancto et ex Virgine natum. |
| Fulfilling your will and gaining for you a holy people, He stretched out His hands and as He endured His Passion, so as to break the bonds of death and manifest the resurrection. | Qui voluntàtem tuam adìmplens et pòpulum tibi sanctum acquirens extèndit manus cum paterètur, ut mortem sòlveret et resurrectiònem manifestàret. |
| And so with all the angels and the saints we declare your glory, as with one voice we acclaim:<br><br>**C.** Holy, Holy, Holy Lord God of hosts. Heaven and earth are full of your glory.<br>Hosanna in the highest. Blessed is He who comes in the name of the Lord. Hosanna in the highest. | Et ìdeo cum Angelis et òmnibus Sanctis glòriam tuam una voce dicèntes:<br><br>**C.** Sanctus, Sanctus, Sanctus, Dóminus Deus Sábaoth. Pleni sunt caeli et terra glória tua. Hosánna in excélsis. Benedíctus qui venit in nómine Domini. Hosánna in excélsis. |
| **P.** You are indeed Holy, O Lord, the fount of all holiness. Make holy, therefore, these gifts, we pray, by sending down Your Spirit upon them like the dewfall, so that they may become for us the Body **+** and Blood of our Lord, Jesus Christ. | **P.** Vere Sanctus es, Domine, fons omnis sanctitatis. Haec ergo dona, quaesumus, Spiritus tui rore sanctifica, ut nobis Corpus et **+** Sanguis fiant Domini nostri Iesu Christi. |
| At the time He was betrayed and entered willingly into His Passion, He took bread and, giving thanks, | Qui, pridie quam pateretur, accepit panem in sanctas ac venerabiles manus suas, et elevatis oculis in |

| | |
|---|---|
| broke it and gave it to His disciples, saying: | caelum ad te Deum Patrem suum omnipotentem, tibi gratias agens benedixit, fregit, deditque discipulis suis, dicens: |
| **TAKE THIS, ALL OF YOU, AND EAT OF IT: FOR THIS IS MY BODY WHICH WILL BE GIVEN UP FOR YOU.** | **ACCIPITE ET MANDUCATE EX HOC OMNES: HOC EST ENIM CORPUS MEUM, QUOD PRO VOBIS TRADETUR.** |
| In a similar way when supper was ended, he took the chalice and, once more giving thanks He gave it to His disciples, saying: | Simili modo, postquam cenatum est, accipiens et hunc praeclarum calicem in sanctas ac venerabiles manus suas, item tibi grtias agens benedixit, deditque discipulis suis, dicens: |
| **TAKE THIS ALL OF YOU AND DRINK FROM IT: FOR THIS IS THE CHALICE OF MY BLOOD, THE BLOOD OF THE NEW AND EVERLASTING COVENANT, WHICH WILL BE POURED OUT FOR YOU AND FOR MANY FOR THE FORGIVENESS OF SINS. DO THIS IN MEMORY OF ME.** | **ACCIPITE ET BIBITE EX EO OMNES: HIC EST ENIM CALIX SANGUINIS MEI NOVI ET AETERNI TESTAMENTI, QUI PRO VOBIS ET PRO MULTIS EFFUNDETUR IN REMISSIONEM PECCATORUM. HOC FACITE IN MEAM COMMEMORATIONEM.** |
| | |
| **P:** The mystery of faith: | **P:** Mystérium fídei. |
| **A.** we proclaim your Death, O Lord, and profess your resurrection until you come again<br>**Or:**<br>**B.** When we eat this bread and drink this cup, we proclaim your death, Lord Jesus, until you come in glory.<br><br>**Or:**<br>**C.** Save us Saviour of the world, for by Your by your cross and resurrection you have set us free. | **A.** Mortem tuam annuntiamus, Domine, et tuam resurrectionem confitemur, donec venias.<br>**Vel:**<br>**B.** Quotiescumque manducamus panem hunc et calicem bibimus, mortem tuam annuntiamus, Domine, donec venias.<br><br>**Vel:**<br>**C.** Salvator mundi, salva nos, qui per crucem et resurrectionem tuam liberasti nos. |
| | |

| | |
|---|---|
| **P.** Therefore, as we celebrate the memorial of His Death and Resurrection, we offer You, Lord the Bread of Life and the Chalice of salvation, giving thanks that you have held us worthy to be in Your presence and minister to You. | **P. M**emores igitur mortis et resurrectionis eius, tibi, Domine, panem vitae et calicem salutis afferimus, gratias agentes quia nos dignos habuisti astare coram te et tibi ministrare. |
| Humbly we pray that, partaking of the Body and Blood of Christ, we may be gathered into one by the Holy Spirit. | Et supplices deprecamur ut Corporis et Sanguinis Christi participes a Spiritu Sancto congregemur in unum. |
| **R**emember, Lord, Your Church spread throughout the world; and bring her to the fullness of charity, together with **N.** our Pope, **N.** our bishop, and all the clergy. | **R**ecordare, Domine, Ecclesiae tuae toto orbe diffusae, ut eam in caritate perficias una cum Papa nostro **N.** et Episcopo nostro **N.** et universo clero. |
| **IN MASSES FOR THE DEAD THE FOLLOWING MAY BE ADDED:** Remember your servant **N.**, whom you have called (today) from this world to yourself. Grant that he (she) who was united with your Son in a death like his, may also be one with him in his Resurrection. | **IN MISSIS PRO DEFUNCTIS ADDI POTEST:** Meménto fámuli tui (fámulae tuae) **N.**, quem (quam) (hódie) ad te ex hoc mundo vocásti. Concéde, ut, qui (quae) complantátus (complantáta) fuit similitúdini mortis Fílii tui, simul fiat et resurrectiónis ipsíus. |
| | |
| **R**emember also our brothers and sisters who have fallen asleep in the hope of the resurrection, and all who have died in Your mercy: welcome them into the light of Your face. | **M**emento etiam fratrum nostrorum, qui in spe resurrectionis dormierunt, omniumque in tua miseratione defunctorum, et eos in lumen vultus tui admitte. |
| Have mercy on us all, we pray, that with the Blessed Virgin Mary, Mother of God, with blessed | Omnium nostrum, quaesumus, miserere, ut cum beata Dei Genetrice Virgine Maria, beatis |

| | |
|---|---|
| Joseph, her Spouse, with the blessed Apostles, and all the Saints who have pleased you throughout the ages, we may merit to be coheirs to eternal life, and may praise and glorify You through Your Son Jesus Christ. | Apostolis et omnibus Sanctis, qui tibi a saeculo placuerunt, aeternae vitae mereamur esse consortes, et te laudemus et glorificemus per Fílium tuum Iesum Christum. |
| | |
| **CONCLUDING DOXOLGY** | |
| **P.** Through him, and with him, and in him, O God, almighty Father, in the unity of the Holy Spirit, all glory and honor is yours, for ever and ever.<br>**C.** Amen. | **P.** Per ipsum, et cum ipso, et in ipso, est tibi Deo Patri omnipoténti, in unitáte Spíritus Sancti, omnis honor et glória per ómnia saecula saeculórum.<br>**C.** Amen. |
| | |

## 4.0 EUCHARISTIC PRAYER III WITH THE PREFACE II OF THE SUNDAYS IN ORDINARY TIME

*Please note that this Eucharistic Prayer does not have its own proper preface. Therefore, the **Preface II of the Sundays in Ordinary Time** that is selected here is subject to change depending on the salvific mystery that is being celebrated and what the rubrics indicate, alongside the initiative of the officiating priest.*

**P:** It is truly right and just, our duty and our salvation, always and everywhere to give you thanks, Lord holy father, almighty and eternal God, through Christ our Lord, amen. For out of compassion for the waywardness that is ours, he humbled himself and was born of the Virgin; by the passion of the Cross he freed us from unending death and by rising from the dead he gave us life eternal. And so, with Angels and Archangels, with Thrones and Dominions, and with all the hosts and Powers of heaven, we sing the hymn of your glory, as without end we acclaim:

**C.** Holy, Holy, Holy Lord God of hosts. Heaven and earth are full of your glory. Hosanna in the highest. Blessed is He who comes in the name of the Lord. Hosanna in the highest.

You are indeed Holy o Lord, and all you have created rightly gives you praise, for through your Son our Lord Jesus Christ, by the power and working of the Holy Spirit, you give life to all things and make them holy, and you never cease to gather a people to yourself, so that from the rising of the sun to its setting a pure sacrifice may be offered to your name.

Therefore, O Lord, we humbly implore you: by the same Spirit graciously make holy these gifts we have brought to you for consecration, that they may become the Body and + Blood of your Son our Lord Jesus Christ, at whose command we celebrate these mysteries.

For on the night he was betrayed he himself took bread, and, giving you thanks, he said the blessing, broke the bread and gave it to his disciples, saying:
**TAKE THIS, ALL OF YOU, AND EAT OF IT: FOR THIS IS MY BODY, WHICH WILL BE GIVEN UP FOR YOU.**

In a similar way, when supper was ended, he took the chalice and, giving you thanks, he said the blessing, and gave the chalice to his disciples, saying:
**TAKE THIS, ALL OF YOU AND DRINK FROM IT, FOR THIS IS THE CHALICE OF MY BLOOD, THE BLOOD OF THE NEW AND ETERNAL COVENANT, WHICH WILL BE POURED OUT FOR YOU AND FOR MANY FOR THE FORGIVENESS OF SINS. DO THIS IN MEMORY OF ME.**

**P:** Let us proclaim the mystery of faith:

**A.** we proclaim your Death, O Lord, and profess your resurrection until you come again

**B.** When we eat this bread and drink this cup, we proclaim your death, Lord Jesus, until you come in glory.

**C.** Save us Saviour of the world, for by Your by your cross and resurrection you have set us free.

Therefore, O Lord, as we celebrate the memorial of the saving Passion of your Son, his wondrous Resurrection and Ascension into heaven, and as we look forward to his second coming, we offer you in thanksgiving this holy and living sacrifice.

Look, we pray, upon the oblation of your Church and, recognizing the sacrificial Victim by whose death you willed to reconcile us to yourself, grant that we, who are nourished by the Body and Blood of your Son and filled with his Holy Spirit, may become one body, one spirit in Christ.

May he make of us an eternal offering to you, so that we may obtain an inheritance with your elect, especially with the most Blessed Virgin Mary, Mother of God, with blessed Joseph, her spouse, and with your blessed Apostles and glorious Martyrs (with Saint **N.**) and with all the Saints, on whose constant intercession in your presence we rely for unfailing help.

May this Sacrifice of our reconciliation, we pray, O Lord, advance the peace and salvation of all the world. Be pleased to confirm in faith and charity your pilgrim Church on earth, with your servant **N.** our Pope and **N.** our Bishop, and the Order of Bishops, all the clergy, and the entire people you have gained for your own.

Listen graciously to the prayers of this family, whom you have summoned before you: in your compassion, O merciful Father, gather to yourself all your children scattered throughout the world.

+To our departed brothers and sisters and to all who were pleasing to you at their passing from this life, give kind admittance to your kingdom. There we hope to enjoy forever the fullness of your glory through Christ our Lord, through whom you bestow on the world all that is good. +

## CONCLUDING DOXOLGY
**P.** Through him, and with him, and in him, O God, almighty Father, in the unity of the Holy Spirit, all glory and honor is yours, for ever and ever.
**C.** Amen.

*****When this Eucharistic Prayer is used in Masses for the dead, the following may be said instead:* *****

+ Remember your servant **N.** whom you have called (today) from this world to yourself. Grant that (she) who was united with your Son in a death like his, may also be one with him in his Resurrection, when from the earth he will raise up in the flesh those who have died, and transform our lowly body after the pattern of his own glorious body.

To our departed brothers and sisters, too, and to all who were pleasing to you at their passing from this life, give kind admittance to your kingdom. There we hope to enjoy forever the fullness of your glory, when you will wipe away every tear from our eyes. For seeing you, our God, as you are, we shall be like you for all ages and praise you without end, through Christ our Lord, through whom you bestow on the world all that is good.

## 5.0 EUCHARISTIC PRAYER IV WITH ITS PROPER PREFACE

| | |
|---|---|
| It is truly right to give you thanks, truly just to give you glory, Father most holy, for you are the one God living and true, existing before all ages and abiding for all eternity, dwelling in unapproachable light; yet you, who alone are good, the source of life, have made all that is, so that you might fill your creatures with blessings and bring joy to many of them by the glory of your light. | Vere dignum est tibi grátias ágere, vere iustum est te glorificáre, Pater sancte, quia unus es Deus vivus et verus, qui es ante saecula et pérmanes in aetérnum, inaccessíbilem lucem inhábitans; sed et qui unus bonus atque fons vitae cuncta fecísti, ut creatúras tuas benedictiónibus adimpléres multásque laetificáres tui lúminis claritáte. |
| And so, in your presence are countless hosts of Angels, who serve you day and night and, gazing upon the glory of your face, glorify you without ceasing. | Et ídeo coram te innúmerae astant turbae angelórum, qui die ac nocte sérviunt tibi et, vultus tui glóriam contemplántes, te incessánter gloríficant. |
| With them we, too, confess your name in exultation, giving voice to every creature under heaven, as we acclaim:<br>**C.** Holy, Holy, Holy Lord God of | Cum quibus et nos et, per nostram vocem, omnis quae sub caelo est creatúra nomen tuum in exsultatióne confitémur, canéntes:<br>**C.** Sanctus, Sanctus, Sanctus, |

| | |
|---|---|
| hosts. Heaven and earth are full of your glory. Hosanna in the highest. Blessed is He who comes in the name of the Lord. Hosanna in the highest. | Dóminus Deus Sábaoth. Pleni sunt caeli et terra glória tua. Hosánna in excélsis. Benedíctus qui venit in nómine Domini. Hosánna in excélsis. |
| **P.** We give you praise, Father most holy, for you are great and you have fashioned all your works in wisdom and in love. | **P.** Confitémur tibi, Pater sancte, quia magnus es et ómnia ópera tua in sapiéntia et caritáte fecísti. |
| You formed man in your own image and entrusted the whole world to his care, so that in serving you alone, the Creator, he might have dominion over all creatures. And when through disobedience he had lost your friendship, you did not abandon him to the domain of death. For you came in mercy to the aid of all, so that those who seek might find you. Time and again you offered them covenants and through the prophets taught them to look forward to salvation. | Hóminem ad tuam imáginem condidísti, eíque commisísti mundi curam univérsi, ut, tibi soli Creatóri sérviens, creatúris omnibus imperáret. Et cum amicítiam tuam, non oboédiens, amisísset, non eum dereliquísti in mortis império. Omnibus enim misericórditer subvenísti, ut te quaeréntes invenírent. Sed et foédera plúries homínibus obtulísti eósque per prophétas erudísti in exspectatióne salútis. |
| And you so loved the world, Father most holy, that in the fullness of time you sent your only Begotten Son to be our Saviour. Made incarnate by the Holy Spirit and born of the Virgin Mary, he shared our human nature in all things but sin. To the poor he proclaimed the good news of salvation, to prisoners, freedom, and to the sorrowful of heart, joy. To accomplish your plan, he gave himself up to death, and, rising | Et sic, Pater sancte, mundum dilexísti, ut, complete plenitúdine témporum, Unigénitum tuum nobis mítteres Salvatórem. Qui, incarnates de Spíritu Sancto et natus ex María Vírgine, in nostra condiciónis forma est conversátus per ómnia absque peccáto; salútem evangelizávit paupéribus, redemptiónem captívis, maestis corde laetítiam. Ut tuam vero dispensatiónem impléret, in mortem trádidit |

| | |
|---|---|
| from the dead, he destroyed death and restored life. | semetípsum ac, resúrgens a mórtuis, mortem destrúxit vitámque renovávit. |
| And that we might live no longer for ourselves but for him who died and rose again for us, he sent the Holy Spirit from you, Father, as the first fruits for those who believe, so that, bringing to perfection his work in the world, he might sanctify creation to the full. | Et, ut non ámplius nobismetípsis viverémus, sed sibi qui pro nobis mórtuus est atque surréxit, a te, Pater, misit Spíritum Sanctum primítias credéntibus, qui, opus suum in mundo perfíciens, omnem sanctificatiónem compléret. |
| Therefore, O Lord, we pray: may this same Holy Spirit graciously sanctify these offerings, that they may become the Body and + Blood of our Lord Jesus Christ for the celebration of this great mystery, which he himself left for us as an eternal covenant. | Quaesumus ígitur, Dómine, ut idem Spíritus Sanctus haec múnera sanctificáre dignétur, ut Corpus et + Sanguis fiant Dómini nostri Iesu Christi ad hoc magnum mystérium celebríndum, quod ipse nobis relíquit in fodus aetérnum. |
| For when the hour had come for him to be glorified by you, Father most holy, having loved his own who were in the world, he loved them to the end: and while they were at supper, he took bread, blessed and broke it, and gave it to his disciples, saying: **TAKE THIS, ALL OF YOU, AND EAT OF IT, FOR THIS IS MY BODY, WHICH WILL BE GIVEN UP FOR YOU.** | Ipse enim, cum hora venísset ut glorificarétur a te, Pater sancte, ac dilexísset suos qui erant in mundo, in finem diléxit eos: et cenántibus illis accépit panem, benedíxit ac fregit, dedítque discípulis suis, dicens: **ACCÍPITE ET MANDUCÁTE EX HOC OMNES: HOC EST ENIM CORPUS MEUM, QUOD PRO VOBIS TRADÉTUR.** |
| In a similar way, taking the chalice filled with the fruit of the vine, he gave thanks, and gave the chalice to his disciples saying: **TAKE THIS, ALL OF YOU AND** | Símili modo accipit cálicem, accípiens cálicem, ex genímine vitis replétum, grátias egit, dedítque discípulis suis, dicens: **ACCÍPITE ET BÍBITE EX EO OMNES: HIC** |

| | |
|---|---|
| DRINK FROM IT, FOR THIS IS THE CHALICE OF MY BLOOD, THE BLOOD OF THE NEW AND ETERNAL COVENANT, WHICH WILL BE POURED OUT FOR YOU AND FOR MANY FOR THE FORGIVENESS OF SINS. DO THIS IN MEMORY OF ME. | EST ENIM CALIX SÁNGUINIS MEI NOVI ET AETÉRNI TESTAMÉNTI, QUI PRO VOBIS ET PRO MULTIS EFFUNDÉTUR IN REMISSIÓNEM ECCATÓRUM. HOC FÁCITE IN MEAM COMMEMORATIÓNEM. |
| | |
| **P:** The mystery of faith: | **P:** Mystérium fídei. |
| **A.** we proclaim your Death, O Lord, and profess your resurrection until you come again.<br><br>**Or:**<br>**B.** When we eat this bread and drink this cup, we proclaim your death, Lord Jesus, until you come in glory.<br>**Or:**<br>**C.** Save us Saviour of the world, for by Your by your cross and resurrection you have set us free. | **A.** Mortem tuam annuntiamus, Domine, et tuam resurrectionem confitemur, donec venias.<br><br>**Vel:**<br>**B.** Quotiescumque manducamus panem hunc et calicem bibimus, mortem tuam annuntiamus, Domine, donec venias.<br>**Vel:**<br>**C.** Salvator mundi, salva nos, qui per crucem et resurrectionem tuam liberasti nos. |
| | |
| **P.** Therefore, O Lord, as we celebrate the memorial of our redemption, we remember Christ's Death and his descent to the realm of the dead, we proclaim his Resurrection and his Ascension to your right hand, and, as we await his coming in glory, we offer you his Body and Blood, the sacrifice acceptable to you which brings salvation to the whole world. | **P.** Unde et nos, Dómine, redemptiónis nostrae memoriále nunc celebrántes, mortem Christi eiúsque descénsum ad ínferos recólimus, eius resurrectiónem et ascensiónem ad tuam déxteram profitémur, et, exspectántes ipsíus advéntum in glória, offérimus tibi eius Corpus et Sánguinem, sacrifícium tibi acceptábile et toti mundo salutáre. |
| Look, O Lord, upon the Sacrifice which you yourself have provided for your Church, and grant in your | Réspice, Dómine, in Hóstiam, quam Ecclésiae tuae ipse parásti, et concede benígnus omnibus qui ex |

| | |
|---|---|
| loving kindness to all who partake of this one Bread and one Chalice that, gathered into one body by the Holy Spirit, they may truly become a living sacrifice in Christ to the praise of your glory. | hoc uno pane participábunt et cálice, ut, in unum corpus a Sancto Spíritu congregáti, in Christo hóstia viva perficiántur, ad laudem glóriae tuae. |
| Therefore, Lord, remember now all for whom we offer this sacrifice: especially your servant **N.** our Pope, **N.** our Bishop, and the whole Order of Bishops, all the clergy, those who take part in this offering, those gathered here before you, your entire people, and all who seek you with a sincere heart. | Nunc ergo, Dómine, ómnium recordáre, pro quibus tibi hanc oblatiónem offérimus: in primis fámuli tui, Papae nostri **N.**, Epíscopi nostri **N.** (eiusque Epíscopis adiutóribus) et Episcopórum órdinis univérsi, sed et totíus cleri, et offeréntium, et circumstántium, et cuncti pópuli tui, et ómnium, qui te quaerunt corde sincéro. |
| **R**emember also those who have died in the peace of your Christ and all the dead, whose faith you alone have known. | **M**eménto étiam illórum, qui obiérunt in pace Christi tui, et ómnium defunctórum, quorum fidem tu solus cognovísti. |
| To all of us, your children, grant O merciful Father, that we may enter into a heavenly inheritance with the Blessed Virgin Mary, Mother of God, with blessed Joseph, her Spouse, and with your Apostles and Saints in your kingdom. There, with the whole of creation, freed from the corruption of sin and death, may we glorify you through Christ our Lord, through whom you bestow on the world all that is good. | Nobis ómnibus, fíliis tuis, clemens Pater, concéde, ut caeléstem hereditátem cónsequi valeámus cum beáta Vírgine, Dei Genetríce, María, cum beáto Ioseph, eius Sponso, cum Apóstolis et Sanctis tuis in regno tuo, ubi cum univérsa creatúra, a corruptióne peccáti et mortis liberáta, te glorificémus per Christum Dóminum nostrum, per quem mundo bona cuncta largíris. |
| | |
| **CONCLUDING DOXOLGY** | |
| **P.** Through him, and with him, and in him, O God, almighty | **P.** Per ipsum, et cum ipso, et in ipso, est tibi Deo Patri omnipoténti, in |

| | |
|---|---|
| Father, in the unity of the Holy Spirit, all glory and honor is yours, for ever and ever.<br>**C.** Amen. | unitáte Spíritus Sancti, omnis honor et glória per ómnia saecula saeculórum.<br>**C.** Amen. |

| **COMMUNION RITE** | **RITUS COMMUNINIS** |
|---|---|
| **Lord's Prayer**<br>**P**: At the Saviour's command and formed by divine teaching, we dare to say:<br><br>Our Father, who art in heaven, hallowed be Thy name. Thy kingdom come. Thy will be done on earth as it is in heaven.<br>Give us this day our daily bread and forgive us our trespasses as we forgive those who trespass against us. And lead us not into temptation, but deliver us from evil. | **Pater Noster**<br>**P:** Praecèptis salutàribus mòniti et divìna institutiòne formàti, audèmus dicere:<br>Páter nóster, qui es in cáelis, sanctificétur nómen túum. Advéniat regnum túum. Fíat volúntas túa, sícut in cáelo et in térra.<br>Pánem nóstrum quotidiánum da nóbis hódie, et dimítte nóbis débita nóstra, sícut et nos dimíttimus debitóribus nóstris. Et ne nos indúcas in tentatiónem: sed líbera nos a málo. |
| **DOXOLOGY**<br>**P.** Deliver us, Lord, we pray, from every evil, graciously grant peace in our days, that, by the help of your mercy, we may be always free from sin and safe from all distress, as we await the blessed hope and the coming of our Savior, Jesus Christ.<br><br>**C.** For the kingdom, the power and the glory are yours now and forever. | **P:** Líbera nos, quǽsumus, Dómine, ab ómnibus malis, da pro pítius pacem in diébus nostris, ut, ope misericórdiæ tuæ adiúti, et a peccáto simus semper líberi et ab omni perturbatióne secúri: exspectántes beátam spem et advéntum Salvatóris nostri Iesu Christi.<br>**C.** Quia tuum est regnum, et potéstas, et glória in sǽcula. |
| **SIGN OF PEACE** | |

| | |
|---|---|
| **P.** Lord Jesus Christ, who said to your Apostles: Peace I leave you, my peace I give you, look not on our sins, but on the faith of your Church, and graciously grant her peace and unity in accordance with your will. Who live and reign for ever and ever.<br>**C.** Amen | **P.** Dómine Iesu Christe, qui dixí- sti Apóstolis tuis: Pacem relínquo vobis, pacem meam do vobis: ne respícias peccáta nostra, sed fidem Ecclésiæ tuæ; eám que secúndum voluntátem tuam pacificáre et coadunáre digne ris. Qui vivis et regnas in sæcula sæculorum.<br>**C.** Amen |
| **P.** The peace of the Lord be with you always,<br>**C.** and with your spirit.<br>**P:** Let us offer each other the sign of peace. | **P.** Pax Dòmini sit semper;<br><br>**C.** Et cum spiritu tuo.<br>**P:** Offèrte vobis pacem. |
| | |
| **BREAKING OF THE BREAD** | |
| **C:** Lamb of God, you take away the sins of the world, have mercy on us.<br>**A:** Lamb of God, you take away the sins of the world, have mercy on us.<br>**A:** Lamb of God, you take away the sins of the world, grant us peace. | **C:** Agnus Dei, qui tollis peccàta mundi; miserère nobis.<br><br>**A:** Agnus Dei, qui tollis peccàta mundi; miserère nobis.<br><br>**A:** Agnus Dei, qui tollis peccàta mundi; dona nobis pacem. |
| **P.** Behold the Lamb of God, behold Him who takes away the sins of the world. Blessed are those called to the supper of the Lamb.<br>**C.** Lord, I am not worthy that you should enter under my roof, but only say the word and my soul shall be healed.<br><br>**P.** May the Body and Blood of Christ keep me safe for eternal life.<br>**C.** Amen | **P.** Ecce Agnus Dei, ecce qui tollis peccáta mundi. Beáti qui ad cenam Agni vocáti sunt.<br><br>**C.** Dómine, non sum dignus, ut intres sub tectum meum, sed tantum dic verbo et sanábitur ánima mea.<br><br>**P.** Corpus et Sanguis Christi custódiat me in vitam ætérnam.<br>**C.** Amen |
| **COMMUNION** | |

| | |
|---|---|
| **P.** The Body of Christ. | **P.** Corpus Christi. |
| **C.** Amen | **C.** Amen |
| **P.** The Blood of Christ. | **P.** Sanguis Christi. |
| **C.** Amen | **C.** Amen |
| | |
| **Prayer After Communion** | **Postcommunio** |
| **P.** Let us pray. | **P.** Oremus |
| (Prayer) | (Prayer) |
| **C:** Amen. | **C:** Amen. |
| | |
| **Concluding Rite** | **Ritus Conclusionis** |
| **P:** The Lord be with you. | **P:** Dòminus vobìscum. |
| **C:** And with your spirit. | **C:** Et cum spìritu tuo. |
| | |
| **BLESSING** | |
| **(Form A)** | **(Form A)** |
| **P:** May almighty God bless you: the Father, and the Son, + and the Holy Spirit. | **P:** Benedícat vos omnípotens Deus, Pater, et Filius, + et Spíritus Sanctus. |
| **C:** Amen. | **C:** Amen. |
| | |
| **DISMISSAL** | |
| **P:** Go forth, the Mass is ended. | **P:** Ite, missa est. |
| **C:** Thanks be to God. | **C:** Deo gratias. |

## 6.0                    JANUARY

### 01 JANUARY 2021, THE OCTAVE DAY OF CHRISTMAS: SOLEMNITY OF MARY, MOTHER OF GOD

**ENTRANCE ANTIPHON**

Hail, Holy Mother, who gave birth to the King, who rules heaven and earth for ever.

**OR**                                        **Cf. Is 9: 1, 5; Lk 1: 33**

Today a light will shine upon us, for the Lord is born for us; and he will be called Wondrous God, Prince of peace, Father of future ages: and his reign will be without end.

## COLLECT

O God, who through the fruitful virginity of Blessed Mary bestowed on the human race the grace of eternal salvation, grant, we pray, that we may experience the intercession of her, through whom we were found worthy to receive the author of life, our Lord Jesus Christ, your Son. Who lives and reigns with you in the unity of the Holy Spirit, one God, for ever and ever.

## FIRST READING                                              *Numbers 6:22—27*

The LORD said to Moses: "Speak to Aaron and his sons and tell them: This is how you shall bless the Israelites. Say to them:
The LORD bless you and keep you! The LORD let his face shine upon you, and be gracious to you! The LORD look upon you kindly and give you peace! So shall they invoke my name upon the Israelites, and I will bless them."

## RESPONSORIAL PSALM                              *Psalm 67:2—3, 5, 6, 8*

**R. May God bless us in his mercy.**
May God have pity on us and bless us; **/** may he let his face shine upon us. **/** So may your way be known upon earth; **/** among all nations, your salvation. **R.**
May the nations be glad and exult **/** because you rule the peoples in equity; **/** the nations on the earth you guide. **R.**
May the peoples praise you, O God; **/** may all the peoples praise you! **/** May God bless us, **/** and may all the ends of the earth fear him! **R.**

## SECOND READING                                          *Galatians 4:4—7*

Brothers and sisters: When the fullness of time had come, God sent his Son, born of a woman, born under the law, to ransom those under the law, so that we might receive adoption as sons. As proof that you are sons, God sent the Spirit of his Son into our hearts, crying out, "Abba, Father!" So you are no longer a slave but a son, and if a son then also an heir, through God.

## ALLELUIA                                                      *Hebrews 1:1—2*

**R. Alleluia, alleluia.** In the past God spoke to our ancestors through the prophets; in these last days, he has spoken to us through the Son. **R.**

## GOSPEL                                                          *Luke 2:16—21*

The shepherds went in haste to Bethlehem and found Mary and Joseph, and the infant lying in the manger. When they saw this, they made known the message that had been told them about this child. All who heard it were amazed by what had been told them by the shepherds. And Mary kept all these things, reflecting on them in her heart. Then the shepherds returned, glorifying and praising God for all they had heard and seen, just as it had been told to them.

When eight days were completed for his circumcision, he was named Jesus, the name given him by the angel before he was conceived in the womb.

**PRAYER OVER THE OFFERINGS**

O God, who in your kindness begin all good things and bring them to fulfilment, grant to us, who find joy in the Solemnity of the holy Mother of God, that, just as we glory in the beginnings of your grace, so one day we may rejoice in its completion. Through Christ our Lord.

**COMMUNION ANTIPHON**          **Heb 13:8**

Jesus Christ is the same yesterday, today, and for ever.

**PRAYER AFTER COMMUNION**

We have received this heavenly Sacrament with joy, O Lord: grant, we pray, that it may lead us to eternal life, for we rejoice to proclaim the blessed ever-Virgin Mary Mother of your Son and Mother of the Church. Through Christ our Lord.

**LESSONS LEARNT FROM THE READINGS / HOMILY**

| 1 | 2 |
|---|---|
| 3 | 4 |
| 5 | 6 |

**ACTION POINTS FOR THE WEEK**

| 1 | 2 |
|---|---|
| 3 | 4 |
| 5 | 6 |

**PRAYER POINTS FOR THE WEEK**

| 1 | 2 |
|---|---|
| 3 | 4 |
| 5 | 6 |

**THIS WEEK, I AM GRATEFUL FOR**

1 _____  2 _____

3 _____  4 _____

5 _____  6 _____

## 03 JANUARY 2021, THE EPIPHANY OF THE LORD

*Please note that the readings for vigil mass and mass of the day are the same. Their liturgical prayers however differ. The liturgical prayers for mass of the day could be found after the vigil mass.*

### THE EPIPHANY OF THE LORD – VIGIL MASS

**ENTRANCE ANTIPHON**                                    **Cf. Bar 5: 5**

Arise, Jerusalem, and look to the East and see your children gathered from the rising to the setting of the sun.

**COLLECT**

May the splendour of your majesty, O Lord, we pray, shed its light upon our hearts, that we may pass through the shadows of this world and reach the brightness of our eternal home. Through our Lord Jesus Christ, your Son, who lives and reigns with you in the unity of the Holy Spirit, one God, for ever and ever.

**FIRST READING**                                        *Isaiah 60:1—6*

Rise up in splendor, Jerusalem! Your light has come, the glory of the Lord shines upon you. See, darkness covers the earth, and thick clouds cover the peoples; but upon you the LORD shines, and over you appears his glory. Nations shall walk by your light, and kings by your shining radiance. Raise your eyes and look about; they all gather and come to you: your sons come from afar, and your daughters in the arms of their nurses.

Then you shall be radiant at what you see, your heart shall throb and overflow, for the riches of the sea shall be emptied out before you, the wealth of nations shall be brought to you. Caravans of camels shall fill you, dromedaries from Midian and Ephah; all from Sheba shall come bearing gold and frankincense, and proclaiming the praises of the LORD.

**PSALM:**                          *Psalm 72:1—2, 7—8, 10—11, 12—13 (see 11)*
R. Lord, every nation on earth will adore you.

O God, with your judgment endow the king, / and with your justice, the king's son; / he shall govern your people with justice / and your afflicted ones with judgment. **R.**

Justice shall flower in his days, / and profound peace, till the moon be no more. / May he rule from sea to sea, / and from the River to the ends of the earth. **R.**

The kings of Tarshish and the Isles shall offer gifts; / the kings of Arabia and Seba shall bring tribute. / All kings shall pay him homage, / all nations shall serve him. **R.**

For he shall rescue the poor when he cries out, / and the afflicted when he has no one to help him. / He shall have pity for the lowly and the poor; / the lives of the poor he shall save. **R.**

**SECOND READING** *Ephesians 3:2—3a, 5—6*

Brothers and sisters: You have heard of the stewardship of God's grace that was given to me for your benefit, namely, that the mystery was made known to me by revelation. It was not made known to people in other generations as it has now been revealed to his holy apostles and prophets by the Spirit: that the Gentiles are coheirs, members of the same body, and copartners in the promise in Christ Jesus through the gospel.

**ALLELUIA** *Matthew 2:2*

**R. Alleluia, alleluia.** We saw his star at its rising and have come to do him homage. **R.**

**GOSPEL** *Matthew 2:1—12*

When Jesus was born in Bethlehem of Judea, in the days of King Herod, behold, magi from the east arrived in Jerusalem, saying, "Where is the newborn king of the Jews? We saw his star at its rising and have come to do him homage." When

King Herod heard this, he was greatly troubled, and all Jerusalem with him. Assembling all the chief priests and the scribes of the people, he inquired of them where the Christ was to be born. They said to him, "In Bethlehem of Judea, for thus it has been written through the prophet:

*And you, Bethlehem, land of Judah, are by no means least among the rulers of Judah; since from you shall come a ruler, who is to shepherd my people Israel."*

Then Herod called the magi secretly and ascertained from them the time of the star's appearance. He sent them to Bethlehem and said, "Go and search diligently for the child. When you have found him, bring me word, that I too may go and do him homage." After their audience with the king they set out. And behold, the star that they had seen at its rising preceded them, until it came and stopped over the place where the child was. They were overjoyed at seeing the star, and on entering the house they saw the child with Mary his mother. They prostrated themselves and did him homage. Then they opened their treasures and offered him gifts of gold, frankincense, and myrrh. And having been warned in a dream not to return to Herod, they departed for their country by another way.

**PRAYER OVER THE OFFERINGS**
Accept we pray, O Lord, our offerings, in honour of the appearing of your Only Begotten Son and the first fruits of the nations, that to you praise may be rendered and eternal salvation be ours. Through Christ our Lord.

**COMMUNION ANTIPHON**          **Cf. Rv 21: 23**
The brightness of God illumined the holy city Jerusalem, and the nations will walk by its light.

**PRAYER AFTER COMMUNION**
Renewed by sacred nourishment, we implore your mercy, O Lord, that the star of your justice may shine always bright in our minds and that our true treasure may ever consist in our confession of you. Through Christ our Lord.

## THE EPIPHANY OF THE LORD – MASS OF THE DAY
**ENTRANCE ANTIPHON Cf. Mal 3: 1:1**
Behold, the Lord, the Mighty One, has come; and kingship is in his grasp, and power and dominion.

**COLLECT**
O God, who on this day revealed your Only Begotten Son to the nations by the guidance of a star, grant in your mercy, that we, who know you already by faith, may be brought to behold the beauty of your sublime glory. Through our Lord Jesus Christ, your Son, who lives and reigns with you in the unity of the Holy Spirit, one God, for ever and ever.

*Please note that the readings of the Mass of the Day are the same with those of Vigil as shown above.*

**PRAYER OVER THE OFFERINGS**
Look with favour, Lord, we pray, on these gifts of your Church, in which are offered now not gold or frankincense or myrrh, but he who by them is

proclaimed, sacrificed and received, Jesus Christ. Who lives and reigns for ever and ever.

**COMMUNION ANTIPHON**                                                        **Cf. Mt. 2:2**

We have seen his star in the East, and have come with gifts to adore the Lord.

**PRAYER AFTER COMMUNION**

Go before us with heavenly light, O Lord, always and everywhere, that we may perceive with clear sight and revere with true affection the mystery in which you have willed us to participate. Through Christ our Lord.

**LESSONS LEARNT FROM THE READINGS / HOMILY**

| 1 | 2 |
|---|---|
| 3 | 4 |
| 5 | 6 |

**ACTION POINTS FOR THE WEEK**

| 1 | 2 |
|---|---|
| 3 | 4 |
| 5 | 6 |

**PRAYER POINTS FOR THE WEEK**

| 1 | 2 |
|---|---|
| 3 | 4 |
| 5 | 6 |

**THIS WEEK, I AM GRATEFUL FOR**

| 1 | 2 |
|---|---|
| 3 | 4 |
| 5 | 6 |

## 10 JANUARY 2021, THE BAPTISM OF THE LORD

**ENTRANCE**                                    **ANTIPHON Cf. Mt 3: 16 – 17**

After the Lord was baptized, the heavens were opened, and the Spirit descended upon him like a dove, and the voice of the Father thundered: This is my beloved Son, with whom I am well pleased.

## COLLECT

Almighty ever-living God, who, when Christ had been baptized in the River Jordan and as the Holy Spirit descended upon him, solemnly declared him your beloved Son, grant that your children by adoption, reborn of water and the Holy Spirit, may always be well pleasing to you. Through our Lord Jesus Christ, your Son, who lives and reigns with you in the unity of the Holy Spirit, one God, for ever and ever.

*OR*

O God, whose Only Begotten Son has appeared in our very flesh, grant, we pray, that we may be inwardly transformed through him whom we recognize as outwardly like ourselves. Who lives and reigns with you in the unity of the Holy Spirit, one God, for ever and ever.

## FIRST READING                                                    *Isaiah 55:1—11*

Thus says the LORD: All you who are thirsty, come to the water! You who have no money, come, receive grain and eat; come, without paying and without cost, drink wine and milk! Why spend your money for what is not bread, your wages for what fails to satisfy? Heed me, and you shall eat well, you shall delight in rich fare. Come to me heedfully, listen, that you may have life. I will renew with you the everlasting covenant, the benefits assured to David. As I made him a witness to the peoples, a leader and commander of nations, so shall you summon a nation you knew not, and nations that knew you not shall run to you, because of the LORD, your God, the Holy One of Israel, who has glorified you.

Seek the LORD while he may be found, call him while he is near. Let the scoundrel forsake his way, and the wicked man his thoughts; let him turn to the LORD for mercy; to our God, who is generous in forgiving. For my thoughts are not your thoughts, nor are your ways my ways, says the LORD. As high as the heavens are above the earth so high are my ways above your ways and my thoughts above your thoughts.

For just as from the heavens the rain and snow come down and do not return there till they have watered the earth, making it fertile and fruitful, giving seed to the one who sows and bread to the one who eats, so shall my word be that goes forth from my mouth; my word shall not return to me void, but shall do my will, achieving the end for which I sent it.

**OR:**                                                          *Isaiah 42:1—4, 6—7*

Thus says the LORD: Here is my servant whom I uphold, my chosen one with whom I am pleased, upon whom I have put my spirit; he shall bring forth justice to the nations, not crying out, not shouting, not making his voice heard in the street. A bruised reed he shall not break, and a smoldering wick he shall not quench, until he establishes justice on the earth; the coastlands will wait for his teaching.

I, the LORD, have called you for the victory of justice, I have grasped you by the hand; I formed you, and set you as a covenant of the people, a light for the nations, to open the eyes of the blind, to bring out prisoners from confinement, and from the dungeon, those who live in darkness.

**PSALM EITHER:**                                   *Isaiah 12:2—3, 4bcd, 5—6 (3)*
**R. You will draw water joyfully from the springs of salvation.**
God indeed is my savior; **/** I am confident and unafraid. **/** My strength and my courage is the LORD, **/** and he has been my savior. **/** With joy you will draw water **/** at the fountain of salvation. **R.**
Give thanks to the LORD, acclaim his name; **/** among the nations make known his deeds, **/** proclaim how exalted is his name. **R.**
Sing praise to the LORD for his glorious achievement; **/** let this be known throughout all the earth. **/** Shout with exultation, O city of Zion, **/** for great in your midst is the Holy One of Israel! **R**

**OR:**                                                          *Psalm 29:1-2,3-4,3,9-10*
**R. The Lord will bless his people with peace.**
Give to the LORD, you sons of God, **/** give to the LORD glory and praise, **/** Give to the LORD the glory due his name; **/** adore the LORD in holy attire. **R.**
The voice of the LORD is over the waters, **/** the LORD, over vast waters. **/** The voice of the LORD is mighty; **/** the voice of the LORD is majestic. **R.**
The God of glory thunders, **/** and in his temple all say, "Glory!" **/** The LORD is enthroned above the flood; **/** the LORD is enthroned as king forever. **R.**

**SECOND READING**                                        *1 John 5:1—9*
Beloved: Everyone who believes that Jesus is the Christ is begotten by God, and everyone who loves the Father loves also the one begotten by him. In this way we know that we love the children of God when we love

41

God and obey his commandments. For the love of God is this, that we keep his commandments. And his commandments are not burdensome, for whoever is begotten by God conquers the world. And the victory that conquers the world is our faith. Who indeed is the victor over the world but the one who believes that Jesus is the Son of God?

This is the one who came through water and blood, Jesus Christ, not by water alone, but by water and blood. The Spirit is the one who testifies, and the Spirit is truth. So there are three that testify, the Spirit, the water and the blood, and the three are of one accord. If we accept human testimony, the testimony of God is surely greater. Now the testimony of God is this, that he has testified on behalf of his Son.

**OR:**                                                                                   *Acts 10:34—38*
Peter proceeded to speak to those gathered in the house of Cornelius, saying: "In truth, I see that God shows no partiality. Rather, in every nation whoever fears him and acts uprightly is acceptable to him. You know the word that he sent to the Israelites as he proclaimed peace through Jesus Christ, who is Lord of all, what has happened all over Judea, beginning in Galilee after the baptism that John preached, how God anointed Jesus of Nazareth with the Holy Spirit and power. He went about doing good and healing all those oppressed by the devil, for God was with him."

**ALLELUIA**                                                                           *see John 1:29*
R. Alleluia, alleluia. John saw Jesus approaching him, and said: Behold the Lamb of God who takes away the sin of the world. **R.**

**GOSPEL**                                                                             *Mark 1:7—11*
This is what John the Baptist proclaimed: "One mightier than I is coming after me. I am not worthy to stoop and loosen the thongs of his sandals. I have baptized you with water; he will baptize you with the Holy Spirit."

It happened in those days that Jesus came from Nazareth of Galilee and was baptized in the Jordan by John. On coming up out of the water he saw the heavens being torn open and the Spirit, like a dove, descending upon him. And a voice came from the heavens, "You are my beloved Son; with you I am well pleased."

**PRAYER OVER THE OFFERINGS**
Accept, O Lord, the offerings we have brought to honour the revealing of

your beloved Son, so that the oblation of your faithful may be transformed into the sacrifice of him who willed in his compassion to wash away the sins of the world.

Who lives and reigns for ever and ever.

## COMMUNION ANTIPHON                                      Jn 1: 32, 34

Behold the One of whom John said: I have seen and testified that this is the Son of God.

## PRAYER AFTER COMMUNION

Nourished with these sacred gifts, we humbly entreat your mercy, O Lord, that, faithfully listening to your Only Begotten Son, we may be your children in name and in truth. Through Christ our Lord.

## LESSONS LEARNT FROM THE READINGS / HOMILY

1 _____ 2 _____
3 _____ 4 _____
5 _____ 6 _____

## ACTION POINTS FOR THE WEEK

1 _____ 2 _____
3 _____ 4 _____
5 _____ 6 _____

## PRAYER POINTS FOR THE WEEK

1 _____ 2 _____
3 _____ 4 _____
5 _____ 6 _____

## THIS WEEK, I AM GRATEFUL FOR

1 _____ 2 _____
3 _____ 4 _____
5 _____ 6 _____

## 17 JANUARY 2021, 2ND SUNDAY IN ORDINARY TIME

### ENTRANCE ANTIPHON                                      Ps 65: 4

All the earth shall bow down before you, O God, and shall sing to you, shall sing to your name, O Most High!

## COLLECT

Almighty ever-living God, who govern all things, both in heaven and on earth, mercifully hear the pleading of your people and bestow your peace on our times. Through our Lord Jesus Christ, your Son, who lives and reigns with you in the unity of the Holy Spirit, one God, for ever and ever.

## FIRST READING                                    *1 Samuel 3:3b—10, 19*

Samuel was sleeping in the temple of the LORD where the ark of God was. The LORD called to Samuel, who answered, "Here I am." Samuel ran to Eli and said, "Here I am. You called me." "I did not call you," Eli said. "Go back to sleep." So he went back to sleep. Again the LORD called Samuel, who rose and went to Eli. "Here I am," he said. "You called me." But Eli answered, "I did not call you, my son. Go back to sleep."

At that time Samuel was not familiar with the LORD, because the LORD had not revealed anything to him as yet. The LORD called Samuel again, for the third time. Getting up and going to Eli, he said, "Here I am. You called me." Then Eli understood that the LORD was calling the youth. So he said to Samuel, "Go to sleep, and if you are called, reply, 'Speak, LORD, for your servant is listening.'" When Samuel went to sleep in his place, the LORD came and revealed his presence, calling out as before, "Samuel, Samuel!" Samuel answered, "Speak, for your servant is listening."

Samuel grew up, and the LORD was with him, not permitting any word of his to be without effect.

## PSALM                          *Psalm 40:2, 4, 7—8, 8—9, 10 (8a and 9a)*
**R. Here am I, Lord; I come to do your will.**

I have waited, waited for the LORD, **/** and he stooped toward me and heard my cry. **/** And he put a new song into my mouth, **/** a hymn to our God. **R.**

Sacrifice or offering you wished not, **/** but ears open to obedience you gave me. **/** Holocausts or sin–offerings you sought not; **/** then said I, "Behold I come." **R.**

"In the written scroll it is prescribed for me, **/** to do your will, O my God, is my delight, **/** and your law is within my heart!" **R.**

I announced your justice in the vast assembly; **/** I did not restrain my lips, as you, O LORD, know. **R.**

**SECOND READING**                    *1 Corinthians 6:13c—15a, 17—20*

Brothers and sisters: The body is not for immorality, but for the Lord, and the Lord is for the body; God raised the Lord and will also raise us by his power. Do you not know that your bodies are members of Christ? But whoever is joined to the Lord becomes one Spirit with him. Avoid immorality. Every other sin a person commits is outside the body, but the immoral person sins against his own body.

Do you not know that your body is a temple of the Holy Spirit within you, whom you have from God, and that you are not your own? For you have been purchased at a price. Therefore glorify God in your body.

**ALLELUIA**                              *John 1:41, 17b*

**R. Alleluia, alleluia.** We have found the Messiah: Jesus Christ, who brings us truth and grace. **R.**

**GOSPEL**                                *John 1:35—42*

John was standing with two of his disciples, and as he watched Jesus walk by, he said, "Behold, the Lamb of God." The two disciples heard what he said and followed Jesus. Jesus turned and saw them following him and said to them, "What are you looking for?" They said to him, "Rabbi"—which translated means Teacher—, "where are you staying?" He said to them, "Come, and you will see." So they went and saw where Jesus was staying, and they stayed with him that day. It was about four in the afternoon. Andrew, the brother of Simon Peter, was one of the two who heard John and followed Jesus. He first found his own brother Simon and told him, "We have found the Messiah" —which is translated Christ—. Then he brought him to Jesus. Jesus looked at him and said, "You are Simon the son of John; you will be called Cephas"—which is translated Peter.

**PRAYER OVER THE OFFERINGS**

Grant us, O Lord, we pray, that we may participate worthily in these mysteries, for whenever the memorial of this sacrifice is celebrated the work of our redemption is accomplished. Through Christ our Lord.

**COMMUNION ANTIPHON**                    **Cf. Ps. 22: 5**

You have prepared a table before me, and how precious is the chalice that quenches my thirst.

**OR:** 1 Jn 4: 16

We have come to know and to believe in the love that God has for us.

**PRAYER AFTER COMMUNION**

Pour on us, O Lord, the Spirit of your love, and in your kindness make those you have nourished by this one heavenly Bread one in mind and heart. Through Christ our Lord.

**LESSONS LEARNT FROM THE READINGS / HOMILY**

1 _____ 2 _____

3 _____ 4 _____

5 _____ 6 _____

**ACTION POINTS FOR THE WEEK**

1 _____ 2 _____

3 _____ 4 _____

5 _____ 6 _____

**PRAYER POINTS FOR THE WEEK**

1 _____ 2 _____

3 _____ 4 _____

5 _____ 6 _____

**THIS WEEK, I AM GRATEFUL FOR**

1 _____ 2 _____

3 _____ 4 _____

5 _____ 6 _____

## 24 JANUARY 2021, SECOND SUNDAY IN ORDINARY TIME

**ENTRANCE ANTIPHON** **Cf. Ps 95: 1, 6**

O sing a new song to the Lord; sing to the Lord, all the earth. In his presence are majesty and splendour, strength and honour in his holy place.

**COLLECT**

Almighty ever-living God, direct our actions according to your good pleasure, that in the name of your beloved Son we may abound in good works. Through our Lord Jesus Christ, your Son, who lives and reigns with you in the unity of the Holy Spirit, one God, for ever and ever.

**FIRST READING**                                    *Jonah 3:1—5, 10*

The word of the LORD came to Jonah, saying: "Set out for the great city of Nineveh, and announce to it the message that I will tell you." So Jonah made ready and went to Nineveh, according to the LORD's bidding. Now Nineveh was an enormously large city; it took three days to go through it. Jonah began his journey through the city, and had gone but a single day's walk announcing, "Forty days more and Nineveh shall be destroyed," when the people of Nineveh believed God; they proclaimed a fast and all of them, great and small, put on sackcloth.

When God saw by their actions how they turned from their evil way, he repented of the evil that he had threatened to do to them; he did not carry it out.

**PSALM**                                *Psalm 25:4—5, 6—7, 8—9 (4a)*

**R. Teach me your ways, O Lord.**

Your ways, O LORD, make known to me; **/** teach me your paths, **/** guide me in your truth and teach me, **/** for you are God my savior. **R.**

Remember that your compassion, O LORD, **/** and your love are from of old. **/** In your kindness remember me, **/** because of your goodness, O LORD. **R.**

Good and upright is the LORD; **/** thus he shows sinners the way. **/** He guides the humble to justice **/** and teaches the humble his way. **R.**

**SECOND READING**                                    *1 Corinthians 7:29—31*

I tell you, brothers and sisters, the time is running out. From now on, let those having wives act as not having them, those weeping as not weeping, those rejoicing as not rejoicing, those buying as not owning, those using the world as not using it fully. For the world in its present form is passing away.

**ALLELUIA**                                    *Mark 1:15*

**R. Alleluia, alleluia.** The kingdom of God is at hand. Repent and believe in the Gospel. **R.**

**GOSPEL**                                    *Mark 1:14—20*

After John had been arrested, Jesus came to Galilee proclaiming the gospel of God: "This is the time of fulfillment. The kingdom of God is at hand. Repent, and believe in the gospel."

As he passed by the Sea of Galilee, he saw Simon and his brother Andrew casting their nets into the sea; they were fishermen. Jesus said to them, "Come after me, and I will make you fishers of men." Then they abandoned their nets and followed him. He walked along a little farther and saw James, the son of Zebedee, and his brother John. They too were in a boat mending their nets. Then he called them. So they left their father Zebedee in the boat along with the hired men and followed him.

**PRAYER OVER THE OFFERINGS**
Accept our offerings, O Lord, we pray, and in sanctifying them grant that they may profit us for salvation. Through Christ our Lord.

**COMMUNION ANTIPHON Cf.** **Ps. 33: 6**
Look toward the Lord and be radiant; let your faces not be abashed.

**OR:** **Jn 8: 12**
I am the light of the world, says the Lord; whoever follows me will not walk in darkness, but will have the light of life.

**PRAYER AFTER COMMUNION**
Grant, we pray, almighty God, that, receiving the grace by which you bring us to new life, we may always glory in your gift.

**LESSONS LEARNT FROM THE READINGS / HOMILY**

| 1 | 2 |
|---|---|
| 3 | 4 |
| 5 | 6 |

**ACTION POINTS FOR THE WEEK**

| 1 | 2 |
|---|---|
| 3 | 4 |
| 5 | 6 |

**PRAYER POINTS FOR THE WEEK**

| 1 | 2 |
|---|---|
| 3 | 4 |
| 5 | 6 |

**THIS WEEK, I AM GRATEFUL FOR**

| 1 | 2 |
|---|---|

## 31 JANUARY 2021, 4TH SUNDAY IN ORDINARY TIME

**ENTRANCE ANTIPHON**                                         Ps. 105: 47

Save us, O Lord our God! And gather us from the nations, to give thanks to your holy name, and make it our glory to praise you.

**COLLECT**

Grant us, Lord our God, that we may honour you with all our mind, and love everyone in truth of heart. Through our Lord Jesus Christ, your Son, who lives and reigns with you in the unity of the Holy Spirit, one God, for ever and ever.

**FIRST READING**                                    *Deuteronomy 18:15—20*

Moses spoke to all the people, saying: "A prophet like me will the LORD, your God, raise up for you from among your own kin; to him you shall listen. This is exactly what you requested of the LORD, your God, at Horeb on the day of the assembly, when you said, 'Let us not again hear the voice of the LORD, our God, nor see this great fire any more, lest we die.' And the LORD said to me, 'This was well said. I will raise up for them a prophet like you from among their kin, and will put my words into his mouth; he shall tell them all that I command him. Whoever will not listen to my words which he speaks in my name, I myself will make him answer for it. But if a prophet presumes to speak in my name an oracle that I have not commanded him to speak, or speaks in the name of other gods, he shall die.'"

**PSALM**                                        *Psalm 95:1—2, 6—7, 7—9*

**R. If today you hear his voice, harden not your hearts.**

Come, let us sing joyfully to the LORD; **/** let us acclaim the rock of our salvation. **/** Let us come into his presence with thanksgiving; **/** let us joyfully sing psalms to him. **R**

Come, let us bow down in worship; **/** let us kneel before the LORD who made us. **/** For he is our God, **/** and we are the people he shepherds, the flock he guides. **R.**

Oh, that today you would hear his voice: **/** "Harden not your hearts as at Meribah, **/** as in the day of Massah in the desert, **/** where your fathers tempted me; **/** they tested me though they had seen my works." **R.**

**SECOND READING**                                *1 Corinthians 7:32—35*
Brothers and sisters: I should like you to be free of anxieties. An unmarried man is anxious about the things of the Lord, how he may please the Lord. But a married man is anxious about the things of the world, how he may please his wife, and he is divided. An unmarried woman or a virgin is anxious about the things of the Lord, so that she may be holy in both body and spirit. A married woman, on the other hand, is anxious about the things of the world, how she may please her husband. I am telling you this for your own benefit, not to impose a restraint upon you, but for the sake of propriety and adherence to the Lord without distraction.

**ALLELUIA**                                         *Matthew 4:16*
**R. Alleluia, alleluia.** The people who sit in darkness have seen a great light; on those dwelling in a land overshadowed by death, light has arisen. **R.**

**GOSPEL**                                         *Mark 1:21—28*
Then they came to Capernaum, and on the sabbath Jesus entered the synagogue and taught. The people were astonished at his teaching, for he taught them as one having authority and not as the scribes. In their synagogue was a man with an unclean spirit; he cried out, "What have you to do with us, Jesus of Nazareth? Have you come to destroy us? I know who you are—the Holy One of God!" Jesus rebuked him and said, "Quiet! Come out of him!" The unclean spirit convulsed him and with a loud cry came out of him. All were amazed and asked one another, "What is this? A new teaching with authority. He commands even the unclean spirits and they obey him." His fame spread everywhere throughout the whole region of Galilee.

**PRAYER OVER THE OFFERINGS**
O Lord, we bring to your altar these offerings of our service: be pleased to receive them, we pray, and transform them into the Sacrament of our redemption. Through Christ our Lord.

## COMMUNION ANTIPHON

Let your face shine on your servant. Save me in your merciful love. O Lord, let me never be put to shame, for I call on you.

**OR**                                                    **Mt 5: 3 – 4**

Blessed are the poor in spirit, for theirs is the kingdom of heaven. Blessed are the meek, for they shall possess the land.

## PRAYER AFTER COMMUNION

Nourished by these redeeming gifts, we pray, O Lord, that through this help to eternal salvation true faith may ever increase. Through Christ our Lord.

## LESSONS LEARNT FROM THE READINGS / HOMILY

1 _____  2 _____
3 _____  4 _____
5 _____  6 _____

## ACTION POINTS FOR THE WEEK

1 _____  2 _____
3 _____  4 _____
5 _____  6 _____

## PRAYER POINTS FOR THE WEEK

1 _____  2 _____
3 _____  4 _____
5 _____  6 _____

## THIS WEEK, I AM GRATEFUL FOR

1 _____  2 _____
3 _____  4 _____
5 _____  6 _____

## 7                          *FEBRUARY*

## 07 FEBRUARY 2021, 5TH SUNDAY IN ORDINARY TIME

**ENTRANCE ANTIPHON**                              **Ps. 94: 6 – 7**

O come, let us worship God and bow low before the God who made us, for he is the Lord our God.

## COLLECT

Keep your family safe, O Lord, with unfailing care, that, relying solely on the hope of heavenly grace, they may be defended always by your protection. Through our Lord Jesus Christ, your Son, who lives and reigns with you in the unity of the Holy Spirit, one God, for ever and ever.

## FIRST READING                                               *Job 7:1—4, 6—7*

Job spoke, saying: Is not man's life on earth a drudgery? Are not his days those of hirelings? He is a slave who longs for the shade, a hireling who waits for his wages. So I have been assigned months of misery, and troubled nights have been allotted to me. If in bed I say, "When shall I arise?" then the night drags on; I am filled with restlessness until the dawn. My days are swifter than a weaver's shuttle; they come to an end without hope. Remember that my life is like the wind; I shall not see happiness again.

## PSALM                                               *Psalm 147:1—2, 3—4, 5—6*
**R. Praise the Lord, who heals the brokenhearted. OR Alleluia.**

Praise the LORD, for he is good; / sing praise to our God, for he is gracious; / it is fitting to praise him. / The LORD rebuilds Jerusalem; / the dispersed of Israel he gathers. **R.**

He heals the brokenhearted / and binds up their wounds. / He tells the number of the stars; / he calls each by name. **R.**

Great is our Lord and mighty in power; / to his wisdom there is no limit. / The LORD sustains the lowly; / the wicked he casts to the ground. **R**

## SECOND READING                                     *1 Corinthians 9:16—19, 22—23*

Brothers and sisters: If I preach the gospel, this is no reason for me to boast, for an obligation has been imposed on me, and woe to me if I do not preach it! If I do so willingly, I have a recompense, but if unwillingly, then I have been entrusted with a stewardship. What then is my recompense? That, when I preach, I offer the gospel free of charge so as not to make full use of my right in the gospel.

Although I am free in regard to all, I have made myself a slave to all so as to win over as many as possible. To the weak I became weak, to win over the weak. I have become all things to all, to save at least some. All this I do for the sake of the gospel, so that I too may have a share in it.

**ALLELUIA**                                                         *Matthew 8:17*

**R. Alleluia, alleluia.** Christ took away our infirmities and bore our diseases. **R.**

## GOSPEL                                                      *Mark 1:29—39*

On leaving the synagogue Jesus entered the house of Simon and Andrew with James and John. Simon's mother–in–law lay sick with a fever. They immediately told him about her. He approached, grasped her hand, and helped her up. Then the fever left her and she waited on them.

When it was evening, after sunset, they brought to him all who were ill or possessed by demons. The whole town was gathered at the door. He cured many who were sick with various diseases, and he drove out many demons, not permitting them to speak because they knew him.

Rising very early before dawn, he left and went off to a deserted place, where he prayed. Simon and those who were with him pursued him and on finding him said, "Everyone is looking for you." He told them, "Let us go on to the nearby villages that I may preach there also. For this purpose have I come." So he went into their synagogues, preaching and driving out demons throughout the whole of Galilee.

## PRAYER OVER THE OFFERINGS

O Lord, our God, who once established these created things to sustain us in our frailty, grant, we pray, that they may become for us now the Sacrament of eternal life. Through Christ our Lord.

## COMMUNION ANTIPHON                                    **Cf. Ps. 106: 8 – 9**

Let them thank the Lord for his mercy, his wonders for the children of men, for he satisfies the thirsty soul, and the hungry he fills with good things.

## OR                                                           **Mt 5: 5 – 6**

Blessed are those who mourn, for they shall be consoled. Blessed are those who hunger and thirst for righteousness, for they shall have their fill.

## PRAYER AFTER COMMUNION

O God, who have willed that we be partakers in the one Bread and the one Chalice, grant us, we pray, so to live that, made one in Christ, we may joyfully bear fruit for the salvation of the world. Through Christ our Lord.

## LESSONS LEARNT FROM THE READINGS / HOMILY

**1**_____          **2**_____

| 3 | 4 |
|---|---|
| 5 | 6 |

## ACTION POINTS FOR THE WEEK

| 1 | 2 |
|---|---|
| 3 | 4 |
| 5 | 6 |

## PRAYER POINTS FOR THE WEEK

| 1 | 2 |
|---|---|
| 3 | 4 |
| 5 | 6 |

## THIS WEEK, I AM GRATEFUL FOR

| 1 | 2 |
|---|---|
| 3 | 4 |
| 5 | 6 |

# 14 FEBRUARY 2021, 6TH SUNDAY IN ORDINARY TIME

**ENTRANCE ANTIPHON**                                    Cf. Ps 30: 3 – 4

Be my protector, O God, a mighty stronghold to save me. For you are my rock, my stronghold! Lead me, guide me, for the sake of your name.

**COLLECT**

O God, who teach us that you abide in hearts that are just and true, grant that we may be so fashioned by your grace as to become a dwelling pleasing to you. Through our Lord Jesus Christ, your Son, who lives and reigns with you in the unity of the Holy Spirit, one God, for ever and ever.

**FIRST READING**                                    *Leviticus 13:1—2, 44—46*

The LORD said to Moses and Aaron, "If someone has on his skin a scab or pustule or blotch which appears to be the sore of leprosy, he shall be brought to Aaron, the priest, or to one of the priests among his descendants. If the man is leprous and unclean, the priest shall declare him unclean by reason of the sore on his head.

"The one who bears the sore of leprosy shall keep his garments rent and his head bare, and shall muffle his beard; he shall cry out,

'Unclean, unclean!' As long as the sore is on him he shall declare himself unclean, since he is in fact unclean. He shall dwell apart, making his abode outside the camp."

**RESPONSORIAL PSALM**                    *Psalm 32:1—2, 5, 11*
**R. I turn to you, Lord, in time of trouble, and you fill me with the joy of salvation.**
Blessed is he whose fault is taken away, **/** whose sin is covered. **/** Blessed the man to whom the LORD imputes not guilt, **/** in whose spirit there is no guile. **R.**
Then I acknowledged my sin to you, **/** my guilt I covered not. **/** I said, "I confess my faults to the LORD," **/** and you took away the guilt of my sin.**R.**
Be glad in the LORD and rejoice, you just; **/** exult, all you upright of heart. **R.**

**SECOND READING**                    *1 Corinthians 10:31—11:1*
Brothers and sisters, whether you eat or drink, or whatever you do, do everything for the glory of God. Avoid giving offense, whether to the Jews or Greeks or the church of God, just as I try to please everyone in every way, not seeking my own benefit but that of the many, that they may be saved. Be imitators of me, as I am of Christ.

**ALLELUIA**                    *Luke 7:16*
**R. Alleluia, alleluia.** A great prophet has arisen in our midst, God has visited his people. **R.**

**GOSPEL**                    *Mark 1:40—45*
A leper came to Jesus and kneeling down begged him and said, "If you wish, you can make me clean." Moved with pity, he stretched out his hand, touched him, and said to him, "I do will it. Be made clean." The leprosy left him immediately, and he was made clean. Then, warning him sternly, he dismissed him at once.

He said to him, "See that you tell no one anything, but go, show yourself to the priest and offer for your cleansing what Moses prescribed; that will be proof for them."

The man went away and began to publicize the whole matter. He spread the report abroad so that it was impossible for Jesus to enter a town openly. He remained outside in deserted places, and people kept coming to him from everywhere.

**PRAYER OVER THE OFFERINGS**

May this oblation, O Lord, we pray, cleanse and renew us and may it become for those who do your will the source of eternal reward. Through Christ our Lord.

**COMMUNION ANTIPHON**                                    **Cf. Ps 77: 29 – 30**

They ate and had their fill, and what they craved the Lord gave them; they were not disappointed in what they craved.

**OR**                                                              **Jn 3: 16**

God so loved the world that he gave his Only Begotten Son, so that all who believe in him may not perish, but may have eternal life.

**PRAYER AFTER COMMUNION**

Having fed upon these heavenly delights, we pray, O Lord, so that we may always long for that food by which we truly live. Through Christ our Lord.

**LESSONS LEARNT FROM THE READINGS / HOMILY**

1 _____ 2 _____

3 _____ 4 _____

5 _____ 6 _____

**ACTION POINTS FOR THE WEEK**

1 _____ 2 _____

3 _____ 4 _____

5 _____ 6 _____

**PRAYER POINTS FOR THE WEEK**

1 _____ 2 _____

3 _____ 4 _____

5 _____ 6 _____

**THIS WEEK, I AM GRATEFUL FOR**

1 _____ 2 _____

3 _____ 4 _____

5 _____ 6 _____

**ENTRANCE ANTIPHON**                    *Wis 11: 24, 25, 27*

You are merciful to all, O Lord, and despise nothing that you have made. You overlook people's sins, to bring them to repentance, and you spare them, for you are the Lord our God.

**COLLECT**

Grant, O Lord, that we may begin with holy fasting this campaign of Christian service, so that, as we take up battle against spiritual evils, we may be armed with weapons of self-restraint. Through our Lord Jesus Christ, your Son, who lives and reigns with you in the unity of the Holy Spirit, one God, for ever and ever.

**FIRST READING**                    *Joel 2:12–18*

Even now, says the LORD, return to me with your whole heart, with fasting, and weeping, and mourning; Rend your hearts, not your garments, and return to the LORD, your God. For gracious and merciful is he, slow to anger, rich in kindness, and relenting in punishment. Perhaps he will again relent and leave behind him a blessing, Offerings and libations for the LORD, your God.

Blow the trumpet in Zion! proclaim a fast, call an assembly; Gather the people, notify the congregation; Assemble the elders, gather the children and the infants at the breast; Let the bridegroom quit his room and the bride her chamber. Between the porch and the altar let the priests, the ministers of the LORD, weep, And say, "Spare, O LORD, your people, and make not your heritage a reproach, with the nations ruling over them! Why should they say among the peoples, 'Where is their God?'"

Then the LORD was stirred to concern for his land and took pity on his people.

**PSALM**                    *Psalm 51:3–4, 5–6ab, 12–13, 14 and 17*

R. (see 3a) Be merciful, O Lord, for we have sinned.

Have mercy on me, O God, in your goodness; / in the greatness of your compassion wipe out my offense. / Thoroughly wash me from my guilt / and of my sin cleanse me. **R.**

For I acknowledge my offense, / and my sin is before me always: / "Against you only have I sinned, / and done what is evil in your sight." **R.**

A clean heart create for me, O God, / and a steadfast spirit renew within me. / Cast me not out from your presence, / and your Holy Spirit take not from me. **R.**

Give me back the joy of your salvation, / and a willing spirit sustain in me. / O Lord, open my lips, / and my mouth shall proclaim your praise. **R.**

## SECOND READING                                    *2 Corinthians 5:20–6:2*

Brothers and sisters: We are ambassadors for Christ, as if God were appealing through us. We implore you on behalf of Christ, be reconciled to God. For our sake he made him to be sin who did not know sin, so that we might become the righteousness of God in him.

Working together, then, we appeal to you not to receive the grace of God in vain. For he says: *In an acceptable time I heard you, and on the day of salvation I helped you.*

Behold, now is a very acceptable time; behold, now is the day of salvation.

## VERSE BEFORE THE GOSPEL                              *See Psalm 95:8*

If today you hear his voice, harden not your hearts.

## GOSPEL                                              *Matthew 6:1–6, 16–18*

Jesus said to his disciples: "Take care not to perform righteous deeds in order that people may see them; otherwise, you will have no recompense from your heavenly Father. When you give alms, do not blow a trumpet before you, as the hypocrites do in the synagogues and in the streets to win the praise of others. Amen, I say to you, they have received their reward. But when you give alms, do not let your left hand know what your right is doing, so that your almsgiving may be secret. And your Father who sees in secret will repay you.

"When you pray, do not be like the hypocrites, who love to stand and pray in the synagogues and on street corners so that others may see them. Amen, I say to you, they have received their reward. But when you pray, go to your inner room, close the door, and pray to your Father in secret. And your Father who sees in secret will repay you.

"When you fast, do not look gloomy like the hypocrites. They neglect their appearance, so that they may appear to others to be fasting. Amen, I say to you, they have received their reward. But when you fast, anoint your head and wash your face, so that you may not appear to be fasting, except to your Father who is hidden. And your Father who sees what is hidden will repay you."

**PRAYER OVER THE OFFERINGS**

As we solemnly offer the annual sacrifice for the beginning of Lent, we entreat you, O Lord, that, through works of penance and charity, we may turn away from harmful pleasures and, cleansed from our sins, may become worthy to celebrate devoutly the Passion of your Son. Who lives and reigns for ever and ever.

**COMMUNION ANTIPHON**                                    **Cf. Ps 1: 2 – 3**

He who ponders the law of the Lord day and night will yield fruit in due season.

**PRAYER AFTER COMMUNION**

May the Sacrament we have received sustain us, O Lord, that our Lenten fast may be pleasing to you and be for us a healing remedy. Through Christ our Lord.

**PRAYER OVER THE PEOPLE**

Pour out a spirit of compunction, O God, on those who bow before your majesty, and by your mercy may they merit the rewards you promise to those who do penance. Through Christ our Lord. **Amen.**

**LESSONS LEARNT FROM THE READINGS / HOMILY**

| 1 | 2 |
|---|---|
| 3 | 4 |
| 5 | 6 |

**ACTION POINTS FOR THE WEEK**

| 1 | 2 |
|---|---|
| 3 | 4 |
| 5 | 6 |

**PRAYER POINTS FOR THE WEEK**

| 1 | 2 |
|---|---|
| 3 | 4 |
| 5 | 6 |

**THIS WEEK, I AM GRATEFUL FOR**

| 1 | 2 |
|---|---|
| 3 | 4 |
| 5 | 6 |

## 21 FEBRUARY 2021, 1ST SUNDAY OF LENT

**ENTRANCE ANTIPHON**                                    Cf. Ps 90: 15 – 16

When he calls on me, I will answer him; I will deliver him and give him glory, I will grant him length of days.

**COLLECT**

Grant, almighty God, through the yearly observances of holy Lent, that we may grow in understanding of the riches hidden in Christ and by worthy conduct pursue their effects. Through our Lord Jesus Christ, your Son, who lives and reigns with you in the unity of the Holy Spirit, one God, for ever and ever.

**FIRST READING**                                       *Genesis 9:8—15*

God said to Noah and to his sons with him: "See, I am now establishing my covenant with you and your descendants after you and with every living creature that was with you: all the birds, and the various tame and wild animals that were with you and came out of the ark. I will establish my covenant with you, that never again shall all bodily creatures be destroyed by the waters of a flood; there shall not be another flood to devastate the earth." God added: "This is the sign that I am giving for all ages to come, of the covenant between me and you and every living creature with you: I set my bow in the clouds to serve as a sign of the covenant between me and the earth. When I bring clouds over the earth, and the bow appears in the clouds, I will recall the covenant I have made between me and you and all living beings, so that the waters shall never again become a flood to destroy all mortal beings."

**PSALM**                          *Psalm 25:4—5, 6—7, 8—9*

**R. Your ways, O Lord, are love and truth to those who keep your covenant.**

Your ways, O LORD, make known to me; / teach me your paths, / guide me in your truth and teach me, / for you are God my savior. **R.**

Remember that your compassion, O LORD, / and your love are from of old. / In your kindness remember me, / because of your goodness, O LORD. **R.**

Good and upright is the LORD, / thus he shows sinners the way. / He guides the humble to justice, / and he teaches the humble his way. **R.**

## SECOND READING

1 Peter 3:18—22

Beloved: Christ suffered for sins once, the righteous for the sake of the unrighteous, that he might lead you to God. Put to death in the flesh, he was brought to life in the Spirit. In it he also went to preach to the spirits in prison, who had once been disobedient while God patiently waited in the days of Noah during the building of the ark, in which a few persons, eight in all, were saved through water. This prefigured baptism, which saves you now. It is not a removal of dirt from the body but an appeal to God for a clear conscience, through the resurrection of Jesus Christ, who has gone into heaven and is at the right hand of God, with angels, authorities, and powers subject to him.

## VERSE BEFORE THE GOSPEL                    *Matthew 4:4b*

One does not live on bread alone, but on every word that comes forth from the mouth of God.

## GOSPEL                                      *Mark 1:12—15*

The Spirit drove Jesus out into the desert, and he remained in the desert for forty days, tempted by Satan. He was among wild beasts, and the angels ministered to him.

After John had been arrested, Jesus came to Galilee proclaiming the gospel of God: "This is the time of fulfillment. The kingdom of God is at hand. Repent, and believe in the gospel."

## PRAYER OVER THE OFFERINGS

Give us the right dispositions, O Lord, we pray, to make these offerings, for with them we celebrate the beginning of this venerable and sacred time. Through Christ our Lord.

## COMMUNION ANTIPHON                         Mt 4: 4

One does not live by bread alone, but by every word that comes forth from the mouth of God.

## OR                          Cf. Ps 90: 4

The Lord will conceal you with his pinions, and under his wings you will trust.

## PRAYER AFTER COMMUNION

Renewed now with heavenly bread, by which faith is nourished, hope increased, and charity strengthened, we pray, O Lord, that we may learn to hunger for Christ, the true and living Bread, and strive to live by every word which proceeds from your mouth. Through Christ our Lord.

## PRAYER OVER THE PEOPLE

May bountiful blessing, O Lord, we pray, come down upon your people, that hope may grow in tribulation, virtue be strengthened in temptation, and eternal redemption be assured. Through Christ our Lord. **Amen.**

## LESSONS LEARNT FROM THE READINGS / HOMILY

| | |
|---|---|
| 1 | 2 |
| 3 | 4 |
| 5 | 6 |

## ACTION POINTS FOR THE WEEK

| | |
|---|---|
| 1 | 2 |
| 3 | 4 |
| 5 | 6 |

## PRAYER POINTS FOR THE WEEK

| | |
|---|---|
| 1 | 2 |
| 3 | 4 |
| 5 | 6 |

## THIS WEEK, I AM GRATEFUL FOR

| | |
|---|---|
| 1 | 2 |
| 3 | 4 |
| 5 | 6 |

# 28 FEBRUARY 2021, 2ND SUNDAY OF LENT

**ENTRANCE ANTIPHON**                                      Cf Ps 26: 8 – 9

Of you my heart has spoken, Seek his face. It is your face, O Lord, that I seek; hide not your face from me.

**OR**                                                            Cf. Ps 24: 6, 2, 22

Remember your compassion, O Lord, and your merciful love, for they are from of old. Let not our enemies exult over us. Redeem us, O God of Israel, from all our distress.

**COLLECT**

O God, who have commanded us to listen to your beloved Son, be pleased, we pray, to nourish us inwardly by your word, that, with spiritual sight made pure, we may rejoice to behold your glory. Through our Lord Jesus Christ, your Son, who lives and reigns with you in the unity of the Holy Spirit, one God, for ever and ever.

**FIRST READING** *Genesis 22:1—2, 9a, 10—13,15—18*

God put Abraham to the test. He called to him, "Abraham!" "Here I am!" he replied. Then God said: "Take your son Isaac, your only one, whom you love, and go to the land of Moriah. There you shall offer him up as a holocaust on a height that I will point out to you."

When they came to the place of which God had told him, Abraham built an altar there and arranged the wood on it. Then he reached out and took the knife to slaughter his son. But the LORD's messenger called to him from heaven, "Abraham, Abraham!" "Here I am!" he answered. "Do not lay your hand on the boy," said the messenger. "Do not do the least thing to him. I know now how devoted you are to God, since you did not withhold from me your own beloved son." As Abraham looked about, he spied a ram caught by its horns in the thicket. So he went and took the ram and offered it up as a holocaust in place of his son.

Again the LORD's messenger called to Abraham from heaven and said: "I swear by myself, declares the LORD, that because you acted as you did in not withholding from me your beloved son, I will bless you abundantly and make your descendants as countless as the stars of the sky and the sands of the seashore; your descendants shall take possession of the gates of their enemies, and in your descendants all the nations of the earth shall find blessing— all this because you obeyed my command."

**PSALM** *Psalm 116:10, 15, 16—17, 18—19*

**R. I will walk before the Lord, in the land of the living.**

I believed, even when I said, **/** "I am greatly afflicted." **/** Precious in the eyes of the LORD **/** is the death of his faithful ones. **R.**

O LORD, I am your servant; I am your servant, **/** the son of your handmaid; **/** you have loosed my bonds. **/** To you will I offer sacrifice of thanksgiving, **/** and I will call upon the name of the LORD. **R.**

My vows to the LORD I will pay**/** in the presence of all his people, **/** in the courts of the house of the LORD, **/** in your midst, O Jerusalem. **R.**

## SECOND READING                                    *Romans 8:31b—34*

Brothers and sisters: If God is for us, who can be against us? He who did not spare his own Son but handed him over for us all, how will he not also give us everything else along with him?

Who will bring a charge against God's chosen ones? It is God who acquits us, who will condemn? Christ Jesus it is who died—or, rather, was raised— who also is at the right hand of God, who indeed intercedes for us.

## VERSE BEFORE THE GOSPEL                           *See Matthew 17:5*

From the shining cloud the Father's voice is heard: This is my beloved Son, listen to him.

## GOSPEL                                             *Mark 9:2—10*

Jesus took Peter, James, and John and led them up a high mountain apart by themselves. And he was transfigured before them, and his clothes became dazzling white, such as no fuller on earth could bleach them. Then Elijah appeared to them along with Moses, and they were conversing with Jesus. Then Peter said to Jesus in reply, "Rabbi, it is good that we are here! Let us make three tents: one for you, one for Moses, and one for Elijah." He hardly knew what to say, they were so terrified. Then a cloud came, casting a shadow over them; from the cloud came a voice, "This is my beloved Son. Listen to him." Suddenly, looking around, they no longer saw anyone but Jesus alone with them.

As they were coming down from the mountain, he charged them not to relate what they had seen to anyone, except when the Son of Man had risen from the dead. So they kept the matter to themselves, questioning what rising from the dead meant.

## PRAYER OVER THE OFFERINGS

May this sacrifice, O Lord, we pray, cleanse us of our faults and sanctify your faithful in body and mind for the celebration of the paschal festivities. Through Christ our Lord.

## COMMUNION ANTIPHON                                 Mt 17: 5

This is my beloved Son, with whom I am well pleased; listen to him.

## PRAYER AFTER COMMUNION

As we receive these glorious mysteries, we make thanksgiving to you, O Lord, for allowing us while still on earth to be partakers even now of the things of heaven. Through Christ our Lord.

## PRAYER OVER THE PEOPLE

Bless your faithful, we pray, O Lord, with a blessing that endures for ever, and keep them faithful to the Gospel of your Only Begotten Son, so that they may always desire and at last attain that glory whose beauty he showed in his own Body, to the amazement of his Apostles. Through Christ our Lord. **Amen.**

## LESSONS LEARNT FROM THE READINGS / HOMILY

1 _____ 2 _____
3 _____ 4 _____
5 _____ 6 _____

### ACTION POINTS FOR THE WEEK

1 _____ 2 _____
3 _____ 4 _____
5 _____ 6 _____

### PRAYER POINTS FOR THE WEEK

1 _____ 2 _____
3 _____ 4 _____
5 _____ 6 _____

### THIS WEEK, I AM GRATEFUL FOR

1 _____ 2 _____
3 _____ 4 _____
5 _____ 6 _____

## LESSONS LEARNT FROM THE READINGS / HOMILY

1 _____ 2 _____
3 _____ 4 _____
5 _____ 6 _____

### ACTION POINTS FOR THE WEEK

1 _____ 2 _____
3 _____ 4 _____
5 _____ 6 _____

## PRAYER POINTS FOR THE WEEK

| 1 | 2 |
|---|---|
| 3 | 4 |
| 5 | 6 |

## THIS WEEK, I AM GRATEFUL FOR

| 1 | 2 |
|---|---|
| 3 | 4 |
| 5 | 6 |

# 8.0 MARCH

## 07 MARCH 2021, 3RD SUNDAY OF LENT

**ENTRANCE ANTIPHON**                                    **Cf. Ps 24: 15 – 16**

My eyes are always on the Lord, for he rescues my feet from the snare. Turn to me and have mercy on me, for I am alone and poor.

**OR**                                                  **Cf. Ezk 36: 23 – 26**

When I prove my holiness among you, I will gather you from all the foreign lands; and I will pour clean water upon you and cleanse you from all your impurities, and I will give you a new spirit, says the Lord.

**COLLECT**

O God, author of every mercy and of all goodness, who in fasting, prayer and almsgiving have shown us a remedy for sin, look graciously on this confession of our lowliness, that we, who are bowed down by our conscience, may always be lifted up by your mercy. Through our Lord Jesus Christ, your Son, who lives and reigns with you in the unity of the Holy Spirit, one God, for ever and ever.

**EITHER:**                          **FIRST READING** *Exodus 20:1—17*

In those days, God delivered all these commandments: "I, the LORD, am your God, who brought you out of the land of Egypt, that place of slavery. You shall not have other gods besides me. You shall not carve idols for yourselves in the shape of anything in the sky above or on the earth below or in the waters beneath the earth; you shall not bow down before them or worship them. For I, the LORD, your God, am a jealous God, inflicting punishment for their fathers' wickedness on the children of those who hate me, down to the third and fourth generation; but bestowing mercy down to the thousandth generation on the children of those who love me and keep my commandments.

"You shall not take the name of the LORD, your God, in vain. For the LORD will not leave unpunished the one who takes his name in vain.

"Remember to keep holy the sabbath day. Six days you may labor and do all your work, but the seventh day is the sabbath of the LORD, your God. No work may be done then either by you, or your son or daughter, or your male or female slave, or your beast, or by the alien who lives with you. In six days the LORD made the heavens and the earth, the sea and all that is in them; but on the seventh day he rested. That is why the LORD has blessed the sabbath day and made it holy.

"Honor your father and your mother, that you may have a long life in the land which the LORD, your God, is giving you. You shall not kill. You shall not commit adultery. You shall not steal. You shall not bear false witness against your neighbor. You shall not covet your neighbor's house. You shall not covet your neighbor's wife, nor his male or female slave, nor his ox or ass, nor anything else that belongs to him."

**OR:** *Exodus 20:1—3, 7—8, 12—17*

In those days, God delivered all these commandments: "I, the LORD am your God, who brought you out of the land of Egypt, that place of slavery. You shall not have other gods besides me.

"You shall not take the name of the LORD, your God, in vain. For the LORD will not leave unpunished the one who takes his name in vain.

"Remember to keep holy the sabbath day. Honor your father and your mother, that you may have a long life in the land which the LORD, your God, is giving you. You shall not kill. You shall not commit adultery. You shall not steal. You shall not bear false witness against your neighbor. You shall not covet your neighbor's house. You shall not covet your neighbor's wife, nor his male or female slave, nor his ox or ass, nor anything else that belongs to him."

**RESPONSORIAL PSALM** *Psalm 19:8, 9, 10, 11*
**R. Lord, you have the words of everlasting life.**
The law of the LORD is perfect, / refreshing the soul; / the decree of the LORD is trustworthy, / giving wisdom to the simple. **R.**
The precepts of the LORD are right, / rejoicing the heart; / the command of the LORD is clear, / enlightening the eye. **R.**

The fear of the LORD is pure, / enduring forever; / the ordinances of the LORD are true, / all of them just. **R.**

They are more precious than gold, / than a heap of purest gold; / sweeter also than syrup / or honey from the comb. **R.**

**SECOND READING**                                                      *1 Corinthians 1:22—25*

Brothers and sisters: Jews demand signs and Greeks look for wisdom, but we proclaim Christ crucified, a stumbling block to Jews and foolishness to Gentiles, but to those who are called, Jews and Greeks alike, Christ the power of God and the wisdom of God. For the foolishness of God is wiser than human wisdom, and the weakness of God is stronger than human strength.

**VERSE BEFORE THE GOSPEL**                                             *John 3:16*

God so loved the world that he gave his only Son, so that everyone who believes in him might have eternal life.

**GOSPEL**                                                             *John 2:13—25*

Since the Passover of the Jews was near, Jesus went up to Jerusalem. He found in the temple area those who sold oxen, sheep, and doves, as well as the money changers seated there. He made a whip out of cords and drove them all out of the temple area, with the sheep and oxen, and spilled the coins of the money changers and overturned their tables, and to those who sold doves he said, "Take these out of here, and stop making my Father's house a marketplace." His disciples recalled the words of Scripture, *Zeal for your house will consume me.* At this the Jews answered and said to him, "What sign can you show us for doing this?" Jesus answered and said to them, "Destroy this temple and in three days I will raise it up." The Jews said, "This temple has been under construction for forty–six years, and you will raise it up in three days?" But he was speaking about the temple of his body. Therefore, when he was raised from the dead, his disciples remembered that he had said this, and they came to believe the Scripture and the word Jesus had spoken.

While he was in Jerusalem for the feast of Passover, many began to believe in his name when they saw the signs he was doing. But Jesus would not trust himself to them because he knew them all, and did not need anyone to testify about human nature. He himself understood it well.

## PRAYER OVER THE OFFERINGS

Be pleased, O Lord, with these sacrificial offerings, and grant that we who beseech pardon for our own sins, may take care to forgive our neighbour. Through Christ our Lord.

## COMMUNION ANTIPHON

The sparrow finds a home, and the swallow a nest for her young: by your altars, O Lord of hosts, my King and my God. Blessed are they who dwell in your house, for ever singing your praise.

## PRAYER AFTER COMMUNION

As we receive the pledge of things yet hidden in heaven and are nourished while still on earth with the Bread that comes from on high, we humbly entreat you, O Lord, that what is being brought about in us in mystery may come to true completion. Through Christ our Lord.

## PRAYER OVER THE PEOPLE

Direct, O Lord, we pray, the hearts of your faithful, and in your kindness grant your servants this grace: that, abiding in the love of you and their neighbour, they may fulfil the whole of your commands. Through Christ our Lord. **Amen.**

## LESSONS LEARNT FROM THE READINGS / HOMILY

1 _____ 2 _____
3 _____ 4 _____
5 _____ 6 _____

## ACTION POINTS FOR THE WEEK

1 _____ 2 _____
3 _____ 4 _____
5 _____ 6 _____

## PRAYER POINTS FOR THE WEEK

1 _____ 2 _____
3 _____ 4 _____
5 _____ 6 _____

## THIS WEEK, I AM GRATEFUL FOR

1 _____ 2 _____
3 _____ 4 _____

## 14 MARCH 2021, 4TH SUNDAY OF LENT

**ENTRANCE ANTIPHON**                    Cf. Is 66: 10 – 11

Rejoice, Jerusalem, and all who love her. Be joyful, all who were in mourning; exult and be satisfied at her consoling breast.

**COLLECT**

O God, who through your Word reconcile the human race to yourself in a wonderful way, grant, we pray, that with prompt devotion and eager faith the Christian people may hasten toward the solemn celebrations to come. Through our Lord Jesus Christ, your Son, who lives and reigns with you in the unity of the Holy Spirit, one God, for ever and ever.

**FIRST READING**                    *2 Chronicles 36:14—16, 19—23*

In those days, all the princes of Judah, the priests, and the people added infidelity to infidelity, practicing all the abominations of the nations and polluting the LORD's temple which he had consecrated in Jerusalem.

Early and often did the LORD, the God of their fathers, send his messengers to them, for he had compassion on his people and his dwelling place. But they mocked the messengers of God, despised his warnings, and scoffed at his prophets, until the anger of the LORD against his people was so inflamed that there was no remedy. Their enemies burnt the house of God, tore down the walls of Jerusalem, set all its palaces afire, and destroyed all its precious objects. Those who escaped the sword were carried captive to Babylon, where they became servants of the king of the Chaldeans and his sons until the kingdom of the Persians came to power. All this was to fulfill the word of the LORD spoken by Jeremiah: "Until the land has retrieved its lost sabbaths, during all the time it lies waste it shall have rest while seventy years are fulfilled."

In the first year of Cyrus, king of Persia, in order to fulfill the word of the LORD spoken by Jeremiah, the LORD inspired King Cyrus of Persia to issue this proclamation throughout his kingdom, both by word of mouth and in writing: "Thus says Cyrus, king of Persia: All the kingdoms of the earth the LORD, the God of heaven, has given to me, and he has also charged me to build him a house in Jerusalem, which is in Judah. Whoever, therefore, among you belongs to any part of his people, let him go up, and may his God be with him!"

## PSALM

**R. Let my tongue be silenced, if I ever forget you!**

By the streams of Babylon **/** we sat and wept **/** when we remembered Zion. **/** On the aspens of that land **/** we hung up our harps. **R.**

For there our captors asked of us **/** the lyrics of our songs, **/** and our despoilers urged us to be joyous: **/** "Sing for us the songs of Zion!" **R.**

How could we sing a song of the LORD **/** in a foreign land? **/** If I forget you, Jerusalem, **/** may my right hand be forgotten! **R.**

May my tongue cleave to my palate **/** if I remember you not, **/** if I place not Jerusalem **/** ahead of my joy. **R.**

## SECOND READING                    *Ephesians 2:4—10*

Brothers and sisters: God, who is rich in mercy, because of the great love he had for us, even when we were dead in our transgressions, brought us to life with Christ—by grace you have been saved—, raised us up with him, and seated us with him in the heavens in Christ Jesus, that in the ages to come He might show the immeasurable riches of his grace in his kindness to us in Christ Jesus. For by grace you have been saved through faith, and this is not from you; it is the gift of God; it is not from works, so no one may boast. For we are his handiwork, created in Christ Jesus for the good works that God has prepared in advance, that we should live in them.

## VERSE BEFORE THE GOSPEL                    *John 3:16*

God so loved the world that he gave his only Son, so everyone who believes in him might have eternal life.

## GOSPEL                    *John 3:14—21*

Jesus said to Nicodemus: "Just as Moses lifted up the serpent in the desert, so must the Son of Man be lifted up, so that everyone who believes in him may have eternal life."

For God so loved the world that he gave his only Son, so that everyone who believes in him might not perish but might have eternal life. For God did not send his Son into the world to condemn the world, but that the world might be saved through him. Whoever believes in him will not be condemned, but whoever does not believe has already been condemned, because he has not believed in the name of the only Son of God. And this is the verdict, that the light came into the world, but people preferred darkness to light, because their works were evil. For everyone who does wicked things hates the light and does not come toward the light, so that his works might not be exposed. But whoever lives the truth comes to the light, so that his works may be clearly seen as done in God.

## PRAYER OVER THE OFFERINGS
We place before you with joy these offerings, which bring eternal remedy, O Lord, praying that we may both faithfully revere them and present them to you, as is fitting, for the salvation of all the world. Through Christ our Lord.

## COMMUNION ANTIPHON
Jerusalem is built as a city bonded as one together. It is there that the tribes go up, the tribes of the Lord, to praise the name of the Lord.

## PRAYER AFTER COMMUNION
O God, who enlighten everyone who comes into this world, illuminate our hearts, we pray, with the splendour of your grace, that we may always ponder what is worthy and pleasing to your majesty and love you in all sincerity. Through Christ our Lord.

## PRAYER OVER THE PEOPLE
Look upon those who call to you, O Lord, and sustain the weak; give life by your unfailing light to those who walk in the shadow of death, and bring those rescued by your mercy from every evil to reach the highest good. Through Christ our Lord. **Amen.**

## LESSONS LEARNT FROM THE READINGS / HOMILY

| | |
|---|---|
| 1 | 2 |
| 3 | 4 |
| 5 | 6 |

## ACTION POINTS FOR THE WEEK

| | |
|---|---|
| 1 | 2 |
| 3 | 4 |
| 5 | 6 |

## PRAYER POINTS FOR THE WEEK

| | |
|---|---|
| 1 | 2 |
| 3 | 4 |
| 5 | 6 |

## THIS WEEK, I AM GRATEFUL FOR

1 _____  2 _____
3 _____  4 _____
5 _____  6 _____

# 19 MARCH 2021, SOLEMNITY OF SAINT JOSEPH, HUSBAND OF THE BLESSED VIRGIN MARY

**ENTRANCE ANTIPHON**                                    Cf. Lk 12: 42

Behold, a faithful and prudent steward, whom the Lord set over his household.

**COLLECT**

Grant, we pray, almighty God, that by Saint Joseph's intercession your Church may constantly watch over the unfolding of the mysteries of human salvation, whose beginnings you entrusted to his faithful care. Through our Lord Jesus Christ, your Son, who lives and reigns with you in the unity of the Holy Spirit, one God, for ever and ever.

**FIRST READING**              *2 Samuel 7:4—5a, 12—14a, 16*

The LORD spoke to Nathan and said: "Go, tell my servant David, 'When your time comes and you rest with your ancestors, I will raise up your heir after you, sprung from your loins, and I will make his kingdom firm. It is he who shall build a house for my name. And I will make his royal throne firm forever. I will be a father to him, and he shall be a son to me. Your house and your kingdom shall endure forever before me; your throne shall stand firm forever.'"

**PSALM:**                            *Psalm 89:2—3, 4—5, 27, 29*

**R. The son of David will live for ever.**

The promises of the LORD I will sing for ever, / through all generations my mouth will proclaim your faithfulness, / For you have said, "My kindness is established forever";/in heaven you have confirmed your faithfulness.**R.**
"I have made a covenant with my chosen one, / I have sworn to David my servant: / Forever will I confirm your posterity / and establish your throne for all generations." **R.**
"He shall say of me, 'You are my father, / my God, the Rock, my savior.' / Forever I will maintain my kindness toward him, / And my covenant with him stands firm."**R**

**SECOND READING**                                        *Romans 4:13, 16—18, 22*

Brothers and sisters: It was not through the law that the promise was made to Abraham and his descendants that he would inherit the world, but through the righteousness that comes from faith. For this reason, it depends on faith, so that it may be a gift, and the promise may be guaranteed to all his descendants, not to those who only adhere to the law but to those who follow the faith of Abraham, who is the father of all of us, as it is written, I have made you father of many nations. He is our father in the sight of God, in whom he believed, who gives life to the dead and calls into being what does not exist. He believed, hoping against hope, that he would become the father of many nations, according to what was said, Thus shall your descendants be. That is why it was credited to him as righteousness.

**ALLELUIA**                                                    *Psalm 84:5*

**R. Alleluia, alleluia.** Blessed are those who dwell in your house, O Lord; they never cease to praise you. **R.**

**GOSPEL**                                          *Matthew 1:16, 18—21, 24a*

Jacob was the father of Joseph, the husband of Mary. Of her was born Jesus who is called the Christ.

Now this is how the birth of Jesus Christ came about. When his mother Mary was betrothed to Joseph, but before they lived together, she was found with child through the Holy Spirit. Joseph her husband, since he was a righteous man, yet unwilling to expose her to shame, decided to divorce her quietly. Such was his intention when, behold, the angel of the Lord appeared to him in a dream and said, "Joseph, son of David, do not be afraid to take Mary your wife into your home. For it is through the Holy Spirit that this child has been conceived in her. She will bear a son and you are to name him Jesus, because he will save his people from their sins." When Joseph awoke, he did as the angel of the Lord had commanded him and took his wife into his home.

**OR:**                                                    *Luke 2:41—51A*

Each year Jesus' parents went to Jerusalem for the feast of Passover, and when he was twelve years old, they went up according to festival custom. After they had completed its days, as they were returning, the boy Jesus remained behind in Jerusalem, but his parents did not know it. Thinking that he was in the caravan, they journeyed for a day and looked for him among their relatives and acquaintances, but not finding him, they returned to Jerusalem to look for him. After three days they found him in the temple, sitting in the midst of the teachers, listening to them and asking them questions, and all who heard him were astounded at his understanding and his answers. When his parents saw him, they were astonished, and his mother said to him, "Son, why have you done this to us? Your father and I have been looking for you with great anxiety." And he said to them, "Why were you looking for me? Did you not know that I must be in my Father's house?" But they did not understand what he said to them. He went down with them and came to Nazareth, and was obedient to them.

## PRAYER OVER THE OFFERINGS
We pray, O Lord, that, just as Saint Joseph served with loving care your Only Begotten Son, born of the Virgin Mary, so we may be worthy to minister with a pure heart at your altar. Through Christ our Lord.

## COMMUNION ANTIPHON                                    Mt 25: 21
Well done, good and faithful servant. Come, share your master's joy.

## PRAYER AFTER COMMUNION
Defend with unfailing protection, O Lord, we pray, the family you have nourished with food from this altar, as they rejoice at the Solemnity of Saint Joseph, and graciously keep safe your gifts among them. Through Christ our Lord.

## PRAYER OVER THE PEOPLE
Look upon your servants, O Lord, and in your goodness protect with heavenly assistance those who trust in your mercy. Through Christ our Lord. **Amen.**

## LESSONS LEARNT FROM THE READINGS / HOMILY
1_____ 2_____
3_____ 4_____
5_____ 6_____

## ACTION POINTS FOR THE WEEK
1_____ 2_____
3_____ 4_____
5_____ 6_____

# 21 MARCH 2021, 5TH SUNDAY OF LENT

**ENTRANCE ANTIPHON**                    Cf. Ps 42: 1 – 2

Give me justice, O God, and plead my cause against a nation that is faithless. From the deceitful and cunning rescue me, for you, O God, are my strength.

**COLLECT**

By your help, we beseech you, Lord our God, may we walk eagerly in that same charity with which, out of love for the world, your Son handed himself over to death. Through our Lord Jesus Christ, your Son, who lives and reigns with you in the unity of the Holy Spirit, one God, for ever and ever.

**FIRST READING**                    *Jeremiah 31:31—34*

The days are coming, says the LORD, when I will make a new covenant with the house of Israel and the house of Judah. It will not be like the covenant I made with their fathers the day I took them by the hand to lead them forth from the land of Egypt; for they broke my covenant, and I had to show myself their master, says the LORD. But this is the covenant that I will make with the house of Israel after those days, says the LORD. I will place my law within them and write it upon their hearts; I will be their God, and they shall be my people. No longer will they have need to teach their friends and relatives how to know the LORD. All, from least to greatest, shall know me, says the LORD, for I will forgive their evildoing and remember their sin no more.

## PSALM

*Psalm 51:3—4, 12—13, 14—15*

**R. Create a clean heart in me, O God.**

Have mercy on me, O God, in your goodness; / in the greatness of your compassion wipe out my offense. / Thoroughly wash me from my guilt / and of my sin cleanse me. **R.**

A clean heart create for me, O God, / and a steadfast spirit renew within me. / Cast me not out from your presence, / and your Holy Spirit take not from me. **R.**

Give me back the joy of your salvation, / and a willing spirit sustain in me. / I will teach transgressors your ways, / and sinners shall return to you. **R.**

## SECOND READING

*Hebrews 5:7—9*

In the days when Christ Jesus was in the flesh, he offered prayers and supplications with loud cries and tears to the one who was able to save him from death, and he was heard because of his reverence. Son though he was, he learned obedience from what he suffered; and when he was made perfect, he became the source of eternal salvation for all who obey him.

## VERSE BEFORE THE GOSPEL

*John 12:26*

Whoever serves me must follow me, says the Lord; and where I am, there also will my servant be.

## GOSPEL

*John 12:20—33*

Some Greeks who had come to worship at the Passover Feast came to Philip, who was from Bethsaida in Galilee, and asked him, "Sir, we would like to see Jesus." Philip went and told Andrew; then Andrew and Philip went and told Jesus. Jesus answered them, "The hour has come for the Son of Man to be glorified. Amen, amen, I say to you, unless a grain of wheat falls to the ground and dies, it remains just a grain of wheat; but if it dies, it produces much fruit. Whoever loves his life loses it, and whoever hates his life in this world will preserve it for eternal life. Whoever serves me must follow me, and where I am, there also will my servant be. The Father will honor whoever serves me.

"I am troubled now. Yet what should I say, 'Father, save me from this hour'? But it was for this purpose that I came to this hour. Father, glorify your name." Then a voice came from heaven, "I have glorified it and will glorify it again." The crowd there heard it and said it was thunder; but others said, "An angel has spoken to him." Jesus answered and said,

"This voice did not come for my sake but for yours. Now is the time of judgment on this world; now the ruler of this world will be driven out. And when I am lifted up from the earth, I will draw everyone to myself." He said this indicating the kind of death he would die.

**PRAYER OVER THE OFFERINGS**
Hear us, almighty God, and, having instilled in your servants the teachings of the Christian faith, graciously purify them by the working of this sacrifice. Through Christ our Lord.

**COMMUNION ANTIPHON**
Amen, Amen I say to you: Unless a grain of wheat falls to the ground and dies, it remains a single grain. But if it dies, it bears much fruit.

**PRAYER AFTER COMMUNION**
We pray, almighty God, that we may always be counted among the members of Christ, in whose Body and Blood we have communion. Who lives and reigns for ever and ever.

**PRAYER OVER THE PEOPLE**
Bless, O Lord, your people, who long for the gift of your mercy, and grant that what, at your prompting, they desire they may receive by your generous gift. Through Christ our Lord. **Amen.**

**LESSONS LEARNT FROM THE READINGS / HOMILY**

| 1 | 2 |
|---|---|
| 3 | 4 |
| 5 | 6 |

**ACTION POINTS FOR THE WEEK**

| 1 | 2 |
|---|---|
| 3 | 4 |
| 5 | 6 |

**PRAYER POINTS FOR THE WEEK**

| 1 | 2 |
|---|---|
| 3 | 4 |
| 5 | 6 |

## THIS WEEK, I AM GRATEFUL FOR

1 _____ 2 _____

3 _____ 4 _____

5 _____ 6 _____

## 25 MARCH 2021, SOLEMNITY OF THE ANNUNCIATION OF THE LORD

**ENTRANCE ANTIPHON** Heb 10: 5, 7

The Lord said, as he entered the world: Behold, I come to do your will, O God.

### COLLECT

O God, who willed that your Word should take on the reality of human flesh in the womb of the Virgin Mary, grant, we pray, that we, who confess our Redeemer to be God and man, may merit to become partakers even in his divine nature. Who lives and reigns with you in the unity of the Holy Spirit, one God, for ever and ever.

### FIRST READING Isaiah 7:10—14; 8:10

The LORD spoke to Ahaz, saying: Ask for a sign from the LORD, your God; let it be deep as the nether world, or high as the sky! But Ahaz answered, "I will not ask! I will not tempt the LORD!" Then Isaiah said: Listen, O house of David! Is it not enough for you to weary people, must you also weary my God? Therefore the Lord himself will give you this sign: the virgin shall be with child, and bear a son, and shall name him Emmanuel, which means "God is with us!"

### PSALM Psalm 40:7—8a, 8b—9, 10, 11

**R. Here I am, Lord; I come to do your will.**

Sacrifice or oblation you wished not, / but ears open to obedience you gave me. / Holocausts or sin—offerings you sought not; / then said I, "Behold I come." **R.**

"In the written scroll it is prescribed for me, / To do your will, O God, is my delight, / and your law is within my heart!" **R.**

I announced your justice in the vast assembly; / I did not restrain my lips, as you, O LORD, know. **R.**

Your justice I kept not hid within my heart; / your faithfulness and your salvation I have spoken of; / I have made no secret of your kindness and your truth / in the vast assembly. **R.**

## SECOND READING                                        *Hebrews 10:4—10*

Brothers and sisters: It is impossible that the blood of bulls and goats takes away sins. For this reason, when Christ came into the world, he said:

"Sacrifice and offering you did not desire, but a body you prepared for me; in holocausts and sin offerings you took no delight. Then I said, 'As is written of me in the scroll, behold, I come to do your will, O God.'"

First Christ says, "Sacrifices and offerings, holocausts and sin offerings, you neither desired nor delighted in." These are offered according to the law. Then he says, "Behold, I come to do your will." He takes away the first to establish the second. By this "will," we have been consecrated through the offering of the Body of Jesus Christ once for all.

## ALLELUIA                                               *John 1:14ab*

R. **Alleluia, alleluia.** The Word became flesh and made his dwelling among us; and we saw his glory. **R.**


## GOSPEL                                                 *Luke 1:26—38*

The angel Gabriel was sent from God to a town of Galilee called Nazareth, to a virgin betrothed to a man named Joseph, of the house of David, and the virgin's name was Mary. And coming to her, he said, "Hail, full of grace! The Lord is with you." But she was greatly troubled at what was said and pondered what sort of greeting this might be. Then the angel said to her, "Do not be afraid, Mary, for you have found favor with God. Behold, you will conceive in your womb and bear a son, and you shall name him Jesus. He will be great and will be called Son of the Most High, and the Lord God will give him the throne of David his father, and he will rule over the house of Jacob forever, and of his Kingdom there will be no end." But Mary said to the angel, "How can this be, since I have no relations with a man?" And the angel said to her in reply, "The Holy Spirit will come upon you, and the power of the Most High will overshadow you. Therefore the child to be born will be called holy, the Son of God. And behold, Elizabeth, your relative, has also conceived a son in her old age, and this is the sixth month for her who was called barren; for nothing will be impossible for God." Mary said, "Behold, I am the handmaid of the Lord. May it be done to me according to your word." Then the angel departed from her.

## PRAYER OVER THE OFFERINGS

Be pleased, almighty God, to accept your Church's offering, so that she, who is aware that her beginnings lie in the Incarnation of your Only

Begotten Son, may rejoice to celebrate his mysteries on this Solemnity. Who lives and reigns for ever and ever.

**COMMUNION ANTIPHON**                                          Is 7: 14

Behold, a Virgin shall conceive and bear a son; and his name will be called Emmanuel.

**PRAYER AFTER COMMUNION**

Confirm in our minds the mysteries of the true faith, we pray, O Lord, so that, confessing that he who was conceived of the Virgin Mary is true God and true man, we may, through the saving power of his Resurrection, merit to attain eternal joy. Through Christ our Lord.

**PRAYER OVER THE PEOPLE**

Be gracious to your people, Lord, we pray, that, as from day to day they reject what does not please you, they may be filled instead with delight at your commands. Through Christ our Lord. **Amen.**

**LESSONS LEARNT FROM THE READINGS / HOMILY**

1 _____ 2 _____
3 _____ 4 _____
5 _____ 6 _____

**ACTION POINTS FOR THE WEEK**

1 _____ 2 _____
3 _____ 4 _____
5 _____ 6 _____

**PRAYER POINTS FOR THE WEEK**

1 _____ 2 _____
3 _____ 4 _____
5 _____ 6 _____

**THIS WEEK, I AM GRATEFUL FOR**

1 _____ 2 _____
3 _____ 4 _____
5 _____ 6 _____

# 28 MARCH 2021, PALM SUNDAY OF THE LORD'S PASSION
## AT THE PROCESSION WITH PALMS

**GOSPEL**                                         *Mark 11:1—10*

When Jesus and his disciples drew near to Jerusalem, to Bethphage and Bethany at the Mount of Olives, he sent two of his disciples and said to them, "Go into the village opposite you, and immediately on entering it, you will find a colt tethered on which no one has ever sat. Untie it and bring it here. If anyone should say to you, 'Why are you doing this?' reply, 'The Master has need of it and will send it back here at once.'" So they went off and found a colt tethered at a gate outside on the street, and they untied it. Some of the bystanders said to them, "What are you doing, untying the colt?" They answered them just as Jesus had told them to, and they permitted them to do it. So they brought the colt to Jesus and put their cloaks over it. And he sat on it. Many people spread their cloaks on the road, and others spread leafy branches that they had cut from the fields. Those preceding him as well as those following kept crying out: "Hosanna! Blessed is he who comes in the name of the Lord! Blessed is the kingdom of our father David that is to come! Hosanna in the highest!"

**OR:**                                            *John 12:12—16*

When the great crowd that had come to the feast heard that Jesus was coming to Jerusalem, they took palm branches and went out to meet him, and cried out: "Hosanna! Blessed is he who comes in the name of the Lord, the king of Israel."

Jesus found an ass and sat upon it, as is written: *Fear no more, O daughter Zion; see, your king comes, seated upon an ass's colt.* His disciples did not understand this at first, but when Jesus had been glorified they remembered that these things were written about him and that they had done this for him.

## AT THE MASS

**ENTRANCE ANTIPHON**          *Cf. Jn 12: 1, 12 – 13; Ps 23: 9 – 10*

Six days before the Passover, when the Lord came into the city of Jerusalem, the children ran to meet him; in their hands they carried palm branches and with a loud voice cried out:

*Hosanna in the highest! Blessed are you, who have come in your abundant mercy!*

O gates, lift high your heads; grow higher, ancient doors. Let him enter, the king of glory! Who is this king of glory? He, the Lord of hosts, he is the king of glory.

*Hosanna in the highest! Blessed are you, who have come in your abundant mercy!*

## COLLECT
Almighty ever-living God, who as an example of humility for the human race to follow caused our Saviour to take flesh and submit to the Cross, graciously grant that we may heed his lesson of patient suffering and so merit a share in his Resurrection. Who lives and reigns with you in the unity of the Holy Spirit, one God, for ever and ever.

## FIRST READING                              *Isaiah 50:4—7*
The Lord GOD has given me a well-trained tongue, that I might know how to speak to the weary a word that will rouse them. Morning after morning he opens my ear that I may hear; and I have not rebelled, have not turned back. I gave my back to those who beat me, my cheeks to those who plucked my beard; my face I did not shield from buffets and spitting.

The Lord GOD is my help, therefore I am not disgraced; I have set my face like flint, knowing that I shall not be put to shame.

## PSALM                          *Psalm 22:8—9, 17—18, 19—20, 23—24*
**R. My God, my God, why have you abandoned me?**
All who see me scoff at me; they mock me with parted lips, they wag their heads: **/** "He relied on the LORD; let him deliver him, **/** let him rescue him, if he loves him." **R.**
Indeed, many dogs surround me, **/** a pack of evildoers closes in upon me; **/** they have pierced my hands and my feet; **/** I can count all my bones. **R.**
They divide my garments among them, **/** and for my vesture they cast lots. **/** But you, O LORD, be not far from me; **/** O my help, hasten to aid me. **R.**
I will proclaim your name to my brethren; **/** in the midst of the assembly I will praise you: **/** "You who fear the LORD, praise him; **/** all you descendants of Jacob, give glory to him; **/** revere him, all you descendants of Israel!" **R.**

**SECOND READING**                    *Philippians 2:6—11*

Christ Jesus, though he was in the form of God, did not regard equality with God something to be grasped. Rather, he emptied himself, taking the form of a slave, coming in human likeness; and found human in appearance, he humbled himself, becoming obedient to the point of death, even death on a cross. Because of this, God greatly exalted him and bestowed on him the name which is above every name, that at the name of Jesus every knee should bend, of those in heaven and on earth and under the earth, and every tongue confess that Jesus Christ is Lord, to the glory of God the Father.

**VERSE BEFORE THE GOSPEL**              *Philippians 2:8—9*

Christ became obedient to the point of death, even death on a cross. Because of this, God greatly exalted him and bestowed on him the name which is above every name.

**GOSPEL**                      *Longer Form Mark 14:1—15:47*

The Passover and the Feast of Unleavened Bread were to take place in two days' time. So the chief priests and the scribes were seeking a way to arrest him by treachery and put him to death. They said, "Not during the festival, for fear that there may be a riot among the people."

When he was in Bethany reclining at table in the house of Simon the leper, a woman came with an alabaster jar of perfumed oil, costly genuine spikenard. She broke the alabaster jar and poured it on his head. There were some who were indignant. "Why has there been this waste of perfumed oil? It could have been sold for more than three hundred days' wages and the money given to the poor." They were infuriated with her. Jesus said, "Let her alone. Why do you make trouble for her? She has done a good thing for me. The poor you will always have with you, and whenever you wish you can do good to them, but you will not always have me. She has done what she could. She has anticipated anointing my body for burial. Amen, I say to you, wherever the gospel is proclaimed to the whole world, what she has done will be told in memory of her."

Then Judas Iscariot, one of the Twelve, went off to the chief priests to hand him over to them. When they heard him they were pleased and promised to pay him money. Then he looked for an opportunity to hand him over.

On the first day of the Feast of Unleavened Bread, when they sacrificed the Passover lamb, his disciples said to him, "Where do you want us to go and prepare for you to eat the Passover?" He sent two of his disciples and said to them, "Go into the city and a man will meet you, carrying a jar of water. Follow him. Wherever he enters, say to the master of the house, 'The Teacher says, "Where is my guest room where I may eat the Passover with my disciples?"' Then he will show you a large upper room furnished and ready. Make the preparations for us there." The disciples then went off, entered the city, and found it just as he had told them; and they prepared the Passover.

When it was evening, he came with the Twelve. And as they reclined at table and were eating, Jesus said, "Amen, I say to you, one of you will betray me, one who is eating with me." They began to be distressed and to say to him, one by one, "Surely it is not I?" He said to them, "One of the Twelve, the one who dips with me into the dish. For the Son of Man indeed goes, as it is written of him, but woe to that man by whom the Son of Man is betrayed. It would be better for that man if he had never been born."

While they were eating, he took bread, said the blessing, broke it, and gave it to them, and said, "Take it; this is my body." Then he took a cup, gave thanks, and gave it to them, and they all drank from it. He said to them, "This is my blood of the covenant, which will be shed for many. Amen, I say to you, I shall not drink again the fruit of the vine until the day when I drink it new in the kingdom of God." Then, after singing a hymn, they went out to the Mount of Olives.

Then Jesus said to them, "All of you will have your faith shaken, for it is written: *I will strike the shepherd, and the sheep will be dispersed.* But after I have been raised up, I shall go before you to Galilee." Peter said to him, "Even though all should have their faith shaken, mine will not be." Then Jesus said to him, "Amen, I say to you, this very night before the cock crows twice you will deny me three times." But he vehemently replied, "Even though I should have to die with you, I will not deny you." And they all spoke similarly.

Then they came to a place named Gethsemane, and he said to his disciples, "Sit here while I pray." He took with him Peter, James, and John, and began to be troubled and distressed. Then he said to them, "My soul is sorrowful even to death. Remain here and keep watch." He advanced a little and fell to the ground and prayed that if it were possible the hour might pass by him; he said, "Abba, Father, all things are possible to you. Take this cup away from me, but not what I will but what you will." When he returned he found them asleep. He said to Peter, "Simon, are you asleep? Could you not keep watch for one hour? Watch and pray that you may not undergo the test. The spirit is willing but the flesh is weak." Withdrawing again, he prayed, saying the same thing. Then he returned once more and found them asleep, for they could not keep their eyes open and did not know what to answer him. He returned a third time and said to them, "Are you still sleeping and taking your rest? It is enough. The hour has come. Behold, the Son of Man is to be handed over to sinners. Get up, let us go. See, my betrayer is at hand."

Then, while he was still speaking, Judas, one of the Twelve, arrived, accompanied by a crowd with swords and clubs who had come from the chief priests, the scribes, and the elders. His betrayer had arranged a signal with them, saying, "The man I shall kiss is the one; arrest him and lead him away securely." He came and immediately went over to him and said, "Rabbi." And he kissed him. At this they laid hands on him and arrested him. One of the bystanders drew his sword, struck the high priest's servant, and cut off his ear. Jesus said to them in reply, "Have you come out as against a robber, with swords and clubs, to seize me? Day after day I was with you teaching in the temple area, yet you did not arrest me; but that the Scriptures may be fulfilled." And they all left him and fled. Now a young man followed him wearing nothing but a linen cloth about his body. They seized him, but he left the cloth behind and ran off naked.

They led Jesus away to the high priest, and all the chief priests and the elders and the scribes came together. Peter followed him at a distance into the high priest's courtyard and was seated with the guards, warming himself at the fire. The chief priests and the entire Sanhedrin kept trying to obtain testimony against Jesus in order to put him to death, but they found none. Many gave false witness against him, but their testimony did not agree. Some took the stand and testified falsely against him, alleging, "We heard him say, 'I will destroy this temple made with hands and within three days I will build another not made with hands.'" Even so their testimony did not agree. The high priest rose before the assembly and questioned Jesus, saying, "Have you no answer? What are these men testifying against you?" But he was silent and answered nothing. Again the high priest asked him and said to him, "Are you the Christ, the son of the Blessed One?" Then Jesus answered, "I am; and 'you will see the Son of Man seated at the right hand of the Power and coming with the clouds of heaven.'" At that the high priest tore his garments and said, "What further need have we of witnesses? You have heard the blasphemy. What do you think?" They all condemned him as deserving to die. Some began to spit on him. They blindfolded him and struck him and said to him, "Prophesy!" And the guards greeted him with blows.

While Peter was below in the courtyard, one of the high priest's maids came along. Seeing Peter warming himself, she looked intently at him and said, "You too were with the Nazarene, Jesus." But he denied it saying, "I neither know nor understand what you are talking about." So he went out into the outer court. Then the cock crowed. The maid saw him and began again to say to the bystanders, "This man is one of them." Once again he denied it. A little later the bystanders said to Peter once more, "Surely you are one of them; for you too are a Galilean." He began to curse and to swear, "I do not know this man about whom you are talking." And immediately a cock crowed a second time. Then Peter remembered the word that Jesus had said to him, "Before the cock crows twice you will deny me three times." He broke down and wept.

As soon as morning came, the chief priests with the elders and the scribes, that is, the whole Sanhedrin, held a council. They bound Jesus, led him away, and handed him over to Pilate. Pilate questioned him, "Are you the king of the Jews?" He said to him in reply, "You say so." The chief priests accused him of many things. Again Pilate questioned him, "Have you no answer? See how many things they accuse you of." Jesus gave him no further answer, so that Pilate was amazed.

Now on the occasion of the feast he used to release to them one prisoner whom they requested. A man called Barabbas was then in prison along with the rebels who had committed murder in a rebellion. The crowd came forward and began to ask him to do for them as he was accustomed. Pilate answered, "Do you want me to release to you the king of the Jews?" For he knew that it was out of envy that the chief priests had handed him over. But the chief priests stirred up the crowd to have him release Barabbas for them instead. Pilate again said to them in reply, "Then what do you want me to do with the man you call the king of the Jews?" They shouted again, "Crucify him." Pilate said to them, "Why? What evil has he done?" They only shouted the louder, "Crucify him." So Pilate, wishing to satisfy the crowd, released Barabbas to them and, after he had Jesus scourged, handed him over to be crucified.

The soldiers led him away inside the palace, that is, the praetorium, and assembled the whole cohort. They clothed him in purple and, weaving a crown of thorns, placed it on him. They began to salute him with, "Hail, King of the Jews!" and kept striking his head with a reed and spitting upon him. They knelt before him in homage. And when they had mocked him, they stripped him of the purple cloak, dressed him in his own clothes, and led him out to crucify him.

They pressed into service a passer–by, Simon, a Cyrenian, who was coming in from the country, the father of Alexander and Rufus, to carry his cross.

They brought him to the place of Golgotha —which is translated Place of the Skull—. They gave him wine drugged with myrrh, but he did not take it. Then they crucified him and divided his garments by casting lots for them to see what each should take. It was nine o'clock in the morning when they crucified him. The inscription of the charge against him read, "The King of the Jews." With him they crucified two revolutionaries, one on his right and one on his left. Those passing by reviled him, shaking their heads and saying, "Aha! You who would destroy the temple and rebuild it in three days, save yourself by coming down from the cross." Likewise the chief priests, with the scribes, mocked him among themselves and said, "He saved others; he cannot save himself. Let the Christ, the King of Israel, come down now from the cross that we may see and believe." Those who were crucified with him also kept abusing him. At noon darkness came over the whole land until three in the afternoon. And at three o'clock Jesus cried out in a loud voice, *"Eloi, Eloi, lema sabachthani?"* which is translated, "My God, my God, why have you forsaken me?" Some of the bystanders who heard it said, "Look, he is calling Elijah." One of them ran, soaked a sponge with wine, put it on a reed and gave it to him to drink saying, "Wait, let us see if Elijah comes to take him down." Jesus gave a loud cry and breathed his last.

***Here all kneel and pause for a short time.***
The veil of the sanctuary was torn in two from top to bottom. When the centurion who stood facing him saw how he breathed his last he said, "Truly this man was the Son of God!" There were also women looking on from a distance. Among them were Mary Magdalene, Mary the mother of the younger James and of Joses, and Salome. These women had followed him when he was in Galilee and ministered to him. There were also many other women who had come up with him to Jerusalem.

When it was already evening, since it was the day of preparation, the day before the sabbath, Joseph of Arimathea, a distinguished member of the council, who was himself awaiting the kingdom of God, came and courageously went to Pilate and asked for the body of Jesus. Pilate was amazed that he was already dead. He summoned the centurion and asked him if Jesus had already died. And when he learned of it from the centurion, he gave the body to Joseph. Having bought a linen cloth, he took him down, wrapped him in the linen cloth, and laid him in a tomb that had been hewn out of the rock. Then he rolled a stone against the entrance to the tomb. Mary Magdalene and Mary the mother of Joses watched where he was laid.

## OR: *Shorter Form*                                          *Mark 15:1—39*

As soon as morning came, the chief priests with the elders and the scribes, that is, the whole Sanhedrin, held a council. They bound Jesus, led him away, and handed him over to Pilate. Pilate questioned him, "Are you the king of the Jews?" He said to him in reply, "You say so." The chief priests accused him of many things. Again Pilate questioned him, "Have you no answer? See how many things they accuse you of." Jesus gave him no further answer, so that Pilate was amazed.

Now on the occasion of the feast he used to release to them one prisoner whom they requested. A man called Barabbas was then in prison along with the rebels who had committed murder in a rebellion. The crowd came forward and began to ask him to do for them as he was accustomed. Pilate answered, "Do you want me to release to you the king of the Jews?" For he knew that it was out of envy that the chief priests had handed him over. But the chief priests stirred up the crowd to have him release Barabbas for them instead. Pilate again said to them in reply, "Then what do you want me to do with the man you call the king of the Jews?" They shouted again, "Crucify him." Pilate said to them, "Why? What evil has he done?" They only shouted the louder, "Crucify him." So Pilate, wishing to satisfy the crowd, released Barabbas to them and, after he had Jesus scourged, handed him over to be crucified.

The soldiers led him away inside the palace, that is, the praetorium, and assembled the whole cohort. They clothed him in purple and, weaving a crown of thorns, placed it on him. They began to salute him with, "Hail, King of the Jews!" and kept striking his head with a reed and spitting upon him. They knelt before him in homage. And when they had mocked him, they stripped him of the purple cloak, dressed him in his own clothes, and led him out to crucify him.

They pressed into service a passer–by, Simon, a Cyrenian, who was coming in from the country, the father of Alexander and Rufus, to carry his cross.

They brought him to the place of Golgotha —which is translated Place of the Skull—. They gave him wine drugged with myrrh, but he did not take it. Then they crucified him and divided his garments by casting lots for them to see what each should take. It was nine o'clock in the morning when they crucified him. The inscription of the charge against him read, "The King of the Jews." With him they crucified two revolutionaries, one on his right and one on his left. Those passing by reviled him, shaking their heads and saying, "Aha! You who would destroy the temple and rebuild it in three days, save yourself by coming down from the cross." Likewise the chief priests, with the scribes, mocked him among themselves and said, "He saved others; he cannot save himself. Let the Christ, the King of Israel, come down now from the cross that we may see and believe." Those who were crucified with him also kept abusing him.

At noon darkness came over the whole land until three in the afternoon. And at three o'clock Jesus cried out in a loud voice, *"Eloi, Eloi, lema sabachthani?"* which is translated, "My God, my God, why have you forsaken me?" Some of the bystanders who heard it said, "Look, he is calling Elijah." One of them ran, soaked a sponge with wine, put it on a reed and gave it to him to drink saying, "Wait, let us see if Elijah comes to take him down."

*Here    all    kneel    and    pause    for    a    short    time.* Jesus gave a loud cry and breathed his last. The veil of the sanctuary was torn in two from top to bottom. When the centurion who stood facing him saw how he breathed his last he said, "Truly this man was the Son of God!"

## PRAYER OVER THE OFFERINGS
Through the Passion of your Only Begotten Son, O Lord, may our reconciliation with you be near at hand, so that, though we do not merit it by our own deeds, yet by this sacrifice made once for all, we may feel already the effects of your mercy. Through Christ our Lord.

**COMMUNION ANTIPHON**                                    **Cf Mt 26: 42**

Father, if this chalice cannot pass without my drinking it, your will be done.

**PRAYER AFTER COMMUNION**

Nourished with these sacred gifts, we humbly beseech you, O Lord, that, just as through the death of your Son you have brought us to hope for what we believe, so by his Resurrection you may lead us to where you call. Through Christ our Lord.

**PRAYER OVER THE PEOPLE**

Look, we pray, O Lord, on this your family, for whom our Lord Jesus Christ did not hesitate to be delivered into the hands of the wicked and submit to the agony of the Cross. Who lives and reigns for ever and ever. **Amen.**

**LESSONS LEARNT FROM THE READINGS / HOMILY**

1 _____ 2 _____
3 _____ 4 _____
5 _____ 6 _____

**ACTION POINTS FOR THE WEEK**

1 _____ 2 _____
3 _____ 4 _____
5 _____ 6 _____

**PRAYER POINTS FOR THE WEEK**

1 _____ 2 _____
3 _____ 4 _____
5 _____ 6 _____

**THIS WEEK, I AM GRATEFUL FOR**

1 _____ 2 _____
3 _____ 4 _____
5 _____ 6 _____

*APRIL*

## 9.1    *EASTER TRIDIUM LITURGY*
### 01 APRIL 2021

## 9.2    HOLY THURSDAY, CHRISM MASS

**ENTRANCE ANTIPHON**                                    **Rv 1: 6**

Jesus Christ has made us into a kingdom, priests for his God and Father. To him be glory and power for ever and ever. Amen.

**COLLECT**

O God, who anointed your Only Begotten Son with the Holy Spirit and made him Christ and Lord, graciously grant that, being made sharers in his consecration, we may bear witness to your Redemption in the world. Through our Lord Jesus Christ, your Son, who lives and reigns with you in the unity of the Holy Spirit, one God, for ever and ever.


**FIRST READING**                                    *Isaiah 61:1—3a, 6a, 8b—9*

The spirit of the Lord GOD is upon me, because the LORD has anointed me; he has sent me to bring glad tidings to the lowly, to heal the brokenhearted, to proclaim liberty to the captives and release to the prisoners, to announce a year of favor from the LORD and a day of vindication by our God, to comfort all who mourn; to place on those who mourn in Zion a diadem instead of ashes, to give them oil of gladness in place of mourning, a glorious mantle instead of a listless spirit.

You yourselves shall be named priests of the LORD, ministers of our God you shall be called.

I will give them their recompense faithfully, a lasting covenant I will make with them. Their descendants shall be renowned among the nations, and their offspring among the peoples; all who see them shall acknowledge them as a race the LORD has blessed.


**PSALM**                                    *Psalm 89:21—22, 25 and 27 (2)*

**R. For ever I will sing the goodness of the Lord.**

"I have found David, my servant; / with my holy oil I have anointed him. / That my hand may always be with him; / and that my arm may make him strong." **R.**

"My faithfulness and my mercy shall be with him; / and through my name shall his horn be exalted. / He shall say of me, 'You are my father, / my God, the Rock, my savior!'" **R.**

**SECOND READING**                            *Revelation 1:5—8*

[Grace to you and peace] from Jesus Christ who is the faithful witness, the firstborn of the dead and ruler of the kings of the earth. To him who loves us and has freed us from our sins by his Blood, who has made us into a Kingdom, priests for his God and Father, to him be glory and power forever and ever. Amen.

Behold, he is coming amid the clouds, and every eye will see him, even those who pierced him. All the peoples of the earth will lament him. Yes. Amen.

"I am the Alpha and the Omega," says the Lord God, "the one who is and who was and who is to come, the Almighty."

**VERSE BEFORE THE GOSPEL**          *Isaiah 61:1 (cited in Luke 4:18)*

The Spirit of the Lord is upon me for he sent me to bring glad tidings to the poor.

**GOSPEL**                                  *Luke 4:16—21*

Jesus came to Nazareth, where he had grown up, and went according to his custom into the synagogue on the sabbath day. He stood up to read and was handed a scroll of the prophet Isaiah. He unrolled the scroll and found the passage where it was written:

*The Spirit of the Lord is upon me, because he has anointed me to bring glad tidings to the poor. He has sent me to proclaim liberty to captives and recovery of sight to the blind, to let the oppressed go free, and to proclaim a year acceptable to the Lord.*

Rolling up the scroll, he handed it back to the attendant and sat down, and the eyes of all in the synagogue looked intently at him. He said to them, "Today this Scripture passage is fulfilled in your hearing."

## 9.3        RENEWAL OF PRIESTLY PROMISES

*Bishop:*

Beloved sons, on the anniversary of that day when Christ our Lord conferred his priesthood on his Apostles and on us, are you resolved to renew in the presence of your Bishop and God's holy people, the promises you once made?

*Priests Respond:* I am.

*Bishop:*

Are you resolved to be more united with the Lord Jesus and more closely conformed to him, denying yourselves and confirming those promises about sacred duties towards Christ's Church which, prompted by love of him, you willingly and joyfully pledged on the day of your priestly ordination?

*Priests Respond:* I am.
*Bishop:*
Are you resolved to be faithful stewards of the mysteries of God in the Holy Eucharist and the other liturgical rites and to discharge faithfully the sacred office of teaching, following Christ the Head and Shepherd, not seeking any gain, but moved only by zeal for souls?

*Priests Respond:* I am.

*Then, turned towards the people, the Bishop continues:*
*Bishop:*
As for you, dearest sons and daughters, pray for your Priests, that the Lord may pour out his gifts abundantly upon them, and keep them faithful as ministers of Christ, the High Priest, so that they may lead you to him, who is the source of salvation.

*People Respond:* **Christ, hear us. Christ, graciously hear us.**
*Bishop:*
And pray also for me, that I may be faithful to the apostolic office entrusted to me in my lowliness and that in your midst I may be made day by day a living and more perfect image of Christ, the Priest, the Good Shepherd, the Teacher and the Servant of all.
**Christ, hear us. Christ, graciously hear us.**
May the Lord keep us all in his charity and lead all of us, shepherds and flock, to eternal life.
*All respond together:* **Amen.**

**PRAYER OVER THE OFFERINGS**
May the power of this sacrifice, O Lord, we pray, mercifully wipe away what is old in us and increase in us grace of salvation and newness of life. Through Christ our Lord.
**COMMUNION ANTIPHON**          **Ps 88: 2**
I will sing for ever of your mercies, O Lord; through all ages my mouth will proclaim your fidelity.

## COMMUNION ANTIPHON

We beseech you, almighty God, that those you renew by your Sacraments may merit to become the pleasing fragrance of Christ. Who lives and reigns for ever and ever.

# EVENING MASS OF THE LORD'S SUPPER

### ENTRANCE ANTIPHON                                    Cf. Gal 6: 14

We should glory in the Cross of our Lord Jesus Christ, in whom is our salvation, life and resurrection, through whom we are saved and delivered.

### COLLECT

O God, who have called us to participate in this most sacred Supper, in which your Only Begotten Son, when about to hand himself over to death, entrusted to the Church a sacrifice new for all eternity, the banquet of his love, grant, we pray, that we may draw from so great a mystery, the fullness of charity and of life. Through our Lord Jesus Christ, your Son, who lives and reigns with you in the unity of the Holy Spirit, one God, for ever and ever.

### FIRST READING                                    *Exodus 12:1—8, 11—14*

The LORD said to Moses and Aaron in the land of Egypt, "This month shall stand at the head of your calendar; you shall reckon it the first month of the year. Tell the whole community of Israel: On the tenth of this month every one of your families must procure for itself a lamb, one apiece for each household. If a family is too small for a whole lamb, it shall join the nearest household in procuring one and shall share in the lamb in proportion to the number of persons who partake of it. The lamb must be a year–old male and without blemish. You may take it from either the sheep or the goats. You shall keep it until the fourteenth day of this month, and then, with the whole assembly of Israel present, it shall be slaughtered during the evening twilight. They shall take some of its blood and apply it to the two doorposts and the lintel of every house in which they partake of the lamb. That same night they shall eat its roasted flesh with unleavened bread and bitter herbs.

"This is how you are to eat it: with your loins girt, sandals on your feet and your staff in hand, you shall eat like those who are in flight. It is the Passover of the Lord. For on this same night I will go through Egypt, striking down every firstborn of the land, both man and beast, and executing judgment on all the gods of Egypt—I, the Lord! But the blood will mark the houses where you are. Seeing the blood, I will pass over you; thus, when I strike the land of Egypt, no destructive blow will come upon you.

"This day shall be a memorial feast for you, which all your generations shall celebrate with pilgrimage to the LORD, as a perpetual institution."

**PSALM**                                   *Psalm 116:12—13, 15—16bc, 17—18*
**R. Our blessing–cup is a communion with the Blood of Christ.**
How shall I make a return to the LORD / for all the good he has done for me? / The cup of salvation I will take up,/ and I will call upon the name of the LORD. **R.**
Precious in the eyes of the LORD / is the death of his faithful ones. / I am your servant, the son of your handmaid; / you have loosed my bonds. **R.**
To you will I offer sacrifice of thanksgiving, / and I will call upon the name of the LORD. / My vows to the LORD I will pay / in the presence of all his people. **R.**

**SECOND READING**                                   *1 Corinthians 11:23—26*
Brothers and sisters: I received from the Lord what I also handed on to you, that the Lord Jesus, on the night he was handed over, took bread, and, after he had given thanks, broke it and said, "This is my body that is for you. Do this in remembrance of me." In the same way also the cup, after supper, saying, "This cup is the new covenant in my blood. Do this, as often as you drink it, in remembrance of me." For as often as you eat this bread and drink the cup, you proclaim the death of the Lord until he comes.
**VERSE BEFORE THE GOSPEL**                                   *John 13:34*
I give you a new commandment, says the Lord: Love one another as I have loved you.

**GOSPEL**                                   *John 13:1—15*
Before the feast of Passover, Jesus knew that his hour had come to pass from this world to the Father. He loved his own in the world and he loved them to the end. The devil had already induced Judas, son of Simon the Iscariot, to hand him over. So, during supper, fully aware that the Father had put everything into his power and that he had come from God and

was returning to God, he rose from supper and took off his outer garments. He took a towel and tied it around his waist. Then he poured water into a basin and began to wash the disciples' feet and dry them with the towel around his waist. He came to Simon Peter, who said to him, "Master, are you going to wash my feet?" Jesus answered and said to him, "What I am doing, you do not understand now, but you will understand later." Peter said to him, "You will never wash my feet." Jesus answered him, "Unless I wash you, you will have no inheritance with me." Simon Peter said to him, "Master, then not only my feet, but my hands and head as well." Jesus said to him, "Whoever has bathed has no need except to have his feet washed, for he is clean all over; so you are clean, but not all." For he knew who would betray him; for this reason, he said, "Not all of you are clean."

So when he had washed their feet and put his garments back on and reclined at table again, he said to them, "Do you realize what I have done for you? You call me 'teacher' and 'master,' and rightly so, for indeed I am. If I, therefore, the master and teacher, have washed your feet, you ought to wash one another's feet. I have given you a model to follow, so that as I have done for you, you should also do."

### THE WASHING OF FEET

*After the Homily, where a pastoral reason suggests it, the Washing of Feet follows. Those who have been chosen are led by the ministers to seats prepared in a suitable place. Then the Priest (removing his chasuble if necessary) goes to each one, and, with the help of the ministers, pours water over each one's feet and then dries them.*

*Meanwhile some of the following antiphons or other appropriate chants are sung.*

**ANTIPHON 1**                              Cf. Jn 13: 4, 5, 16

After the Lord had risen from supper, he poured water into a basin and began to wash the feet of his disciples: he left them this example.

**ANTIPHON 2**                              Cf. Jn 13: 12, 13, 15

The Lord Jesus, after eating supper with his disciples, washed their feet and said to them: Do you know what I, your Lord and Master, have done for you? I have given you an example, that you should do likewise.

## ANTIPHON 3
Jn 13: 6, 7, 8

**R.** Lord, are you to wash my feet? Jesus said to him in answer: If I do not wash your feet, you will have no share with me.

**V.** So he came to Simon Peter and Peter said to him:

**R.** Lord, are you to wash my feet? Jesus said to him in answer: If I do not wash your feet, you will have no share with me.

**V.** What I am doing, you do not know for now, but later you will come to know.

**R.** Lord, are you to wash my feet? Jesus said to him in answer: If I do not wash your feet, you will have no share with me.

## ANTIPHON 4
Cf. Jn 13: 14

If I, your Lord and Master, have washed your feet, / how much more should you wash each other's feet?

## ANTIPHON 5
Jn 13: 35

**R.** This is how all will know that you are my disciples: if you have love for one another.

**V.** Jesus said to his disciples:

**R.** This is how all will know that you are my disciples: if you have love for one another.

## ANTIPHON 6
Cf. Jn 13: 34

I give you a new commandment, that you love one another as I have loved you, says the Lord.

ANTIPHON 7 1Cor 13: 13

**R.** Let faith, hope and charity, these three, remain among you, but the greatest of these is charity.

**V.** Now faith, hope and charity, these three, remain; but the greatest of these is charity.

**R.** Let faith, hope and charity, these three, remain among you, but the greatest of these is charity.

## PRAYER OVER THE OFFERINGS
Grant us, O Lord, we pray, that we may participate worthily in these mysteries, for whenever the memorial of this sacrifice is celebrated the work of our redemption is accomplished. Through Christ our Lord.

## COMMUNION ANTIPHON            1Cor 11: 24 – 25

This is the Body that will be given up for you; this is the Chalice of the new covenant in my Blood, says the Lord; do this, whenever you receive it, in memory of me.

## PRAYER AFTER COMMUNION

Grant, almighty God, that, just as we are renewed by the Supper of your Son in this present age, so we may enjoy his banquet for all eternity. Who lives and reigns for ever and ever.

## LESSONS LEARNT FROM THE READINGS / HOMILY

1 _____ 2 _____
3 _____ 4 _____
5 _____ 6 _____

### ACTION POINTS FOR THE WEEK

1 _____ 2 _____
3 _____ 4 _____
5 _____ 6 _____

### PRAYER POINTS FOR THE WEEK

1 _____ 2 _____
3 _____ 4 _____
5 _____ 6 _____

### THIS WEEK, I AM GRATEFUL FOR

1 _____ 2 _____
3 _____ 4 _____
5 _____ 6 _____

## 02 APRIL 2021

### 9.4                 GOOD FRIDAY

## COLLECT

Remember your mercies, O Lord, and with your eternal protection sanctify your servants, for whom Christ your Son, by the shedding of his Blood, established the Paschal Mystery. Who lives and reigns with you in the unity of the Holy Spirit, God for ever and ever.

*OR:*

O God, who by the Passion of Christ your Son, our Lord, abolished the death inherited from ancient sin by every succeeding generation, grant that just as, being conformed to him, we have borne by the law of nature the image of the man of earth, so by the sanctification of grace we may bear the image of the Man of heaven. Through our Lord Jesus Christ, your Son, who lives and reigns with you in the unity of the Holy Spirit, one God, for ever and ever. **Amen.**

## FIRST READING                          *Isaiah 52:13—53:12*

See, my servant shall prosper, he shall be raised high and greatly exalted. Even as many were amazed at him— so marred was his look beyond human semblance and his appearance beyond that of the sons of man— so shall he startle many nations, because of him kings shall stand speechless; for those who have not been told shall see, those who have not heard shall ponder it.

Who would believe what we have heard? To whom has the arm of the LORD been revealed? He grew up like a sapling before him, like a shoot from the parched earth; there was in him no stately bearing to make us look at him, nor appearance that would attract us to him. He was spurned and avoided by people, a man of suffering, accustomed to infirmity, one of those from whom people hide their faces, spurned, and we held him in no esteem.

Yet it was our infirmities that he bore, our sufferings that he endured, while we thought of him as stricken, as one smitten by God and afflicted. But he was pierced for our offenses, crushed for our sins; upon him was the chastisement that makes us whole, by his stripes we were healed. We had all gone astray like sheep, each following his own way; but the LORD laid upon him the guilt of us all.

Though he was harshly treated, he submitted and opened not his mouth; like a lamb led to the slaughter or a sheep before the shearers, he was silent and opened not his mouth. Oppressed and condemned, he was taken away, and who would have thought any more of his destiny? When he was cut off from the land of the living, and smitten for the sin of his people, a grave was assigned him among the wicked and a burial place with evildoers, though he had done no wrong nor spoken any falsehood. But the LORD was pleased to crush him in infirmity.

If he gives his life as an offering for sin, he shall see his descendants in a long life, and the will of the LORD shall be accomplished through him.

Because of his affliction he shall see the light in fullness of days; through his suffering, my servant shall justify many, and their guilt he shall bear. Therefore I will give him his portion among the great, and he shall divide the spoils with the mighty, because he surrendered himself to death and was counted among the wicked; and he shall take away the sins of many, and win pardon for their offenses.

## PSALM
Psalm 31:2, 6, 12—13, 15—16, 17, 25

**R. Father, into your hands I commend my spirit.**

In you, O LORD, I take refuge; **/** let me never be put to shame. **/** In your justice rescue me. **/** Into your hands I commend my spirit; **/** you will redeem me, O LORD, O faithful God. **R.**

For all my foes I am an object of reproach, **/** a laughingstock to my neighbors, and a dread to my friends; **/** they who see me abroad flee from me. **/** I am forgotten like the unremembered dead; I am like a dish that is broken. **R.**

But my trust is in you, O LORD; **/** I say, "You are my God. **/** In your hands is my destiny; rescue me **/** from the clutches of my enemies and my persecutors." **R.**

Let your face shine upon your servant; **/** save me in your kindness. **/** Take courage and be stouthearted, **/** all you who hope in the LORD. **R.**

## SECOND READING
Hebrews 4:14—16; 5:7—9

Brothers and sisters: Since we have a great high priest who has passed through the heavens, Jesus, the Son of God, let us hold fast to our confession. For we do not have a high priest who is unable to sympathize with our weaknesses, but one who has similarly been tested in every way, yet without sin. So let us confidently approach the throne of grace to receive mercy and to find grace for timely help.

In the days when Christ was in the flesh, he offered prayers and supplications with loud cries and tears to the one who was able to save him from death, and he was heard because of his reverence. Son though he was, he learned obedience from what he suffered; and when he was made perfect, he became the source of eternal salvation for all who obey him.

Christ became obedient to the point of death, even death on a cross. Because of this, God greatly exalted him and bestowed on him the name which is above every other name.

## THE PASSION OF OUR LORD JESUS CHRIST ACCORDING TO JOHN.
### *John 18:1—19:42*

Jesus went out with his disciples across the Kidron valley to where there was a garden, into which he and his disciples entered. Judas his betrayer also knew the place, because Jesus had often met there with his disciples. So Judas got a band of soldiers and guards from the chief priests and the Pharisees and went there with lanterns, torches, and weapons. Jesus, knowing everything that was going to happen to him, went out and said to them, "Whom are you looking for?" They answered him, "Jesus the Nazorean." He said to them, "I AM." Judas his betrayer was also with them. When he said to them, "I AM," they turned away and fell to the ground. So he again asked them, "Whom are you looking for?" They said, "Jesus the Nazorean." Jesus answered, "I told you that I AM. So if you are looking for me, let these men go." This was to fulfill what he had said, "I have not lost any of those you gave me." Then Simon Peter, who had a sword, drew it, struck the high priest's slave, and cut off his right ear. The slave's name was Malchus. Jesus said to Peter, "Put your sword into its scabbard. Shall I not drink the cup that the Father gave me?"

So the band of soldiers, the tribune, and the Jewish guards seized Jesus, bound him, and brought him to Annas first. He was the father–in–law of Caiaphas, who was high priest that year. It was Caiaphas who had counseled the Jews that it was better that one man should die rather than the people.

Simon Peter and another disciple followed Jesus. Now the other disciple was known to the high priest, and he entered the courtyard of the high priest with Jesus. But Peter stood at the gate outside. So the other disciple, the acquaintance of the high priest, went out and spoke to the gatekeeper and brought Peter in. Then the maid who was the gatekeeper said to Peter, "You are not one of this man's disciples, are you?" He said, "I am not." Now the slaves and the guards were standing around a charcoal fire that they had made, because it was cold, and were warming themselves. Peter was also standing there keeping warm.

The high priest questioned Jesus about his disciples and about his doctrine. Jesus answered him, "I have spoken publicly to the world. I have always taught in a synagogue or in the temple area where all the Jews gather, and in secret I have said nothing. Why ask me? Ask those who heard me what I said to them. They know what I said." When he had said this, one of the temple guards standing there struck Jesus and said, "Is this the way you answer the high priest?" Jesus answered him, "If I have spoken wrongly, testify to the wrong; but if I have spoken rightly, why do you strike me?" Then Annas sent him bound to Caiaphas the high priest.

Now Simon Peter was standing there keeping warm. And they said to him, "You are not one of his disciples, are you?" He denied it and said, "I am not." One of the slaves of the high priest, a relative of the one whose ear Peter had cut off, said, "Didn't I see you in the garden with him?" Again Peter denied it. And immediately the cock crowed.

Then they brought Jesus from Caiaphas to the praetorium. It was morning. And they themselves did not enter the praetorium, in order not to be defiled so that they could eat the Passover. So Pilate came out to them and said, "What charge do you bring against this man?" They answered and said to him, "If he were not a criminal, we would not have handed him over to you." At this, Pilate said to them, "Take him yourselves, and judge him according to your law." The Jews answered him, "We do not have the right to execute anyone," in order that the word of Jesus might be fulfilled that he said indicating the kind of death he would die. So Pilate went back into the praetorium and summoned Jesus and said to him, "Are you the King of the Jews?" Jesus answered, "Do you say this on your own or have others told you about me?" Pilate answered, "I am not a Jew, am I? Your own nation and the chief priests handed you over to me. What have you done?" Jesus answered, "My kingdom does not belong to this world. If my kingdom did belong to this world, my attendants would be fighting to keep me from being handed over to the Jews. But as it is, my kingdom is not here." So Pilate said to him, "Then you are a king?" Jesus answered, "You say I am a king. For this I was born and for this I came into the world, to testify to the truth. Everyone who belongs to the truth listens to my voice." Pilate said to him, "What is truth?"

When he had said this, he again went out to the Jews and said to them, "I find no guilt in him. But you have a custom that I release one prisoner to you at Passover. Do you want me to release to you the King of the Jews?" They cried out again, "Not this one but Barabbas!" Now

Barabbas was a revolutionary.

Then Pilate took Jesus and had him scourged. And the soldiers wove a crown out of thorns and placed it on his head, and clothed him in a purple cloak, and they came to him and said, "Hail, King of the Jews!" And they struck him repeatedly. Once more Pilate went out and said to them, "Look, I am bringing him out to you, so that you may know that I find no guilt in him." So Jesus came out, wearing the crown of thorns and the purple cloak. And he said to them, "Behold, the man!" When the chief priests and the guards saw him they cried out, "Crucify him, crucify him!" Pilate said to them, "Take him yourselves and crucify him. I find no guilt in him." The Jews answered, "We have a law, and according to that law he ought to die, because he made himself the Son of God." Now when Pilate heard this statement, he became even more afraid, and went back into the praetorium and said to Jesus, "Where are you from?" Jesus did not answer him. So Pilate said to him, "Do you not speak to me? Do you not know that I have power to release you and I have power to crucify you?" Jesus answered him, "You would have no power over me if it had not been given to you from above. For this reason the one who handed me over to you has the greater sin." Consequently, Pilate tried to release him; but the Jews cried out, "If you release him, you are not a Friend of Caesar. Everyone who makes himself a king opposes Caesar."

When Pilate heard these words he brought Jesus out and seated him on the judge's bench in the place called Stone Pavement, in Hebrew, Gabbatha. It was preparation day for Passover, and it was about noon. And he said to the Jews, "Behold, your king!" They cried out, "Take him away, take him away! Crucify him!" Pilate said to them, "Shall I crucify your king?" The chief priests answered, "We have no king but Caesar." Then he handed him over to them to be crucified.

So they took Jesus, and, carrying the cross himself, he went out to what is called the Place of the Skull, in Hebrew, Golgotha. There they crucified him, and with him two others, one on either side, with Jesus in the middle. Pilate also had an inscription written and put on the cross. It read, "Jesus the Nazorean, the King of the Jews." Now many of the Jews read this inscription, because the place where Jesus was crucified was near the city; and it was written in Hebrew, Latin, and Greek. So the chief priests of the Jews said to Pilate, "Do not write 'The King of the Jews,' but that he said, 'I am the King of the Jews'." Pilate answered, "What I have written, I have written."

When the soldiers had crucified Jesus, they took his clothes and divided them into four shares, a share for each soldier. They also took his tunic, but the tunic was seamless, woven in one piece from the top down. So they said to one another, "Let's not tear it, but cast lots for it to see whose it will be," in order that the passage of Scripture might be fulfilled that says: *They divided my garments among them, and for my vesture they cast lots.* This is what the soldiers did. Standing by the cross of Jesus were his mother and his mother's sister, Mary the wife of Clopas, and Mary of Magdala. When Jesus saw his mother and the disciple there whom he loved he said to his mother, "Woman, behold, your son." Then he said to the disciple, "Behold, your mother." And from that hour the disciple took her into his home.

After this, aware that everything was now finished, in order that the Scripture might be fulfilled, Jesus said, "I thirst." There was a vessel filled with common wine. So they put a sponge soaked in wine on a sprig of hyssop and put it up to his mouth. When Jesus had taken the wine, he said, "It is finished." And bowing his head, he handed over the spirit.

**HERE ALL KNEEL AND PAUSE A SHORT TIME.** Now since it was preparation day, in order that the bodies might not remain on the cross on the sabbath, for the sabbath day of that week was a solemn one, the Jews asked Pilate that their legs be broken and that they be taken down. So the soldiers came and broke the legs of the first and then of the other one who was crucified with Jesus. But when they came to Jesus and saw that he was already dead, they did not break his legs, but one soldier thrust his lance into his side, and immediately blood and water flowed out. An eyewitness has testified, and his testimony is true; he knows that he is speaking the truth, so that you also may come to believe. For this happened so that the Scripture passage might be fulfilled: *Not a bone of it will be broken.* And again another passage says: *They will look upon him whom they have pierced.*

After this, Joseph of Arimathea, secretly a disciple of Jesus for fear of the Jews, asked Pilate if he could remove the body of Jesus. And Pilate permitted it. So he came and took his body. Nicodemus, the one who had first come to him at night, also came bringing a mixture of myrrh and aloes weighing about one hundred pounds. They took the body of Jesus and bound it with burial cloths along with the spices, according to the Jewish burial custom. Now in the place where he had been crucified there was a garden, and in the garden a new tomb, in which no one had yet been buried. So they laid Jesus there because of the Jewish preparation day; for the tomb was close by.

## THE SOLEMN INTERCESSION
### FOR HOLY CHURCH

Let us pray, dearly beloved, for the holy Church of God, that our God and Lord be pleased to give her peace, to guard her and to unite her throughout the whole world and grant that, leading our life in tranquility and quiet, we may glorify God the Father almighty.

*Prayer in Silence. Then the priest says:*

Almighty ever-living God, who in Christ revealed your glory to all the nations, watch over the works of your mercy, that your Church, spread throughout all the world, may persevere with steadfast faith in confessing your name. Through Christ our Lord. **Amen.**

### FOR THE POPE

Let us pray also for our most Holy Father Pope **N.**, that our God and Lord, who chose him for the order of Bishops, may keep him safe and unharmed for the Lord's holy Church, to govern the holy People of God.

*Prayer in Silence. Then the priest says:*

Almighty ever-living God, by whose decree all things are founded, look with favour on our prayers and in your kindness protect the Pope chosen for us, that, under him, the Christian people governed by you their maker, may grow in merit by reason of their faith. Through Christ our Lord. **Amen**

### FOR ALL ORDERS AND DEGREES OF THE FAITHFUL

Let us pray also for our Bishop **N.**, for all Bishops, Priests, and Deacons of the Church and for the whole of the faithful people.

*Prayer in silence. Then the Priest says:*

Almighty ever-living God, by whose Spirit the whole body of the Church is sanctified and governed, hear our humble prayer for your ministers, that, by the gift of your grace, all may serve you faithfully. Through Christ our Lord. **Amen.**

### FOR CATECHUMENS

Let us pray also for (our) catechumens, that our God and Lord may open wide the ears of their inmost hearts and unlock the gates of his mercy, that, having received forgiveness of all their sins through the waters of rebirth, they, too, may be one with Christ Jesus our Lord.

*Prayer in silence. Then the Priest says:*

Almighty ever-living God, who make your Church ever fruitful with new offspring, increase the faith and understanding of **(our)** catechumens, that, reborn in the font of Baptism, they may be added to the number of your adopted children. Through Christ our Lord. **Amen.**

## FOR THE UNITY OF CHRISTIANS

Let us pray also for all our brothers and sisters who believe in Christ, that our God and Lord may be pleased, as they live the truth, to gather them together and keep them in his one Church.

*Prayer in silence. Then the Priest says:*

Almighty ever-living God, who gather what is scattered and keep together what you have gathered, look kindly on the flock of your Son, that those whom one Baptism has consecrated may be joined together by integrity of faith and united in the bond of charity. Through Christ our Lord. **Amen.**

## FOR THE JEWISH PEOPLE

Let us pray also for the Jewish people, to whom the Lord our God spoke first, that he may grant them to advance in love of his name and in faithfulness to his covenant.

*Prayer in silence. Then the Priest says:*

Almighty ever-living God, who bestowed your promises on Abraham and his descendants, graciously hear the prayers of your Church, that the people you first made your own may attain the fullness of redemption. Through Christ our Lord. **Amen.**

## FOR THOSE WHO DO NOT BELIEVE IN CHRIST

Let us pray also for those who do not believe in Christ, that, enlightened by the Holy Spirit, they, too, may enter on the way of salvation.

*Prayer in silence. Then the Priest says:*

Almighty ever-living God, grant to those who do not confess Christ that, by walking before you with a sincere heart, they may find the truth and that we ourselves, being constant in mutual love and striving to understand more fully the mystery of your life, may be made more perfect witnesses to your love in the world. Through Christ our Lord. **Amen.**

## FOR THOSE WHO DO NOT BELIEVE IN GOD

Let us pray also for those who do not acknowledge God, that, following what is right in sincerity of heart, they may find the way to God himself.

*Prayer in silence. Then the Priest says:*

Almighty ever-living God, who created all people to seek you always by desiring you and, by finding you, come to rest, grant, we pray, that, despite every harmful obstacle, all may recognize the signs of your fatherly love and the witness of the good works done by those who believe in you, and so in gladness confess you, the one true God and Father of our human race. Through Christ our Lord. **Amen.**

## FOR THOSE IN PUBLIC OFFICE

Let us pray also for those in public office, that our God and Lord may direct their minds and hearts according to his will for the true peace and freedom of all.

*Prayer in silence. Then the Priest says:*

Almighty ever-living God, in whose hand lies every human heart and the rights of peoples, look with favour, we pray, on those who govern with authority over us, that throughout the whole world, the prosperity of peoples, the assurance of peace, and freedom of religion may through your gift be made secure. Through Christ our Lord. **Amen.**

## FOR THOSE IN TRIBULATION

Let us pray, dearly beloved, to God the Father almighty, that he may cleanse the world of all errors, banish disease, drive out hunger, unlock prisons, loosen fetters, granting to travellers safety, to pilgrims return, health to the sick, and salvation to the dying.

*Prayer in silence. Then the Priest says:*

Almighty ever-living God, comfort of mourners, strength of all who toil, may the prayers of those who cry out in any tribulation come before you, that all may rejoice, because in their hour of need your mercy was at hand. **Amen.**

## THE ADORATION OF THE HOLY CROSS

The priest says the following or similar words at each point of the unveiling of the veiled crucifix. The unveiling is done thrice.

**Priest:** This is the Wood of the Cross on which hung the Saviour of the world

**Congregation's Response:** Come and worship.

The priest and all those present will then procede with the adoration of the cross after the unveiling is done. The adoration can be by kissing, genuflecting or similar gesture.

## HOLY COMMUNION

*The congregation stands and the Priest says:*

At the Saviour's command and formed by divine teaching, we dare to say: Our Father, who art in heaven, hallowed be thy name...

## PRAYER AFTER COMMUNION

Almighty ever-living God, who have restored us to life by the blessed Death and Resurrection of your Christ, preserve in us the work of your mercy, that, by partaking of this mystery, we may have a life unceasingly devoted to you. Through Christ our Lord. **Amen.**

## PRAYER OVER THE PEOPLE

May abundant blessing, O Lord, we pray, descend upon your people, who have honoured the Death of your Son in the hope of their resurrection: may pardon come, comfort be given, holy faith increase, and everlasting redemption be made secure. Through Christ our Lord. **Amen.**

*And all, after genuflecting to the Cross, depart in silence.*

## LESSONS LEARNT FROM THE READINGS / HOMILY

1 _____ 2 _____

3 _____ 4 _____

5 _____ 6 _____

### ACTION POINTS FOR THE WEEK

1 _____ 2 _____

3 _____ 4 _____

5 _____ 6 _____

## PRAYER POINTS FOR THE WEEK

1 _____ 2 _____
3 _____ 4 _____
5 _____ 6 _____

## THIS WEEK, I AM GRATEFUL FOR

1 _____ 2 _____
3 _____ 4 _____
5 _____ 6 _____

# 03 APRIL 2021
## 9.5 *HOLY SATURDAY - EASTER VIGIL*

## THE SOLEMN BEGINNING OF THE VIGIL, OR LUCERNARIUM
### The Blessing of the Fire and Preparation of the Candle

*A blazing fire is prepared in a suitable place outside the church. When the people are gathered there, the Priest approaches with the ministers, one of whom carries the paschal candle. The processional cross and candles are not carried.*

*Where, however, a fire cannot be lit outside the church, the rite is carried out within the church and adapted appropriately.*

*All make the Sign of the Cross as the Priest says:*

In the name of the Father, and of the Son, and of the Holy Spirit.

*The people reply:* **Amen.**

*Either of the following is then taken by the priest:*

The grace of our Lord Jesus Christ, and the love of God, and the communion of the Holy Spirit be with you all.

*OR:*

Grace to you and peace from God our Father and the Lord Jesus Christ.

*Or:*

The Lord be with you.

*The people reply:* **And with your spirit.**

*The Priest briefly instructs the people about the night vigil in these or similar words:*

Dear brethren (brothers and sisters), on this most sacred night, in which our Lord Jesus Christ passed over from death to life, the Church calls upon her sons and daughters, scattered throughout the world, to come together to watch and pray. If we keep the memorial of the Lord's paschal solemnity in this way, listening to his word and celebrating his mysteries, then we shall have the sure hope of sharing his triumph over death and living with him in God.

*Then the Priest blesses the fire, saying with hands extended:*
O God, who through your Son bestowed upon upon the faithful the fire of your glory, sanctify + this new fire that, by these paschal celebrations, we may be so inflamed with heavenly desires, that with minds
made pure we may attain festivities of unending splendour. Through Christ our Lord. **Amen.**

*After the blessing of the new fire, one of the ministers brings the paschal candle to the Priest, who cuts a cross into the candle with a stylus. Then he makes the Greek letter Alpha above the cross, the letter Omega below, and the four numerals of the current year between the arms of the cross, saying meanwhile:*
**1.** Christ yesterday and today; *(he cuts a vertical line)*
**2.** the Beginning and the End; *(he cuts a horizontal line)*
**3.** the Alpha; *(he cuts the letter Alpha above the vertical line)*
**4.** and the Omega. *(he cuts the letter Omega below the vertical line)*
**5.** All time belongs to him; *(he cuts the first numeral of the current year in the upper left corner of the cross)*
**6.** and all the ages. *(he cuts the second numeral of the current year in the upper right corner of the cross)*
**7.** To him be glory and power *(he cuts the third numeral of the current year in the lower left corner of the cross)*
**8.** through every age and for ever. Amen. *(he cuts the fourth numeral of the current year in the lower right corner of the cross)*
*When the cutting of the cross and of the other signs has been completed, the Priest may insert five grains*
*of incense into the candle in the form of a cross, while saying:*
**1.** By his holy **2.** and glorious wounds,
**3.** may Christ the Lord **4.** guard us
**5.** and protect us. Amen.
*The Priest lights the paschal candle from the new fire, saying:*
May the light of Christ rising in glory

dispel the darkness of our hearts and minds.

## PROCESSION
*When the candle has been lit, one of the ministers takes burning coals from the fire and places them in the thurible, and the Priest puts incense into it in the usual way. The Deacon or, if there is no Deacon, another suitable minister, takes the paschal candle and a procession forms. The thurifer with the smoking thurible precedes the Deacon or other minister who carries the paschal candle. After them follows the Priest with the ministers and the people, all holding in their hands unlit candles.*
*At the door of the church the Deacon, standing and raising up the candle, sings:*
The Light of Christ.

*And all reply:* **Thanks be to God.**
*The Priest lights his candle from the flame of the paschal candle.*
*Then the Deacon moves forward to the middle of the church and, standing and raising up the candle, sings a second time:*
The Light of Christ.

*And all reply:* **Thanks be to God.**
*All light their candles from the flame of the paschal candle and continue in procession.*
*When the Deacon arrives before the altar, he stands facing the people, raises up the candle and sings a third time:*
The Light of Christ.

*And all reply:* **Thanks be to God.**
*Then the Deacon places the paschal candle on a large candlestand prepared next to the ambo or in the middle of the sanctuary.*
*And lights are lit throughout the church, except for the altar candles.*

## THE EASTER PROCLAMATION (EXULTET)
*Arriving at the altar, the Priest goes to his chair, gives his candle to a minister, puts incense into the thurible and blesses the incense as at the Gospel at Mass.*
*If the Exsultet is to be sung by a Deacon, the Deacon goes to the Priest and saying,* your blessing, Father, *asks for and receives a blessing from*

May the Lord be in your heart and on your lips, that you may proclaim his paschal praise worthily and well, in the name of the Father and of the Son, + and of the Holy Spirit
*The Deacon replies:* **Amen.**
*If the Exsultet is to be sung by a lay cantor, this dialogue is omitted, as are also the words in brackets* **[...]** *below.*

## THE EASTER PROCLAMATION (THE EXULTET)

Exult, let them exult, the hosts of heaven, **/**
exult, let Angel ministers of God exult, **/** let the trumpet of salvation **/** sound aloud our mighty King's triumph! **/** Be glad, let earth be glad, as glory floods her, **/** ablaze with light from her eternal King, **/** let all corners of the earth be glad, **/** knowing an end to gloom and darkness. **/** Rejoice, let Mother Church also rejoice, **/** arrayed with the lightning of his glory, **/** let this holy building shake with joy, **/** filled with the mighty voices of the peoples.

**[** Therefore, dearest friends, standing in the awesome glory of this holy light, **/** invoke with me, I ask you, **/** the mercy of God almighty, **/** that he, who has been pleased to number me, **/** though unworthy, among the Levites, **/** may pour into me his light unshadowed, **/** that I may sing this candle's perfect praises. **]**
**[** The Lord be with you. **]**
**[ And with your spirit. ]**
Lift up your hearts.
**We lift them up to the Lord.**
Let us give thanks to the Lord our God.
**It is right and just.**

It is truly right and just, **/** with ardent love of mind and heart **/** and with devoted service of our voice, **/** to acclaim our God invisible, the almighty Father, **/** and Jesus Christ, our Lord, his Son, his Only Begotten.

Who for our sake paid Adam's debt to the eternal Father, **/** and, pouring out his own dear Blood, **/** wiped clean the record of our ancient sinfulness.

These, then, are the feasts of Passover, / in which is slain the Lamb, the one true Lamb, / whose Blood anoints the doorposts of believers.

This is the night, / when once you led our forebears, Israel's children, / from slavery in Egypt / and made them pass dry-shod through the Red Sea.

This is the night / that with a pillar of fire / banished the darkness of sin.

This is the night / that even now, throughout the world, / sets Christian believers apart from worldly vices / and from the gloom of sin, / leading them to grace / and joining them to his holy ones.

This is the night, / when Christ broke the prison-bars of death / and rose victorious from the underworld.

Our birth would have been no gain, / had we not been redeemed. / O wonder of your humble care for us! / O love, O charity beyond all telling, / to ransom a slave you gave away your Son!

O truly necessary sin of Adam, / destroyed completely by the Death of Christ!

O happy fault / that earned so great, so glorious a Redeemer!
O truly blessed night, / worthy alone to know the time and hour / when Christ rose from the underworld!

This is the night / of which it is written: / The night shall be as bright as day, / dazzling is the night for me, / and full of gladness.

The sanctifying power of this night / dispels wickedness, washes faults away, / restores innocence to the fallen, and joy to mourners, /
drives out hatred, fosters concord, and brings down the mighty.

On this, your night of grace, O holy Father, / accept this candle, a solemn offering, / the work of bees and of your servants' hands, / an evening sacrifice of praise, / this gift from your most holy Church.

But now we know the praises of this pillar, / which glowing fire ignites for God's honour, / a fire into many flames divided, / yet never dimmed by sharing of its light, / for it is fed by melting wax, / drawn out by mother bees / to build a torch so precious.

O truly blessed night, / when things of heaven are wed to those of earth, / and divine to the human.

Therefore, O Lord, / we pray you that this candle, / hallowed to the honour of your name, / may persevere undimmed, / to overcome the darkness of this night. / Receive it as a pleasing fragrance, / and let it mingle with the lights of heaven. / May this flame be found still burning / by the Morning Star: / the one Morning Star who never sets, / Christ your Son, / who, coming back from death's domain, / has shed his peaceful light on humanity, / and lives and reigns for ever and ever. **Amen.**

*If the Exsultet is to be sung by a lay cantor, this dialogue is omitted, as are also the words in brackets [...] below.*

## LITURGY OF THE WORD

**FIRST READING**                    *Longer Form Genesis 1:1—2:2*

In the beginning, when God created the heavens and the earth, the earth was a formless wasteland, and darkness covered the abyss, while a mighty wind swept over the waters.

Then God said, "Let there be light," and there was light. God saw how good the light was. God then separated the light from the darkness. God called the light "day," and the darkness he called "night." Thus evening came, and morning followed—the first day.

Then God said, "Let there be a dome in the middle of the waters, to separate one body of water from the other." And so it happened: God made the dome, and it separated the water above the dome from the water below it. God called the dome "the sky." Evening came, and morning followed—the second day.

Then God said, "Let the water under the sky be gathered into a single basin, so that the dry land may appear." And so it happened: the water under the sky was gathered into its basin, and the dry land appeared. God called the dry land "the earth," and the basin of the water he called "the sea." God saw how good it was.

Then God said, "Let the earth bring forth vegetation: every kind of plant that bears seed and every kind of fruit tree on earth that bears fruit with its seed in it." And so it happened: the earth brought forth every kind of plant that bears seed and every kind of fruit tree on earth that bears fruit with its seed in it. God saw how good it was. Evening came, and morning followed—the third day.

Then God said: "Let there be lights in the dome of the sky, to separate day from night. Let them mark the fixed times, the days and the years, and serve as luminaries in the dome of the sky, to shed light upon the earth." And so it happened: God made the two great lights, the greater one to govern the day, and the lesser one to govern the night; and he made the stars. God set them in the dome of the sky, to shed light upon the earth, to govern the day and the night, and to separate the light from the darkness. God saw how good it was. Evening came, and morning followed—the fourth day.

Then God said, "Let the water teem with an abundance of living creatures, and on the earth let birds fly beneath the dome of the sky." And so it happened: God created the great sea monsters and all kinds of swimming creatures with which the water teems, and all kinds of winged birds. God saw how good it was, and God blessed them, saying, "Be fertile, multiply, and fill the water of the seas; and let the birds multiply on the earth." Evening came, and morning followed—the fifth day.

Then God said, "Let the earth bring forth all kinds of living creatures: cattle, creeping things, and wild animals of all kinds." And so it happened: God made all kinds of wild animals, all kinds of cattle, and all kinds of creeping things of the earth. God saw how good it was.

Then God said: "Let us make man in our image, after our likeness. Let them have dominion over the fish of the sea, the birds of the air, and the cattle, and over all the wild animals and all the creatures that crawl on the ground." God created man in his image; in the image of God he created him; male and female he created them. God blessed them, saying: "Be fertile and multiply; fill the earth and subdue it. Have dominion over the fish of the sea, the birds of the air, and all the living things that move on the earth." God also said: "See, I give you every seed–bearing plant all over the earth and every tree that has seed–bearing fruit on it to be your food; and to all the animals of the land, all the birds of the air, and all the living creatures that crawl on the ground, I give all the green plants for food." And so it happened. God looked at everything he had made, and he found it very good. Evening came, and morning followed—the sixth day.

Thus the heavens and the earth and all their array were completed. Since on the seventh day God was finished with the work he had been doing, he rested on the seventh day from all the work he had undertaken.

## OR: *Shorter Form*              *Genesis 1:1, 26—31a*

In the beginning, when God created the heavens and the earth, God said: "Let us make man in our image, after our likeness. Let them have dominion over the fish of the sea, the birds of the air, and the cattle, and over all the wild animals and all the creatures that crawl on the ground." God created man in his image; in the image of God he created him; male and female he created them. God blessed them, saying: "Be fertile and multiply; fill the earth and subdue it. Have dominion over the fish of the sea, the birds of the air, and all the living things that move on the earth."

God also said: "See, I give you every seed—bearing plant all over the earth and every tree that has seed—bearing fruit on it to be your food; and to all the animals of the land, all the birds of the air, and all the living creatures that crawl on the ground, I give all the green plants for food." And so it happened. God looked at everything he had made, and found it very good.

## PSALM EITHER:       *Psalm 104:1—2,5—6, 10, 12, 13—14, 24, 35 (30)*

**R. Lord, send out your Spirit, and renew the face of the earth.**

Bless the LORD, O my soul! / O LORD, my God, you are great indeed! / You are clothed with majesty and glory, / robed in light as with a cloak. **R.**
You fixed the earth upon its foundation, / not to be moved forever; / with the ocean, as with a garment, you covered it; / above the mountains the waters stood. **R.**
You send forth springs into the watercourses / that wind among the mountains. / Beside them the birds of heaven dwell; / from among the branches they send forth their song **R.**
You water the mountains from your palace; / the earth is replete with the fruit of your works. / You raise grass for the cattle, / and vegetation for man's use, / producing bread from the earth. **R.**

How manifold are your works, O LORD! / In wisdom you have wrought them all— / the earth is full of your creatures. / Bless the LORD, O my soul! **R.**

OR: Psalm 33:4—5, 6—7, 12—13, 20, 22
**R. The earth is full of the goodness of the Lord.**
Upright is the word of the LORD, / and all his works are trustworthy. / He loves justice and right; / of the kindness of the LORD the earth is full. **R.**
By the word of the LORD the heavens were made; / by the breath of his mouth all their host. / He gathers the waters of the sea as in a flask; / in cellars he confines the deep. **R.**
Blessed the nation whose God is the LORD, / the people he has chosen for his own inheritance. / From heaven the LORD looks down; / he sees all mankind. **R.**
Our soul waits for the LORD, / who is our help and our shield. / May your kindness, O LORD, be upon us / who have put our hope in you. **R.**
*Let us pray.*
Almighty ever-living God, who are wonderful in the ordering of all your works, may those you have redeemed understand that there exists nothing more marvellous than the world's creation in the beginning except that, at the end of the ages, Christ our Passover has been sacrificed. Who lives and reigns for ever and ever. **Amen.**

*OR:* O God, who wonderfully created human nature and still more wonderfully redeemed it, grant us, we pray, to set our minds against the enticements of sin, that we may merit to attain eternal joys. Through Christ our Lord. **Amen.**

**SECOND READING EITHER:** *Genesis 22:1—18*
God put Abraham to the test. He called to him, "Abraham!" "Here I am," he replied. Then God said: "Take your son Isaac, your only one, whom you love, and go to the land of Moriah. There you shall offer him up as a holocaust on a height that I will point out to you." Early the next morning Abraham saddled his donkey, took with him his son Isaac and two of his servants as well, and with the wood that he had cut for the holocaust, set out for the place of which God had told him.

On the third day Abraham got sight of the place from afar. Then he said to his servants: "Both of you stay here with the donkey, while the boy and I go on over yonder. We will worship and then come back to you." Thereupon Abraham took the wood for the holocaust and laid it on his son Isaac's shoulders, while he himself carried the fire and the knife. As the two walked on together, Isaac spoke to his father Abraham: "Father!" Isaac said. "Yes, son," he replied. Isaac continued, "Here are the fire and the wood, but where is the sheep for the holocaust?" "Son," Abraham answered, "God himself will provide the sheep for the holocaust." Then the two continued going forward.

When they came to the place of which God had told him, Abraham built an altar there and arranged the wood on it. Next he tied up his son Isaac, and put him on top of the wood on the altar. Then he reached out and took the knife to slaughter his son. But the LORD's messenger called to him from heaven, "Abraham, Abraham!" "Here I am," he answered. "Do not lay your hand on the boy," said the messenger. "Do not do the least thing to him. I know now how devoted you are to God, since you did not withhold from me your own beloved son." As Abraham looked about, he spied a ram caught by its horns in the thicket. So he went and took the ram and offered it up as a holocaust in place of his son. Abraham named the site Yahweh–yireh; hence people now say, "On the mountain the LORD will see."

Again the LORD's messenger called to Abraham from heaven and said: "I swear by myself, declares the Lord, that because you acted as you did in not withholding from me your beloved son, I will bless you abundantly and make your descendants as countless as the stars of the sky and the sands of the seashore; your descendants shall take possession of the gates of their enemies, and in your descendants all the nations of the earth shall find blessing— all this because you obeyed my command."

**OR:**                                    *Genesis 22:1—2, 9a, 10—13, 15—18*
God put Abraham to the test. He called to him, "Abraham!" "Here I am," he replied. Then God said: "Take your son Isaac, your only one, whom you love, and go to the land of Moriah. There you shall offer him up as a holocaust on a height that I will point out to you."

When they came to the place of which God had told him, Abraham built an altar there and arranged the wood on it. Then he reached out and took the knife to slaughter his son. But the Lord's messenger called to him from heaven, "Abraham, Abraham!" "Here I am," he answered. "Do not lay your hand on the boy," said the messenger. "Do not do the least thing to him. I know now how devoted you are to God, since you did not withhold from me your own beloved son." As Abraham looked about, he spied a ram caught by its horns in the thicket. So he went and took the ram and offered it up as a holocaust in place of his son.

Again the LORD's messenger called to Abraham from heaven and said: "I swear by myself, declares the LORD, that because you acted as you did in not withholding from me your beloved son, I will bless you abundantly and make your descendants as countless as the stars of the sky and the sands of the seashore; your descendants shall take possession of the gates of their enemies, and in your descendants all the nations of the earth shall find blessing— all this because you obeyed my command."

**PSALM**                                   *Psalm 16:5, 8, 9—10, 11*
**R. You are my inheritance, O Lord.**
O LORD, my allotted portion and my cup, / you it is who hold fast my lot. / I set the Lord ever before me; / with him at my right hand I shall not be disturbed. **R.**
Therefore my heart is glad and my soul rejoices, / my body, too, abides in confidence; / because you will not abandon my soul to the netherworld, / nor will you suffer your faithful one to undergo corruption. **R.**
You will show me the path to life, / fullness of joys in your presence, / the delights at your right hand forever. **R.**
**Let us pray.**
O God, supreme Father of the faithful, who increase the children of your promise by pouring out the grace of adoption throughout the whole world and who through the Paschal Mystery make your servant Abraham father of nations, as once you swore, grant, we pray, that your peoples may enter worthily into the grace to which you call them. Through Christ our Lord. **Amen.**

**THIRD READING**                           *Exodus 14:15—15:1*
The Lord said to Moses, "Why are you crying out to me? Tell the Israelites to go forward. And you, lift up your staff and, with hand outstretched over the sea, split the sea in two, that the Israelites may pass through it on dry land. But I will make the Egyptians so obstinate that they will go in after them. Then I will receive glory through Pharaoh and all his army, his chariots and charioteers. The Egyptians shall know that I am the LORD, when I receive glory through Pharaoh and his chariots and charioteers."

The angel of God, who had been leading Israel's camp, now moved and went around behind them. The column of cloud also, leaving the front, took up its place behind them, so that it came between the camp of the Egyptians and that of Israel. But the cloud now became dark, and thus the night passed without the rival camps coming any closer together all night long. Then Moses stretched out his hand over the sea, and the LORD swept the sea with a strong east wind throughout the night and so turned it into dry land. When the water was thus divided, the Israelites marched into the midst of the sea on dry land, with the water like a wall to their right and to their left.

The Egyptians followed in pursuit; all Pharaoh's horses and chariots and charioteers went after them right into the midst of the sea. In the night watch just before dawn the LORD cast through the column of the fiery cloud upon the Egyptian force a glance that threw it into a panic; and he so clogged their chariot wheels that they could hardly drive. With that the Egyptians sounded the retreat before Israel, because the LORD was fighting for them against the Egyptians. Then the LORD told Moses, "Stretch out your hand over the sea, that the water may flow back upon the Egyptians, upon their chariots and their charioteers." So Moses stretched out his hand over the sea, and at dawn the sea flowed back to its normal depth. The Egyptians were fleeing head on toward the sea, when the LORD hurled them into its midst. As the water flowed back, it covered the chariots and the charioteers of Pharaoh's whole army which had followed the Israelites into the sea. Not a single one of them escaped. But the Israelites had marched on dry land through the midst of the sea, with the water like a wall to their right and to their left. Thus the LORD saved Israel on that day from the power of the Egyptians. When Israel saw the Egyptians lying dead on the seashore and beheld the great power that the LORD had shown against the Egyptians, they feared the LORD and believed in him and in his servant Moses.

Then Moses and the Israelites sang this song to the LORD: I will sing to the LORD, for he is gloriously triumphant; horse and chariot he has cast into the sea.

**CANTICLE**                    *Exodus 15:1—2, 3—4, 5—6, 17—18*
**R. Let us sing to the Lord; he has covered himself in glory.**
I will sing to the LORD, for he is gloriously triumphant; / horse and chariot he has cast into the sea. / My strength and my courage is the LORD, / and

he has been my savior. / He is my God, I praise him; / the God of my father, I extol him. **R.**

The LORD is a warrior, / LORD is his name! / Pharaoh's chariots and army he hurled into the sea; / the elite of his officers were submerged in the Red Sea. **R.**

The flood waters covered them, / they sank into the depths like a stone. / Your right hand, O LORD, magnificent in power, / your right hand, O LORD, has shattered the enemy. **R.**

You brought in the people you redeemed / and planted them on the mountain of your inheritanc— / the place where you made your seat, O LORD, / the sanctuary, LORD, which your hands established. / The LORD shall reign forever and ever. **R.**

**Let us pray.**
O God, whose ancient wonders remain undimmed in splendour even in our day, for what you once bestowed on a single people, freeing them from Pharaoh's persecution by the power of your right hand now you bring about as the salvation of the nations through the waters of rebirth, grant, we pray, that the whole world may become children of Abraham and inherit the dignity of Israel's birthright. Through Christ our Lord. **Amen.**

*OR:*
O God, who by the light of the New Testament have unlocked the meaning of wonders worked in former times, so that the Red Sea prefigures the sacred font and the nation delivered from slavery foreshadows the Christian people, grant, we pray, that all nations, obtaining the privilege of Israel by merit of faith, may be reborn by partaking of your Spirit. Through Christ our Lord. **Amen.**

**FOURTH READING**                                  *Isaiah 54:5—14*
The One who has become your husband is your Maker; his name is the LORD of hosts; your redeemer is the Holy One of Israel, called God of all the earth. The LORD calls you back, like a wife forsaken and grieved in spirit, a wife married in youth and then cast off, says your God. For a brief moment I abandoned you, but with great tenderness I will take you back. In an outburst of wrath, for a moment I hid my face from you; but with enduring love I take pity on you, says the LORD, your redeemer. This is for

me like the days of Noah, when I swore that the waters of Noah should never again deluge the earth; so I have sworn not to be angry with you, or to rebuke you. Though the mountains leave their place and the hills be shaken, my love shall never leave you nor my covenant of peace be shaken, says the LORD, who has mercy on you. O afflicted one, storm–battered and unconsoled, I lay your pavements in carnelians, and your foundations in sapphires; I will make your battlements of rubies, your gates of carbuncles, and all your walls of precious stones. All your children shall be taught by the LORD, and great shall be the peace of your children. In justice shall you be established, far from the fear of oppression, where destruction cannot come near you.

## PSALM                                   *Psalm 30:2, 4, 5—6, 11—12, 13*

**R. I will praise you, Lord, for you have rescued me.**

I will extol you, O LORD, for you drew me clear **/** and did not let my enemies rejoice over me. **/** O LORD, you brought me up from the netherworld; **/** you preserved me from among those going down into the pit. **R.**

Sing praise to the LORD, you his faithful ones, **/** and give thanks to his holy name. **/** For his anger lasts but a moment; **/** a lifetime, his good will. **/** At nightfall, weeping enters in, **/** but with the dawn, rejoicing. **R.**

Hear, O LORD, and have pity on me; **/** O LORD, be my helper. **/** You changed my mourning into dancing; **/** O LORD, my God, forever will I give you thanks. **R.**

**Let us pray.**

Almighty ever-living God, surpass, for the honour of your name, what you pledged to the Patriarchs by reason of their faith, and through sacred adoption increase the children of your promise, so that what the Saints of old never doubted would come to pass your Church may now see in great part fulfilled. Through Christ our Lord. **Amen.**

## FIFTH READING                                   *Isaiah 55:1—11*

Thus says the LORD: All you who are thirsty, come to the water! You who have no money, come, receive grain and eat; come, without paying and without cost, drink wine and milk! Why spend your money for what is not bread, your wages for what fails to satisfy? Heed me, and you shall eat well, you shall delight in rich fare. Come to me heedfully, listen, that you may have life. I will renew with you the everlasting covenant, the benefits assured to David. As I made him a witness to the peoples, a leader and commander of nations, so shall you summon a nation you knew not, and nations that knew you not shall run to you, because of the LORD, your God, the Holy One of Israel, who has glorified you.

Seek the LORD while he may be found, call him while he is near. Let the scoundrel forsake his way, and the wicked man his thoughts; let him turn to the LORD for mercy; to our God, who is generous in forgiving. For my thoughts are not your thoughts, nor are your ways my ways, says the LORD. As high as the heavens are above the earth, so high are my ways above your ways and my thoughts above your thoughts.

For just as from the heavens the rain and snow come down and do not return there till they have watered the earth, making it fertile and fruitful, giving seed to the one who sows and bread to the one who eats, so shall my word be that goes forth from my mouth; my word shall not return to me void, but shall do my will, achieving the end for which I sent it.

**CANTICLE** *Isaiah 12:2—3, 4, 5—6*
**R. You will draw water joyfully from the springs of salvation.**
God indeed is my savior; **/** I am confident and unafraid. **/** My strength and my courage is the LORD, **/** and he has been my savior. **/** With joy you will draw water **/** at the fountain of salvation. **R.**
Give thanks to the LORD, acclaim his name; **/** among the nations make known his deeds, **/** proclaim how exalted is his name. **R.**
Sing praise to the LORD for his glorious achievement; **/** let this be known throughout all the earth. **/** Shout with exultation, O city of Zion, **/** for great in your midst **/** is the Holy One of Israel! **R.**
**LET US PRAY.**
Almighty ever-living God, sole hope of the world, who by the preaching of your Prophets unveiled the mysteries of this present age, graciously increase the longing of your people, for only at the prompting of your grace do the faithful progress in any kind of virtue. Through Christ our Lord. **Amen.**

**SIXTH READING** *Baruch 3:9—15, 32—4:4*
Hear, O Israel, the commandments of life: listen, and know prudence! How is it, Israel, that you are in the land of your foes, grown old in a foreign land, defiled with the dead, accounted with those destined for the

netherworld? You have forsaken the fountain of wisdom! Had you walked in the way of God, you would have dwelt in enduring peace. Learn where prudence is, where strength, where understanding; that you may know also where are length of days, and life, where light of the eyes, and peace. Who has found the place of wisdom, who has entered into her treasuries?

The One who knows all things knows her; he has probed her by his knowledge— the One who established the earth for all time, and filled it with four–footed beasts; he who dismisses the light, and it departs, calls it, and it obeys him trembling; before whom the stars at their posts shine and rejoice; when he calls them, they answer, "Here we are!" shining with joy for their Maker. Such is our God; no other is to be compared to him: he has traced out the whole way of understanding, and has given her to Jacob, his servant, to Israel, his beloved son.

Since then she has appeared on earth, and moved among people. She is the book of the precepts of God, the law that endures forever; all who cling to her will live, but those will die who forsake her. Turn, O Jacob, and receive her: walk by her light toward splendor. Give not your glory to another, your privileges to an alien race. Blessed are we, O Israel; for what pleases God is known to us!

## RESPONSORIAL PSALM                     *Psalm 19:8, 9, 10, 11*
**R. Lord, you have the words of everlasting life.**
The law of the LORD is perfect, / refreshing the soul; / the decree of the LORD is trustworthy, / giving wisdom to the simple. **R.**
The precepts of the LORD are right, / rejoicing the heart; / the command of the LORD is clear, / enlightening the eye. **R.**
The fear of the LORD is pure, / enduring forever; / the ordinances of the LORD are true, / all of them just. **R.**
They are more precious than gold, / than a heap of purest gold; / sweeter also than syrup / or honey from the comb. **R.**
**LET US PRAY.**
O God, who constantly increase your Church by your call to the nations, graciously grant to those you wash clean in the waters of Baptism the assurance of your unfailing protection. Through Christ our Lord. **Amen.**

## SEVENTH READING                     *Ezekiel 36:16—17a, 18—28*
The word of the LORD came to me, saying: Son of man, when the house of Israel lived in their land, they defiled it by their conduct and deeds.

Therefore I poured out my fury upon them because of the blood that they poured out on the ground, and because they defiled it with idols. I scattered them among the nations, dispersing them over foreign lands; according to their conduct and deeds I judged them. But when they came among the nations wherever they came, they served to profane my holy name, because it was said of them: "These are the people of the LORD, yet they had to leave their land." So I have relented because of my holy name which the house of Israel profaned among the nations where they came. Therefore say to the house of Israel: Thus says the Lord GOD: Not for your sakes do I act, house of Israel, but for the sake of my holy name, which you profaned among the nations to which you came. I will prove the holiness of my great name, profaned among the nations, in whose midst you have profaned it. Thus the nations shall know that I am the Lord, says the LORD GOD, when in their sight I prove my holiness through you. For I will take you away from among the nations, gather you from all the foreign lands, and bring you back to your own land. I will sprinkle clean water upon you to cleanse you from all your impurities, and from all your idols I will cleanse you. I will give you a new heart and place a new spirit within you, taking from your bodies your stony hearts and giving you natural hearts. I will put my spirit within you and make you live by my statutes, careful to observe my decrees. You shall live in the land I gave your fathers; you shall be my people, and I will be your God.

**RESPONSORIAL PSALM**                                    *Psalm 42:3, 5; 43:3, 4*
*This psalm is to be used when baptism is celebrated.*
**R. Like a deer that longs for running streams, my soul longs for you, my God.**
Athirst is my soul for God, the living God. / When shall I go and behold the face of God? **R.**
I went with the throng / and led them in procession to the house of God, / amid loud cries of joy and thanksgiving, / with the multitude keeping festival. **R.**
Send forth your light and your fidelity; / they shall lead me on / and bring me to your holy mountain, / to your dwelling–place. **R.**
Then will I go in to the altar of God, / the God of my gladness and joy; / then will I give you thanks upon the harp, / O God, my God! **R.**

*This following psalm is to be used when there is no baptism.*

*Isaiah* 12:2—3, 4bcd, 5—6

**R. You will draw water joyfully from the springs of salvation.**

God indeed is my savior; / I am confident and unafraid. / My strength and my courage is the LORD, / and he has been my savior. / With joy you will draw water / at the fountain of salvation. **R.**

Give thanks to the LORD, acclaim his name; / among the nations make known his deeds, / proclaim how exalted is his name. **R.**

Sing praise to the LORD for his glorious achievement; / let this be known throughout all the earth. / Shout with exultation, O city of Zion, / for great in your midst / is the Holy One of Israel! **R.**

*OR:* *Psalm 51:12—13, 14—15, 18—19*

*This following psalm is to be used when there is no baptism.*

**R. Create a clean heart in me, O God.**

A clean heart create for me, O God, / and a steadfast spirit renew within me. / Cast me not out from your presence, / and your Holy Spirit take not from me. **R.**

Give me back the joy of your salvation, / and a willing spirit sustain in me. / I will teach transgressors your ways, / and sinners shall return to you. **R.**

For you are not pleased with sacrifices; / should I offer a holocaust, you would not accept it. / My sacrifice, O God, is a contrite spirit; / a heart contrite and humbled, O God, you will not spurn. **R**

**LET US PRAY.**

O God of unchanging power and eternal light, look with favour on the wondrous mystery of the whole Church and serenely accomplish the work of human salvation, which you planned from all eternity; may the whole world know and see that what was cast down is raised up, what had become old is made new, and all things are restored to integrity through Christ, just as by him they came into being. Who lives and reigns for ever and ever. **Amen.**

*OR:*

O God, who by the pages of both Testaments instruct and prepare us to celebrate the Paschal Mystery, grant that we may comprehend your mercy, so that the gifts we receive from you this night may confirm our hope of the gifts to come. Through Christ our Lord. **Amen.**

*At this point, the altar candles are lit.*

## THE GLORIA

*During the Gloria bells are rung, according to local custom.*

**LET US PRAY.**

O God, who make this most sacred night radiant with the glory of the Lord's Resurrection, stir up in your Church a spirit of adoption, so that, renewed in body and mind, we may render you undivided service. Through our Lord Jesus Christ, your Son, who lives and reigns with you in the unity of the Holy Spirit, one God, for ever and ever. **Amen.**

**EPISTLE**                                                    *Romans 6:3—11*

Brothers and sisters: Are you unaware that we who were baptized into Christ Jesus were baptized into his death? We were indeed buried with him through baptism into death, so that, just as Christ was raised from the dead by the glory of the Father, we too might live in newness of life.

For if we have grown into union with him through a death like his, we shall also be united with him in the resurrection. We know that our old self was crucified with him, so that our sinful body might be done away with, that we might no longer be in slavery to sin. For a dead person has been absolved from sin. If, then, we have died with Christ, we believe that we shall also live with him. We know that Christ, raised from the dead, dies no more; death no longer has power over him. As to his death, he died to sin once and for all; as to his life, he lives for God. Consequently, you too must think of yourselves as being dead to sin and living for God in Christ Jesus.

**PSALM**                                          *Psalm 118:1 – 2, 16 – 17, 22 – 23*

**R. Alleluia, alleluia, alleluia.**

Give thanks to the LORD, for he is good, **/** for his mercy endures forever. **/** Let the house of Israel say, **/** "His mercy endures forever." **R.**

"The right hand of the LORD has struck with power; **/** the right hand of the LORD is exalted. **/** I shall not die, but live, **/** and declare the works of the LORD." **R.**

The stone which the builders rejected **/** has become the cornerstone. **/** By the LORD has this been done; **/** it is wonderful in our eyes. **R.**

**GOSPEL**                                                    *Mark 16:1–7*

When the sabbath was over, Mary Magdalene, Mary, the mother of James, and Salome bought spices so that they might go and anoint him.

Very early when the sun had risen, on the first day of the week, they came to the tomb. They were saying to one another, "Who will roll back the stone for us from the entrance to the tomb?" When they looked up, they saw that the stone had been rolled back; it was very large. On entering the tomb they saw a young man sitting on the right side, clothed in a white robe, and they were utterly amazed. He said to them, "Do not be amazed! You seek Jesus of Nazareth, the crucified. He has been raised; he is not here. Behold the place where they laid him. But go and tell his disciples and Peter, 'He is going before you to Galilee; there you will see him, as he told you.'"

**THE HOMILY**

## 9.6  *THE BAPTISMAL LITURGY*

### When there is no baptism

*If no one present is to be baptized and the font is not to be blessed, the Priest introduces the faithful to the blessing of water, saying:*
Dear brothers and sisters, let us humbly beseech
the Lord our God to bless this water he has created, which will be sprinkled upon us as a memorial of our Baptism. May he graciously renew us, that we may remain faithful to the Spirit whom we have received.

***And after a brief pause in silence, he proclaims the following prayer, with hands extended:***
Lord our God, in your mercy be present to your people who keep vigil on this most sacred night, and, for us who recall the wondrous work of our creation and the still greater work of our redemption, graciously bless this water. For you
created water to make the fields fruitful and to refresh and cleanse our bodies. You also made water the instrument of your mercy: for through water you freed your people from slavery and quenched their thirst in the desert; through water the Prophets proclaimed the new covenant you were to enter upon with the human race; and last of all, through water, which Christ made holy in the Jordan, you have renewed our corrupted nature in the bath of regeneration.
Therefore, may this water be for us a memorial of the Baptism we have

received, and grant that we may share in the gladness of our brothers and sisters, who at Easter have received their Baptism. Through Christ our Lord. **Amen.**

## THE RENEWAL OF BAPTISMAL PROMISES

*All stand, holding lighted candles in their hands, and renew the promise of baptismal faith, unless this has already been done together with those to be baptized.*

*The Priest addresses the faithful in these or similar words:*

Dear brethren (brothers and sisters), through the Paschal Mystery we have been buried with Christ in Baptism, so that we may walk with him in newness of life. And so, now that our Lenten observance is concluded, let us renew the promises of Holy Baptism, by which we once renounced Satan and his works and promised to serve God in the holy Catholic Church. And so I ask you:

Do you renounce Satan? **I do.**

And all his works? **I do.**

And all his empty show? **I do.**

*OR:*

Do you renounce sin, so as to live in the freedom of the children of God?

**I do.**

Do you renounce the lure of evil, so that sin may have no mastery over you? **I do.**

Do you renounce Satan, the author and prince of sin?

**I do.**

*Then the Priest continues:*

Do you believe in God, the Father almighty, Creator of heaven and earth?

**I do.**

Do you believe in Jesus Christ, his only Son, our Lord, who was born of the Virgin Mary, suffered death and was buried, rose again from the dead and is seated at the right hand of the Father? **I do.**

Do you believe in the Holy Spirit, the holy Catholic Church, the communion of saints, the forgiveness of sins, the resurrection of the body, and life everlasting? **I do.**

And may almighty God, the Father of our Lord Jesus Christ, who has given us new birth by water and the Holy Spirit and bestowed on us forgiveness of our sins, keep us by his grace, in

Christ Jesus our Lord, for eternal life. **Amen.**

*The Priest sprinkles the people with the blessed water, while all sing:*
I saw water flowing from the Temple, from its right-hand side, alleluia; and all to whom this water came were saved and shall say: Alleluia, alleluia.
*Another chant that is baptismal in character may also be sung.*

### The Prayer of the Faithful (Bidding Prayers)

## WHEN THERE IS A BAPTISM

*After the Homily the Baptismal Liturgy begins. The Priest goes with the ministers to the baptismal font, if this can be seen by the faithful. Otherwise a vessel with water is placed in the sanctuary.*

*Catechumens, if there are any, are called forward and presented by their godparents in front of the assembled Church or, if they are small children, are carried by their parents and godparents.*

*Then, if there is to be a procession to the baptistery or to the font, it forms immediately. A minister with the paschal candle leads off, and those to be baptized follow him with their godparents, then the ministers, the Deacon, and the Priest. During the procession, the Litany is sung. When the Litany is completed, the Priest addresses the people.*

*If, however, the Baptismal Liturgy takes place in the sanctuary, the Priest addresses the people first, in these or similar words, and the Litany follows.*

*If there are candidates to be baptized:*
Dearly beloved, with one heart and one soul, let us by our prayers come to the aid of these our brothers and sisters in their blessed hope, so that, as they approach the font of rebirth, the almighty Father may bestow on them all his merciful help.

*If the font is to be blessed, but no one is to be baptized:*
Dearly beloved, let us humbly invoke upon this font the grace of God the almighty Father, that those who from it are born anew may be numbered among the children of adoption in Christ.

# THE LITANY

*The Litany is sung by two cantors, with all standing (because it is Easter Time) and responding. In the Litany the names of some Saints may be added, especially the Titular Saint of the church and the Patron Saints of the place and of those to be baptized.*

| | |
|---|---|
| Lord, have mercy.    – | **Lord, have mercy.** |
| Christ, have mercy.    – | **Christ, have mercy.** |
| Lord, have mercy. – | **Lord, have mercy.** |
| Holy Mary, Mother of God, – | **pray for us.** |
| Saint Michael, – | **pray for us.** |
| Holy angels of God, – | **pray for us.** |
| Saint John the Baptist, – | **pray for us.** |
| Saint Joseph, – | **pray for us.** |
| Saint Peter and Saint Paul, – | **pray for us.** |
| Saint Andrew, – | **pray for us.** |
| Saint John, – | **pray for us.** |
| Saint Mary Magdalene, – | **pray for us.** |
| Saint Stephen, – | **pray for us.** |
| Saint Ignatius, – | **pray for us.** |
| Saint Laurence, – | **pray for us.** |
| Saint Perpetua and Saint Felicity, – | **pray for us.** |
| Saint Agnes, – | **pray for us.** |
| Saint Gregory, – | **pray for us.** |
| Saint Augustine, – | **pray for us.** |
| Saint Athanasius, – | **pray for us.** |
| Saint Basil, – | **pray for us.** |
| Saint Martin, – | **pray for us.** |
| Saint Benedict, – | **pray for us.** |
| Saint Francis and Saint Dominic, – | **pray for us.** |
| Saint Francis Xavier, – | **pray for us.** |
| Saint John Vianney, – | **pray for us.** |
| Saint Teresa, – | **pray for us.** |
| All holy men and women, – | **pray for us.** |
| Lord, be merciful: – | **Lord, save your people.** |
| From all evil, – | **Lord, save your people.** |
| From every sin, – | **Lord, save your people.** |
| From everlasting death, – | **Lord, save your people.** |
| By your coming as man, – | **Lord, save your people.** |

| | |
|---|---|
| By your death and rising to new life, – | **Lord, save your people.** |
| By your gift of the Holy Spirit, – | **Lord, save your people.** |
| Be merciful to us sinners: – | **Lord, save your people.** |

Give new life to these chosen ones by the grace of baptism: –

**Lord, hear our prayer.**

| | |
|---|---|
| Jesus, Son of the living God, – | **Lord, hear our prayer.** |
| Christ, hear us. – | **Christ, hear us.** |
| Lord Jesus, hear our prayer. – | **Lord Jesus, hear our prayer.** |

## The Blessing of Water

*The Priest then blesses the baptismal water, saying*
*the following prayer with hands extended:*

O God, who by invisible power accomplish a wondrous effect through sacramental signs and who in many ways have prepared water, your creation, to show forth the grace of Baptism;

O God, whose Spirit in the first moments of the world's creation hovered over the waters, so that the very substance of water would even then take to itself the power to sanctify;

O God, who by the outpouring of the flood foreshadowed regeneration, so that from the mystery of one and the same element of water would come an end to vice and a beginning of virtue;

O God, who caused the children of Abraham to pass dry-shod through the Red Sea, so that the chosen people, set free from slavery to Pharaoh, would prefigure the people of the baptized;

O God, whose Son, baptized by John in the waters of the Jordan, was anointed with the Holy Spirit, and, as he hung upon the Cross, gave forth water from his side along with blood, and after his Resurrection, commanded his disciples: "Go forth, teach all nations, baptizing them in the name of the Father and of the Son and of the Holy Spirit," look now, we pray, upon the face of your Church and graciously unseal for her the fountain of Baptism.

May this water receive by the Holy Spirit the grace of your Only Begotten Son, so that human nature, created in your image and washed clean through the Sacrament of Baptism from all the squalor of the life of old, may be found worthy to rise to the life of newborn children through water and the Holy Spirit.

***If appropriate, he lowers the paschal candle into the water either once or three times as he continues:***
May the power of the Holy Spirit, O Lord, we pray, come down through your Son into the fullness of this font,
*Holding the candle in the water, he continues:*
so that all who have been buried with Christ by Baptism into death may rise again to life with him. Who lives and reigns with you in the unity of the Holy Spirit, one God, for ever and ever. **Amen.**
*Then the candle is lifted out of the water, as the people acclaim:*
**Springs of water, bless the Lord; praise and exalt him above all for ever.**
*After the blessing of baptismal water and the acclamation of the people, the baptism or baptisms take place.*

## THE RENEWAL OF BAPTISMAL PROMISE
*Please use the Renewal of Baptismal Promise given on page **130** above.*

## PRAYER OVER THE OFFERINGS
Accept, we ask, O Lord, the prayers of your people with the sacrificial offerings, that what has begun in the paschal mysteries may, by the working of your power, bring us to the healing of eternity. Through Christ our Lord.

## COMMUNION ANTIPHON                    1Corinthians 5: 7 – 8
Christ our Passover has been sacrificed; therefore let us keep the feast with the unleavened bread of purity and truth, alleluia.

## PRAYER AFTER COMMUNION
Pour out on us, O Lord, the Spirit of your love, and in your kindness make those you have nourished by this paschal Sacrament one in mind and heart. Through Christ our Lord. **Amen.**

## LESSONS LEARNT FROM THE READINGS / HOMILY

| 1 | 2 |
|---|---|
| 3 | 4 |
| 5 | 6 |

## ACTION POINTS FOR THE WEEK

1 _____ 2 _____
3 _____ 4 _____
5 _____ 6 _____

## PRAYER POINTS FOR THE WEEK

1 _____ 2 _____
3 _____ 4 _____
5 _____ 6 _____

## THIS WEEK, I AM GRATEFUL FOR

1 _____ 2 _____
3 _____ 4 _____
5 _____ 6 _____

# 04 APRIL 2021, EASTER SUNDAY

**ENTRANCE ANTIPHON**                          Cf. Ps 138: 18, 5 – 6

I have risen, and I am with you still, alleluia. You have laid your hand upon me, alleluia. Too wonderful for me, this knowledge, alleluia, alleluia.

**OR**                          Lk 24: 34; Cf. Rv 1:6

The Lord is truly risen, alleluia. To him be glory and power for all the ages of eternity, alleluia, alleluia.

**COLLECT**

O God, who on this day, through your Only Begotten Son, have conquered death and unlocked for us the path to eternity, grant, we pray, that we who keep the solemnity of the Lord's Resurrection may, through the renewal brought by your Spirit, rise up in the light of life. Through our Lord Jesus Christ, your Son, who lives and reigns with you in the unity of the Holy Spirit, one God, for ever and ever.

**FIRST READING**                          *Acts 10:34a, 37—43*

Peter proceeded to speak and said: "You know what has happened all over Judea, beginning in Galilee after the baptism that John preached, how God anointed Jesus of Nazareth with the Holy Spirit and power. He went about doing good and healing all those oppressed by the devil, for God was with him. We are witnesses of all that he did both in the country of the Jews and in Jerusalem. They put him to death by hanging him on a tree. This man God raised on the third day and granted that he be visible, not to all the people, but to us, the witnesses chosen by God in advance, who ate and drank with him after he rose from the dead. He commissioned us to preach to the people and testify that he is the one appointed by God as judge of the living and the dead. To him all the prophets bear witness, that everyone who believes in him will receive forgiveness of sins through his name."

## PSALM                                    *Psalm 118:1—2, 16—17, 22—23*
**R. This is the day the Lord has made; let us rejoice and be glad. or R. Alleluia.**
Give thanks to the LORD, for he is good, **/** for his mercy endures forever. **/** Let the house of Israel say, **/** "His mercy endures forever." **R.**
"The right hand of the LORD has struck with power; **/** the right hand of the LORD is exalted. **/** I shall not die, but live, **/** and declare the works of the LORD. **R.**
The stone which the builders rejected **/** has become the cornerstone. **/** By the LORD has this been done; **/** it is wonderful in our eyes. **R.**

## SECOND READING                                    *Colossians 3:1—4*
Brothers and sisters: If then you were raised with Christ, seek what is above, where Christ is seated at the right hand of God. Think of what is above, not of what is on earth. For you have died, and your life is hidden with Christ in God. When Christ your life appears, then you too will appear with him in glory.

## OR:                                              *1 Corinthians 5:6b—8*
Brothers and sisters: Do you not know that a little yeast leavens all the dough? Clear out the old yeast, so that you may become a fresh batch of dough, inasmuch as you are unleavened. For our paschal lamb, Christ, has been sacrificed. Therefore, let us celebrate the feast, not with the old yeast, the yeast of malice and wickedness, but with the unleavened bread of sincerity and truth.

## SEQUENCE
**Christians, to the Paschal Victim /** Offer your thankful praises! **/** A Lamb the sheep redeems; **/** Christ, who only is sinless, **/** Reconciles sinners to the Father.

**Death and life have contended /** in that combat stupendous: **/** The Prince of life, who died, reigns immortal. **/** Speak, Mary, declaring what you saw, wayfaring.

**"The tomb of Christ, who is living, /** the glory of Jesus' resurrection;
**Bright angels attesting, /** the shroud and napkin resting.
**Yes, Christ my hope is arisen**; **/** to Galilee he goes before you."
**Christ indeed from death is risen, /** our new life obtaining. **/** Have mercy, victor King, ever reigning! Amen. Alleluia.

**ALLELUIA** *see 1 Corinthians 5:7b—8a*

R. **Alleluia, alleluia.** Christ, our paschal lamb, has been sacrificed; let us then feast with joy in the Lord. **R.**

**GOSPEL EITHER:** *John 20:1—9*

On the first day of the week, Mary of Magdala came to the tomb early in the morning, while it was still dark, and saw the stone removed from the tomb. So she ran and went to Simon Peter and to the other disciple whom Jesus loved, and told them, "They have taken the Lord from the tomb, and we don't know where they put him." So Peter and the other disciple went out and came to the tomb. They both ran, but the other disciple ran faster than Peter and arrived at the tomb first; he bent down and saw the burial cloths there, but did not go in. When Simon Peter arrived after him, he went into the tomb and saw the burial cloths there, and the cloth that had covered his head, not with the burial cloths but rolled up in a separate place. Then the other disciple also went in, the one who had arrived at the tomb first, and he saw and believed. For they did not yet understand the Scripture that he had to rise from the dead.

**OR:** *Mark 16:1—8*

When the sabbath was over, Mary of Magdala, Mary the mother of James, and Salome, bought spices with which to go and anoint him. And very early in the morning on the first day of the week they went to the tomb, just as the sun was rising.

They had been saying to one another, 'Who will roll away the stone for us from the entrance to the tomb?' But when they looked they could see that the stone – which was very big – had already been rolled back. On entering the tomb they saw a young man in a white robe seated on the right-hand side, and they were struck with amazement. But he said to them, 'There is no need for alarm. You are looking for Jesus of

Nazareth, who was crucified: he has risen, he is not here. See, here is the place where they laid him. But you must go and tell his disciples and Peter, "He is going before you to Galilee; it is there you will see him, just as he told you."'

### The following gospel is to be used if the mass is celebrated in the afternoon or evening
### Luke 24:13—35

That very day, the first day of the week, two of Jesus' disciples were going to a village seven miles from Jerusalem called Emmaus, and they were conversing about all the things that had occurred. And it happened that while they were conversing and debating, Jesus himself drew near and walked with them, but their eyes were prevented from recognizing him. He asked them, "What are you discussing as you walk along?" They stopped, looking downcast. One of them, named Cleopas, said to him in reply, "Are you the only visitor to Jerusalem who does not know of the things that have taken place there in these days?" And he replied to them, "What sort of things?" They said to him, "The things that happened to Jesus the Nazarene, who was a prophet mighty in deed and word before God and all the people, how our chief priests and rulers both handed him over to a sentence of death and crucified him. But we were hoping that he would be the one to redeem Israel; and besides all this, it is now the third day since this took place. Some women from our group, however, have astounded us: they were at the tomb early in the morning and did not find his body; they came back and reported that they had indeed seen a vision of angels who announced that he was alive. Then some of those with us went to the tomb and found things just as the women had described, but him they did not see." And he said to them, "Oh, how foolish you are! How slow of heart to believe all that the prophets spoke! Was it not necessary that the Christ should suffer these things and enter into his glory?" Then beginning with Moses and all the prophets, he interpreted to them what referred to him in all the Scriptures. As they approached the village to which they were going, he gave the impression that he was going on farther. But they urged him, "Stay with us, for it is nearly evening and the day is almost over." So he went in to stay with them. And it happened that, while he was with them at table, he took bread, said the blessing, broke it, and gave it to them. With that their eyes were opened and they recognized him, but he vanished from their sight.

Then they said to each other, "Were not our hearts burning within us while he spoke to us on the way and opened the Scriptures to us?" So they set out at once and returned to Jerusalem where they found gathered together the eleven and those with them who were saying, "The Lord has truly been raised and has appeared to Simon!" Then the two recounted what had taken place on the way and how he was made known to them in the breaking of bread.

## PRAYER OVER THE OFFERINGS
Exultant with paschal gladness, O Lord, we offer the sacrifice by which your Church is wondrously reborn and nourished. Through Christ our Lord.

**COMMUNION ANTIPHON**                                        **1Cor 5: 7 – 8**
Christ our Passover has been sacrificed, alleluia; therefore let us keep the feast with the unleavened bread of purity and truth, alleluia, alleluia.

## PRAYER AFTER COMMUNIION
Look upon your Church, O God, with unfailing love and favour, so that, renewed by the paschal mysteries, she may come to the glory of the resurrection. Through Christ our Lord.

**LESSONS LEARNT FROM THE READINGS / HOMILY**

1 _____ 2 _____
3 _____ 4 _____
5 _____ 6 _____

**ACTION POINTS FOR THE WEEK**

1 _____ 2 _____
3 _____ 4 _____
5 _____ 6 _____

**PRAYER POINTS FOR THE WEEK**

1 _____ 2 _____
3 _____ 4 _____
5 _____ 6 _____

**THIS WEEK, I AM GRATEFUL FOR**

1 _____ 2 _____

## 11 APRIL 2021, 2ND SUNDAY OF EASTER
## (DIVINE MERCY SUNDAY)

**ENTRANCE ANTIPHON**                                1Pt 2: 2

Like newborn infants, you must long for the pure, spiritual milk, that in him you may grow to salvation, alleluia.

**OR**                                                    4 Esdras 2: 36 – 37

Receive the joy of your glory, giving thanks to God, who has called you into the heavenly kingdom, alleluia.

**COLLECT**

God of everlasting mercy, who in the very recurrence of the paschal feast kindle the faith of the people you have made your own, increase, we pray, the grace you have bestowed, that all may grasp and rightly understand in what font they have been washed, by whose Spirit they have been reborn, by whose Blood they have been redeemed. Through our Lord Jesus Christ, your Son, who lives and reigns with you in the unity of the Holy Spirit, one God, for ever and ever.

**FIRST READING**                                        *Acts 4:32—35*

The community of believers was of one heart and mind, and no one claimed that any of his possessions was his own, but they had everything in common. With great power the apostles bore witness to the resurrection of the Lord Jesus, and great favor was accorded them all. There was no needy person among them, for those who owned property or houses would sell them, bring the proceeds of the sale, and put them at the feet of the apostles, and they were distributed to each according to need.

**PSALM**                                    *Psalm 118:2—4, 13—15, 22—24 (1)*

**R. Give thanks to the Lord, for he is good; his love is everlasting. or R. Alleluia.**

Let the house of Israel say, **/** "His mercy endures forever." **/** Let the house of Aaron say, **/** "His mercy endures forever." **/** Let those who fear the LORD say, **/** "His mercy endures forever." **R.**

I was hard pressed and was falling, / but the LORD helped me. / My strength and my courage is the LORD, / and he has been my savior. / The joyful shout of victory in the tents of the just. **R.**

The stone which the builders rejected / has become the cornerstone. / By the LORD has this been done; it is wonderful in our eyes. /This is the day the LORD has made; / let us be glad and rejoice in it. **R.**

## SECOND READING                                    1 John 5:1—6

Beloved: Everyone who believes that Jesus is the Christ is begotten by God, and everyone who loves the Father loves also the one begotten by him. In this way we know that we love the children of God when we love God and obey his commandments. For the love of God is this, that we keep his commandments. And his commandments are not burdensome, for whoever is begotten by God conquers the world. And the victory that conquers the world is our faith. Who indeed is the victor over the world but the one who believes that Jesus is the Son of God?

This is the one who came through water and blood, Jesus Christ, not by water alone, but by water and blood. The Spirit is the one that testifies, and the Spirit is truth.

## ALLELUIA                                    John 20:29

**R. Alleluia, alleluia.** You believe in me, Thomas, because you have seen me, says the Lord; blessed are those who have not seen me, but still believe! **R.**

## GOSPEL                                    John 20:19—31

On the evening of that first day of the week, when the doors were locked, where the disciples were, for fear of the Jews, Jesus came and stood in their midst and said to them, "Peace be with you." When he had said this, he showed them his hands and his side. The disciples rejoiced when they saw the Lord. Jesus said to them again, "Peace be with you. As the Father has sent me, so I send you." And when he had said this, he breathed on them and said to them, "Receive the Holy Spirit. Whose sins you forgive are forgiven them, and whose sins you retain are retained."

Thomas, called Didymus, one of the Twelve, was not with them when Jesus came. So the other disciples said to him, "We have seen the Lord." But he said to them, "Unless I see the mark of the nails in his hands and put my finger into the nailmarks and put my hand into his side, I will not believe."

Now a week later his disciples were again inside and Thomas was with them. Jesus came, although the doors were locked, and stood in their midst and said, "Peace be with you." Then he said to Thomas, "Put your finger here and see my hands, and bring your hand and put it into my side, and do not be unbelieving, but believe." Thomas answered and said to him, "My Lord and my God!" Jesus said to him, "Have you come to believe because you have seen me? Blessed are those who have not seen and have believed."

Now Jesus did many other signs in the presence of his disciples that are not written in this book. But these are written that you may come to believe that Jesus is the Christ, the Son of God, and that through this belief you may have life in his name.

## PRAYER OVER THE OFFERINGS
Accept, O Lord, we pray, the oblations of your people (and of those you have brought to new birth), that, renewed by confession of your name and by Baptism, they may attain unending happiness. Through Christ our Lord.

## COMMUNION ANTIPHON          Cf. Jn 20: 27
Bring your hand and feel the place of the nails, and do not be unbelieving but believing, alleluia.

## PRAYER AFTER COMMUNION
Grant, we pray, almighty God, that our reception of this paschal Sacrament may have a continuing effect in our minds and hearts. Through Christ our Lord.


## LESSONS LEARNT FROM THE READINGS / HOMILY
1 _____ 2 _____
3 _____ 4 _____
5 _____ 6 _____


### ACTION POINTS FOR THE WEEK
1 _____ 2 _____
3 _____ 4 _____
5 _____ 6 _____


### PRAYER POINTS FOR THE WEEK

| 1 | 2 |
|---|---|
| 3 | 4 |
| 5 | 6 |

### THIS WEEK, I AM GRATEFUL FOR

| 1 | 2 |
|---|---|
| 3 | 4 |
| 5 | 6 |

# 18 APRIL 2021, 3RD SUNDAY OF EASTER

**ENTRANCE ANTIPHON**                                    Cf. Ps 6: 1 – 2

Cry out with joy to God, all the earth; O sing to the glory of his name. O render him glorious praise, alleluia.

**COLLECT**

May your people exult for ever, O God, in renewed youthfulness of spirit, so that, rejoicing now in the restored glory of our adoption, we may look forward in confident hope to the rejoicing of the day of resurrection. Through our Lord Jesus Christ, your Son, who lives and reigns with you in the unity of the Holy Spirit, one God, for ever and ever.

**FIRST READING**                                    *Acts 3:13—15, 17—19*

Peter said to the people: "The God of Abraham, the God of Isaac, and the God of Jacob, the God of our fathers, has glorified his servant Jesus, whom you handed over and denied in Pilate's presence when he had decided to release him. You denied the Holy and Righteous One and asked that a murderer be released to you. The author of life you put to death, but God raised him from the dead; of this we are witnesses. Now I know, brothers, that you acted out of ignorance, just as your leaders did; but God has thus brought to fulfillment what he had announced beforehand through the mouth of all the prophets, that his Christ would suffer. Repent, therefore, and be converted, that your sins may be wiped away."

**RESPONSORIAL PSALM**                                    *Psalm 4:2, 4, 7—8, 9*

**R. Lord, let your face shine on us. or R. Alleluia.**

When I call, answer me, O my just God, / you who relieve me when I am in distress; / have pity on me, and hear my prayer! **R.**

Know that the LORD does wonders for his faithful one; / the LORD will hear me when I call upon him. **R.**

O LORD, let the light of your countenance shine upon us! / You put gladness into my heart. **R.**

As soon as I lie down, I fall peacefully asleep, / for you alone, O LORD, / bring security to my dwelling. **R.**

## SECOND READING                                          *1 John 2:1—5a*

My children, I am writing this to you so that you may not commit sin. But if anyone does sin, we have an Advocate with the Father, Jesus Christ the righteous one. He is expiation for our sins, and not for our sins only but for those of the whole world. The way we may be sure that we know him is to keep his commandments. Those who say, "I know him," but do not keep his commandments are liars, and the truth is not in them. But whoever keeps his word, the love of God is truly perfected in him.

## ALLELUIA                                                  *see Luke 24:32*

R. Alleluia, alleluia. Lord Jesus, open the Scriptures to us; make our hearts burn while you speak to us. **R.**

## GOSPEL                                                   *Luke 24:35—48*

The two disciples recounted what had taken place on the way, and how Jesus was made known to them in the breaking of bread.

While they were still speaking about this, he stood in their midst and said to them, "Peace be with you." But they were startled and terrified and thought that they were seeing a ghost. Then he said to them, "Why are you troubled? And why do questions arise in your hearts? Look at my hands and my feet, that it is I myself. Touch me and see, because a ghost does not have flesh and bones as you can see I have." And as he said this, he showed them his hands and his feet. While they were still incredulous for joy and were amazed, he asked them, "Have you anything here to eat?" They gave him a piece of baked fish; he took it and ate it in front of them.

He said to them, "These are my words that I spoke to you while I was still with you, that everything written about me in the law of Moses and in the prophets and psalms must be fulfilled." Then he opened their minds to understand the Scriptures. And he said to them, "Thus it is written that the Christ would suffer and rise from the dead on the third day and that repentance, for the forgiveness of sins, would be preached in his name to all the nations, beginning from Jerusalem. You are witnesses of these things."

## PRAYER OVER THE OFFERINGS

Receive, O Lord, we pray, these offerings of your exultant Church, and, as you have given her cause for such great gladness, grant also that the gifts we bring may bear fruit in perpetual happiness. Through Christ our Lord.

## COMMUNION ANTIPHON                    Lk 24: 36

The disciples recognized the Lord Jesus in the breaking of the bread, alleluia.

## OR                                              Lk 24: 46 – 47

The Christ had to suffer and on the third day rise from the dead; in his name repentance and remission of sins must be preached to all the nations, alleluia.

## PRAYER AFTER COMMUNION

Look with kindness upon your people, O Lord, and grant, we pray, that those you were pleased to renew by eternal mysteries may attain in their flesh the incorruptible glory of the resurrection. Through Christ our Lord.

## LESSONS LEARNT FROM THE READINGS / HOMILY

1 _____ 2 _____
3 _____ 4 _____
5 _____ 6 _____

## ACTION POINTS FOR THE WEEK

1 _____ 2 _____
3 _____ 4 _____
5 _____ 6 _____

## PRAYER POINTS FOR THE WEEK

1 _____ 2 _____
3 _____ 4 _____
5 _____ 6 _____

## THIS WEEK, I AM GRATEFUL FOR

1 _____ 2 _____
3 _____ 4 _____

## 25 APRIL 2021, 4TH SUNDAY OF EASTER

**ENTRANCE ANTIPHON**                     **Cf. Ps 32: 5 – 6**

The merciful love of the Lord fills the earth; by the word of the Lord the heavens were made, alleluia.

**COLLECT**

Almighty ever-living God, lead us to a share in the joys of heaven, so that the humble flock may reach where the brave Shepherd has gone before. Who lives and reigns with you in the unity of the Holy Spirit, one God, for ever and ever.

**FIRST READING**                         **Acts 4:8—12**

Peter, filled with the Holy Spirit, said: "Leaders of the people and elders: If we are being examined today about a good deed done to a cripple, namely, by what means he was saved, then all of you and all the people of Israel should know that it was in the name of Jesus Christ the Nazorean whom you crucified, whom God raised from the dead; in his name this man stands before you healed. *He is the stone rejected by you, the builders, which has become the cornerstone.* There is no salvation through anyone else, nor is there any other name under heaven given to the human race by which we are to be saved."

**PSALM**                 *Psalm 118:1, 8—9, 21—23, 26, 28, 29 (22)*

**R. The stone rejected by the builders has become the cornerstone. or R. Alleluia.**

Give thanks to the LORD, for he is good, / for his mercy endures forever. / It is better to take refuge in the LORD / than to trust in man. / It is better to take refuge in the LORD / than to trust in princes. **R.**

I will give thanks to you, for you have answered me / and have been my savior. / The stone which the builders rejected / has become the cornerstone. / By the LORD has this been done; / it is wonderful in our eyes. **R.**

Blessed is he who comes in the name of the LORD; / we bless you from the house of the LORD. / I will give thanks to you, for you have answered me / and have been my savior. / Give thanks to the LORD, for he is good; / for his kindness endures forever. **R.**

## SECOND READING
*1 John 3:1—2*

Beloved: See what love the Father has bestowed on us that we may be called the children of God. Yet so we are. The reason the world does not know us is that it did not know him. Beloved, we are God's children now; what we shall be has not yet been revealed. We do know that when it is revealed we shall be like him, for we shall see him as he is.

## ALLELUIA
*John 10:14*

**R. Alleluia, alleluia.** I am the good shepherd, says the Lord; I know my sheep, and mine know me. **R.**

## GOSPEL
*John 10:11—18*

Jesus said: "I am the good shepherd. A good shepherd lays down his life for the sheep. A hired man, who is not a shepherd and whose sheep are not his own, sees a wolf coming and leaves the sheep and runs away, and the wolf catches and scatters them. This is because he works for pay and has no concern for the sheep. I am the good shepherd, and I know mine and mine know me, just as the Father knows me and I know the Father; and I will lay down my life for the sheep. I have other sheep that do not belong to this fold. These also I must lead, and they will hear my voice, and there will be one flock, one shepherd. This is why the Father loves me, because I lay down my life in order to take it up again. No one takes it from me, but I lay it down on my own. I have power to lay it down, and power to take it up again. This command I have received from my Father."

## PRAYER OVER THE OFFERINGS
Grant, we pray, O Lord, that we may always find delight in these paschal mysteries, so that the renewal constantly at work within us may be the cause of our unending joy. Through Christ our Lord.

## COMMUNION ANTIPHON
The Good Shepherd has risen, who laid down his life for his sheep and willingly died for his flock, alleluia.

## PRAYER AFTER COMMUNION
Look upon your flock, kind Shepherd, and be pleased to settle in eternal pastures the sheep you have redeemed by the Precious Blood of your Son. Who lives and reigns for ever and ever.

## LESSONS LEARNT FROM THE READINGS / HOMILY
1 _____  2 _____

| 3 | 4 |
|---|---|
| 5 | 6 |

### ACTION POINTS FOR THE WEEK

| 1 | 2 |
|---|---|
| 3 | 4 |
| 5 | 6 |

### PRAYER POINTS FOR THE WEEK

| 1 | 2 |
|---|---|
| 3 | 4 |
| 5 | 6 |

### THIS WEEK, I AM GRATEFUL FOR

| 1 | 2 |
|---|---|
| 3 | 4 |
| 5 | 6 |

## 02 MAY 2021, 5TH SUNDAY OF EASTER

**ENTRANCE ANTIPHON**                                      Cf. Ps 97: 1 – 2

O sing a new song to the Lord, for he has worked wonders; in the sight of the nations he has shown his deliverance, alleluia.

**COLLECT**

Almighty ever-living God, constantly accomplish the Paschal Mystery within us, that those you were pleased to make new in Holy Baptism may, under your protective care, bear much fruit and come to the joys of life eternal. Through our Lord Jesus Christ, your Son, who lives and reigns with you in the unity of the Holy Spirit, one God, for ever and ever.

**FIRST READING**                                            *Acts 9:26—31*

When Saul arrived in Jerusalem he tried to join the disciples, but they were all afraid of him, not believing that he was a disciple. Then Barnabas took charge of him and brought him to the apostles, and he reported to them how he had seen the Lord, and that he had spoken to him, and how in Damascus he had spoken out boldly in the name of Jesus. He moved about freely with them in Jerusalem, and spoke out boldly in the name of the Lord. He also spoke and debated with the Hellenists, but they tried to kill him. And when the brothers learned of this, they took him down to Caesarea and sent him on his way to Tarsus. The church throughout all Judea, Galilee, and Samaria was at peace. It was being built up and walked in the fear of the Lord, and with the consolation of the Holy Spirit it grew in numbers.

**PSALM** *Psalm 22:26—27, 28, 30, 31—32 (26a)*
**R. I will praise you, Lord, in the assembly of your people. or R. Alleluia.**
I will fulfill my vows before those who fear the LORD. / The lowly shall eat their fill; / they who seek the LORD shall praise him: / "May your hearts live forever!" **R.**
All the ends of the earth / shall remember and turn to the LORD; / all the families of the nations / shall bow down before him. **R.**
To him alone shall bow down / all who sleep in the earth; / before him shall bend / all who go down into the dust. **R.**
And to him my soul shall live; / my descendants shall serve him. / Let the coming generation be told of the LORD / that they may proclaim to a people yet to be born/the justice he has shown. **R**

**SECOND READING** *1 John 3:18—24*
Children, let us love not in word or speech but in deed and truth. Now this is how we shall know that we belong to the truth and reassure our hearts before him in whatever our hearts condemn, for God is greater than our hearts and knows everything. Beloved, if our hearts do not condemn us, we have confidence in God and receive from him whatever we ask, because we keep his commandments and do what pleases him. And his commandment is this: we should believe in the name of his Son, Jesus Christ, and love one another just as he commanded us. Those who keep his commandments remain in him, and he in them, and the way we know that he remains in us is from the Spirit he gave us.
**ALLELUIA** *John 15:4a, 5b*
**R. Alleluia, alleluia.** Remain in me as I remain in you, says the Lord. Whoever remains in me will bear much fruit. **R.**

## GOSPEL                                         *John 15:1—8*

Jesus said to his disciples: "I am the true vine, and my Father is the vine grower. He takes away every branch in me that does not bear fruit, and every one that does he prunes so that it bears more fruit. You are already pruned because of the word that I spoke to you. Remain in me, as I remain in you. Just as a branch cannot bear fruit on its own unless it remains on the vine, so neither can you unless you remain in me. I am the vine, you are the branches. Whoever remains in me and I in him will bear much fruit, because without me you can do nothing. Anyone who does not remain in me will be thrown out like a branch and wither; people will gather them and throw them into a fire and they will be burned. If you remain in me and my words remain in you, ask for whatever you want and it will be done for you. By this is my Father glorified, that you bear much fruit and become my disciples."

## PRAYER OVER THE OFFERINGS

O God, who by the wonderful exchange effected in this sacrifice have made us partakers of the one supreme Godhead, grant, we pray, that, as we have come to know your truth, we may make it ours by a worthy way of life. Through Christ our Lord.

## COMMUNION ANTIPHON              Cf. Jn 15: 1, 5

I am the true vine and you are the branches, says the Lord. Whoever remains in me, and I in him, bears fruit in plenty, alleluia.

## PRAYER AFTER COMMUNION

Graciously be present to your people, we pray, O Lord, and lead those you have imbued with heavenly mysteries to pass from former ways to newness of life. Through Christ our Lord.


## LESSONS LEARNT FROM THE READINGS / HOMILY

| 1 | 2 |
|---|---|
| 3 | 4 |
| 5 | 6 |


## ACTION POINTS FOR THE WEEK

| 1 | 2 |
|---|---|
| 3 | 4 |
| 5 | 6 |

## PRAYER POINTS FOR THE WEEK

| 1 | 2 |
|---|---|
| 3 | 4 |
| 5 | 6 |

## THIS WEEK, I AM GRATEFUL FOR

| 1 | 2 |
|---|---|
| 3 | 4 |
| 5 | 6 |

## 09 MAY 2021, 6TH SUNDAY OF EASTER

**ENTRANCE ANTIPHON**        **Cf. Is 48: 20**

Proclaim a joyful sound and let it be heard; proclaim to the ends of the earth: The Lord has freed his people, alleluia.

**COLLECT**

Grant, almighty God, that we may celebrate with heartfelt devotion these days of joy, which we keep in honour of the risen Lord, and that what we relive in remembrance we may always hold to in what we do. Through our Lord Jesus Christ, your Son, who lives and reigns with you in the unity of the Holy Spirit, one God, for ever and ever.

**FIRST READING**        *Acts 10:25—26, 34—35, 44—48*

When Peter entered, Cornelius met him and, falling at his feet, paid him homage. Peter, however, raised him up, saying, "Get up. I myself am also a human being."

Then Peter proceeded to speak and said, "In truth, I see that God shows no partiality. Rather, in every nation whoever fears him and acts uprightly is acceptable to him."

While Peter was still speaking these things, the Holy Spirit fell upon all who were listening to the word. The circumcised believers who had accompanied Peter were astounded that the gift of the Holy Spirit should have been poured out on the Gentiles also, for they could hear them speaking in tongues and glorifying God. Then Peter responded, "Can anyone withhold the water for baptizing these people, who have received the Holy Spirit even as we have?" He ordered them to be baptized in the name of Jesus Christ.

## RESPONSORIAL PSALM                    *Psalm 98:1, 2—3, 3—4*

**R. The Lord has revealed to the nations his saving power. or R. Alleluia.**

Sing to the LORD a new song, **/** for he has done wondrous deeds; **/** His right hand has won victory for him, **/** his holy arm. **R.**

The LORD has made his salvation known: **/** in the sight of the nations he has revealed his justice. **/** He has remembered his kindness and his faithfulness **/** toward the house of Israel. **R.**

All the ends of the earth have seen **/** the salvation by our God. **/** Sing joyfully to the LORD, all you lands; **/** break into song; sing praise. **R.**

## SECOND READING                        *1 John 4:7—10*

Beloved, let us love one another, because love is of God; everyone who loves is begotten by God and knows God. Whoever is without love does not know God, for God is love. In this way the love of God was revealed to us: God sent his only Son into the world so that we might have life through him. In this is love: not that we have loved God, but that he loved us and sent his Son as expiation for our sins.

## ALLELUIA                              *John 14:23*

**R. Alleluia, alleluia.** Whoever loves me will keep my word, says the Lord, and my Father will love him and we will come to him. **R.**

## GOSPEL                                *John 15:9—17*

Jesus said to his disciples: "As the Father loves me, so I also love you. Remain in my love. If you keep my commandments, you will remain in my love, just as I have kept my Father's commandments and remain in his love.

"I have told you this so that my joy may be in you and your joy might be complete. This is my commandment: love one another as I love you. No one has greater love than this, to lay down one's life for one's friends. You are my friends if you do what I command you. I no longer call you slaves, because a slave does not know what his master is doing. I have called you friends, because I have told you everything I have heard from my Father. It was not you who chose me, but I who chose you and appointed you to go and bear fruit that will remain, so that whatever you ask the Father in my name he may give you. This I command you: love one another."

**PRAYER OVER THE OFFERINGS**

May our prayers rise up to you, O Lord, together with the sacrificial offerings, so that, purified by your graciousness, we may be conformed to the mysteries of your mighty love. Through Christ our Lord.

**COMMUNION ANTIPHON**                                    **Jn 14: 15 – 16**

If you love me, keep my commandments, says the Lord, and I will ask the Father and he will send you another Paraclete, to abide with you for ever, alleluia.

**PRAYER AFTER COMMUNION**

Almighty ever-living God, who restore us to eternal life in the Resurrection of Christ, increase in us, we pray, the fruits of this paschal Sacrament and pour into our hearts the strength of this saving food. Through Christ our Lord.

**LESSONS LEARNT FROM THE READINGS / HOMILY**

1 _____ 2 _____
3 _____ 4 _____
5 _____ 6 _____

**ACTION POINTS FOR THE WEEK**

1 _____ 2 _____
3 _____ 4 _____
5 _____ 6 _____

**PRAYER POINTS FOR THE WEEK**

1 _____ 2 _____
3 _____ 4 _____
5 _____ 6 _____

**THIS WEEK, I AM GRATEFUL FOR**

1 _____ 2 _____
3 _____ 4 _____
5 _____ 6 _____

*If Ascension is not celebrated on this day in your local church, please consult the readings for Thursday Mass. They are located after the ones for Ascension.*

## ASCENSION OF THE LORD – VIGIL MASS

**ENTRANCE ANTIPHON**                    **Ps 67: 33, 35**

You kingdoms of the earth, sing to God; praise the Lord, who ascends above the highest heavens; his majesty and might are in the skies, alleluia.

**COLLECT**

O God, whose Son today ascended to the heavens as the Apostles looked on, grant, we pray, that, in accordance with his promise, we may be worthy for him to live with us always on earth, and we with him in heaven. Who lives and reigns with you in the unity of the Holy Spirit, one God, for ever and ever.

*The readings for this mass are the same with the ones for Mass of the Day given below.*

**PRAYER OVER THE OFFERINGS**

O God, whose Only Begotten Son, our High Priest, is seated ever-living at your right hand to intercede for us, grant that we may approach with confidence the throne of grace and there obtain your mercy. Through Christ our Lord.

**COMMUNION ANTIPHON**                    **Cf. Heb 10: 12**

Christ, offering a single sacrifice for sins, is seated for ever at God's right hand, alleluia.

**PRAYER AFTER COMMUNION**

May the gifts we have received from your altar, Lord, kindle in our hearts a longing for the heavenly homeland and cause us to press forward, following in the Saviour's footsteps, to the place where for our sake he entered before us. Who lives and reigns for ever and ever.

## MASS OF THE DAY

**ENTRANCE ANTIPHON**                    **Acts 1: 11**

Men of Galilee, why gaze in wonder at the heavens? This Jesus whom you saw ascending into heaven will return as you saw him go, alleluia.

## COLLECT

Gladden us with holy joys, almighty God, and make us rejoice with devout thanksgiving, for the Ascension of Christ your Son is our exaltation, and, where the Head has gone before in glory, the Body is called to follow in hope. Through our Lord Jesus Christ, your Son, who lives and reigns with you in the unity of the Holy Spirit, one God, for ever and ever.

**OR**

Grant, we pray, almighty God, that we, who believe that your Only Begotten Son, our Redeemer, ascended this day to the heavens, may in spirit dwell already in heavenly realms. Who lives and reigns with you in the unity of the Holy Spirit, one God, for ever and ever.

## FIRST READING                                                   Acts 1:1—11

In the first book, Theophilus, I dealt with all that Jesus did and taught until the day he was taken up, after giving instructions through the Holy Spirit to the apostles whom he had chosen. He presented himself alive to them by many proofs after he had suffered, appearing to them during forty days and speaking about the kingdom of God. While meeting with them, he enjoined them not to depart from Jerusalem, but to wait for "the promise of the Father about which you have heard me speak; for John baptized with water, but in a few days you will be baptized with the Holy Spirit."

When they had gathered together they asked him, "Lord, are you at this time going to restore the kingdom to Israel?" He answered them, "It is not for you to know the times or seasons that the Father has established by his own authority. But you will receive power when the Holy Spirit comes upon you, and you will be my witnesses in Jerusalem, throughout Judea and Samaria, and to the ends of the earth." When he had said this, as they were looking on, he was lifted up, and a cloud took him from their sight. While they were looking intently at the sky as he was going, suddenly two men dressed in white garments stood beside them. They said, "Men of Galilee, why are you standing there looking at the sky? This Jesus who has been taken up from you into heaven will return in the same way as you have seen him going into heaven."

## PSALM                                                   Psalm 47:2—3, 6—7, 8—9 (6)
**R. God mounts his throne to shouts of joy: a blare of trumpets for the Lord. or R. Alleluia.**

All you peoples, clap your hands, / shout to God with cries of gladness. / For the LORD, the Most High, the awesome, / is the great king over all the earth. **R.**

God mounts his throne amid shouts of joy; / the LORD, amid trumpet blasts. / Sing praise to God, sing praise; / sing praise to our king, sing praise. **R.**

For king of all the earth is God; / sing hymns of praise. / God reigns over the nations, / God sits upon his holy throne. **R.**

## EITHER: SECOND READING                    *Ephesians 1:17—23*

Brothers and sisters: May the God of our Lord Jesus Christ, the Father of glory, give you a Spirit of wisdom and revelation resulting in knowledge of him. May the eyes of your hearts be enlightened, that you may know what is the hope that belongs to his call, what are the riches of glory in his inheritance among the holy ones, and what is the surpassing greatness of his power for us who believe, in accord with the exercise of his great might, which he worked in Christ, raising him from the dead and seating him at his right hand in the heavens, far above every principality, authority, power, and dominion, and every name that is named not only in this age but also in the one to come. And he put all things beneath his feet and gave him as head over all things to the church, which is his body, the fullness of the one who fills all things in every way.

## OR:                                        *Ephesians 4:1—13*

Brothers and sisters, I, a prisoner for the Lord, urge you to live in a manner worthy of the call you have received, with all humility and gentleness, with patience, bearing with one another through love, striving to preserve the unity of the spirit through the bond of peace: one body and one Spirit, as you were also called to the one hope of your call; one Lord, one faith, one baptism; one God and Father of all, who is over all and through all and in all.

But grace was given to each of us according to the measure of Christ's gift. Therefore, it says: *He ascended on high and took prisoners captive; he gave gifts to men.* What does "he ascended" mean except that he also descended into the lower regions of the earth? The one who descended is also the one who ascended far above all the heavens, that he might fill all things.

And he gave some as apostles, others as prophets, others as evangelists, others as pastors and teachers, to equip the holy ones for the work of ministry, for building up the body of Christ, until we all attain to the unity of faith and knowledge of the Son of God, to mature manhood, to the extent of the full stature of Christ.

**OR: *Shorter Form*** *Ephesians 4:1—7, 11—13*

Brothers and sisters, I, a prisoner for the Lord, urge you to live in a manner worthy of the call you have received, with all humility and gentleness, with patience, bearing with one another through love, striving to preserve the unity of the Spirit through the bond of peace: one body and one Spirit, as you were also called to the one hope of your calling; one Lord, one faith, one baptism; one God and Father of all, who is over all and through all and in all.

But grace was given to each of us according to the measure of Christ's gift.

And he gave some as apostles, others as prophets, others as evangelists, others as pastors and teachers, to equip the holy ones for the work of ministry, for building up the body of Christ, until we all attain to the unity of faith and knowledge of the Son of God, to mature manhood, to the extent of the full stature of Christ.

**ALLELUIA** *Luke 3:4, 6*

**R. Alleluia, alleluia.** Go and teach all nations, says the Lord; I am with you always, until the end of the world. **R.**

**GOSPEL** *Mark 16:15—20*

Jesus said to his disciples: "Go into the whole world and proclaim the gospel to every creature. Whoever believes and is baptized will be saved; whoever does not believe will be condemned. These signs will accompany those who believe: in my name they will drive out demons, they will speak new languages. They will pick up serpents with their hands, and if they drink any deadly thing, it will not harm them. They will lay hands on the sick, and they will recover."

So then the Lord Jesus, after he spoke to them, was taken up into heaven and took his seat at the right hand of God. But they went forth and preached everywhere, while the Lord worked with them and confirmed the word through accompanying signs.

## PRAYER OVER THE OFFERINGS

We offer sacrifice now in supplication, O Lord, to honour the wondrous Ascension of your Son: grant, we pray, that through this most holy exchange we, too, may rise up to the heavenly realms. Through Christ our Lord.

## COMMUNION ANTIPHON                    Mt 28: 20

Behold, I am with you always, even to the end of the age, alleluia.

## PRAYER AFTER COMMUNION

Almighty ever-living God, who allow those on earth to celebrate divine mysteries, grant, we pray, that Christian hope may draw us onward to where our nature is united with you. Through Christ our Lord.

## LESSONS LEARNT FROM THE READINGS / HOMILY

| 1 | 2 |
|---|---|
| 3 | 4 |
| 5 | 6 |

### ACTION POINTS FOR THE WEEK

| 1 | 2 |
|---|---|
| 3 | 4 |
| 5 | 6 |

### PRAYER POINTS FOR THE WEEK

| 1 | 2 |
|---|---|
| 3 | 4 |
| 5 | 6 |

### THIS WEEK, I AM GRATEFUL FOR

| 1 | 2 |
|---|---|
| 3 | 4 |
| 5 | 6 |

## 16 MAY 2021, 7TH SUN OF EASTER OR ASCENSION OF THE LORD

*Please consult the readings of Ascension given on the 13th of May if the celebration of Ascension is shifted to this Sunday in your local church*

# SEVENTH SUNDAY OF EASTER

**ENTRANCE ANTIPHON**     Cf. Ps 26: 7 – 9

O Lord, hear my voice, for I have called to you; of you my heart has spoken: Seek his face; hide not your face from me, alleluia.

**COLLECT**

Graciously hear our supplications, O Lord, so that we, who believe that the Saviour of the human race is with you in your glory, may experience, as he promised, until the end of the world, his abiding presence among us. Who lives and reigns with you in the unity of the Holy Spirit, one God, for ever and ever.

**FIRST READING**                    *Acts 1:15—17, 20a, 20c—26*

Peter stood up in the midst of the brothers —there was a group of about one hundred and twenty persons in the one place—. He said, "My brothers, the Scripture had to be fulfilled which the Holy Spirit spoke beforehand through the mouth of David, concerning Judas, who was the guide for those who arrested Jesus. He was numbered among us and was allotted a share in this ministry.

"For it is written in the Book of Psalms: *May another take his office.*

"Therefore, it is necessary that one of the men who accompanied us the whole time the Lord Jesus came and went among us, beginning from the baptism of John until the day on which he was taken up from us, become with us a witness to his resurrection." So they proposed two, Judas called Barsabbas, who was also known as Justus, and Matthias. Then they prayed, "You, Lord, who know the hearts of all, show which one of these two you have chosen to take the place in this apostolic ministry from which Judas turned away to go to his own place." Then they gave lots to them, and the lot fell upon Matthias, and he was counted with the eleven apostles.

**PSALM**                    *Psalm 103:1—2, 11—12, 19—20 (19a)*

**R. The Lord has set his throne in heaven. or R. Alleluia.**

Bless the LORD, O my soul; / and all my being, bless his holy name. / Bless the LORD, O my soul, / and forget not all his benefits. **R.**

For as the heavens are high above the earth, / so surpassing is his kindness toward those who fear him. / As far as the east is from the west, / so far has he put our transgressions from us. **R.**

The LORD has established his throne in heaven, **/** and his kingdom rules over all. **/** Bless the LORD, all you his angels,**/** you mighty in strength, who do his bidding. **R.**

## SECOND READING                                    *1 John 4:11—16*

Beloved, if God so loved us, we also must love one another. No one has ever seen God. Yet, if we love one another, God remains in us, and his love is brought to perfection in us.

This is how we know that we remain in him and he in us, that he has given us of his Spirit. Moreover, we have seen and testify that the Father sent his Son as savior of the world. Whoever acknowledges that Jesus is the Son of God, God remains in him and he in God. We have come to know and to believe in the love God has for us.

God is love, and whoever remains in love remains in God and God in him.

## ALLELUIA                                          *see John 14:18*

**R. Alleluia, alleluia.** I will not leave you orphans, says the Lord. I will come back to you, and your hearts will rejoice. **R.**

## GOSPEL                                            *John 17:11b—19*

Lifting up his eyes to heaven, Jesus prayed, saying: "Holy Father, keep them in your name that you have given me, so that they may be one just as we are one. When I was with them I protected them in your name that you gave me, and I guarded them, and none of them was lost except the son of destruction, in order that the Scripture might be fulfilled. But now I am coming to you. I speak this in the world so that they may share my joy completely. I gave them your word, and the world hated them, because they do not belong to the world any more than I belong to the world. I do not ask that you take them out of the world but that you keep them from the evil one. They do not belong to the world any more than I belong to the world. Consecrate them in the truth. Your word is truth. As you sent me into the world, so I sent them into the world. And I consecrate myself for them, so that they also may be consecrated in truth."

## PRAYER OVER THE OFFERINGS

Accept, O Lord, the prayers of your faithful with the sacrificial offerings, that through these acts of devotedness we may pass over to the glory of heaven. Through Christ our Lord.

**COMMUNION ANTIPHON**     **Jn 17: 22**

Father, I pray that they may be one as we also are one, alleluia.

**PRAYER AFTER COMMUNION**

Hear us, O God our Saviour, and grant us confidence, that through these sacred mysteries there will be accomplished in the body of the whole Church what has already come to pass in Christ her Head. Who lives and reigns for ever and ever.

**LESSONS LEARNT FROM THE READINGS / HOMILY**

1        2

3        4

5        6

**ACTION POINTS FOR THE WEEK**

1        2

3        4

5        6

**PRAYER POINTS FOR THE WEEK**

1        2

3        4

5        6

**THIS WEEK, I AM GRATEFUL FOR**

1        2

3        4

5        6

## 23 MAY 2021, PENTECOST – SOLEMNITY, VIGIL MASS

**ENTRANCE ANTIPHON**     **Rm 5: 5; Cf. 8: 11**

The love of God has been poured into our hearts through the Spirit of God dwelling within us, alleluia.

**COLLECT**

Almighty ever-living God, who willed the Paschal Mystery to be encompassed as a sign in fifty days, grant that from out of the scattered nations the confusion of many tongues may be gathered by heavenly grace into one great confession of your name. Through our Lord Jesus Christ, your Son, who lives and reigns with you in the unity of the Holy Spirit, one God, for ever and ever.

**OR**

Grant, we pray, almighty God, that the splendour of your glory may shine forth upon us and that, by the bright rays of the Holy Spirit, the light of your light may confirm the hearts of those born again by your grace. Through our Lord Jesus Christ, your Son, who lives and reigns with you in the unity of the Holy Spirit, one God, for ever and ever.

**FIRST READING**                                                  *Genesis 11:1—9*

The whole world spoke the same language, using the same words. While the people were migrating in the east, they came upon a valley in the land of Shinar and settled there. They said to one another, "Come, let us mold bricks and harden them with fire." They used bricks for stone, and bitumen for mortar. Then they said, "Come, let us build ourselves a city and a tower with its top in the sky, and so make a name for ourselves; otherwise we shall be scattered all over the earth."

The LORD came down to see the city and the tower that the people had built. Then the LORD said: "If now, while they are one people, all speaking the same language, they have started to do this, nothing will later stop them from doing whatever they presume to do. Let us then go down there and confuse their language, so that one will not understand what another says." Thus the LORD scattered them from there all over the earth, and they stopped building the city. That is why it was called Babel, because there the LORD confused the speech of all the world. It was from that place that he scattered them all over the earth.

**OR:**                                                  *Exodus 19:3—8a, 16—20b*

Moses went up the mountain to God. Then the LORD called to him and said, "Thus shall you say to the house of Jacob; tell the Israelites: You have seen for yourselves how I treated the Egyptians and how I bore you up on eagle wings and brought you here to myself. Therefore, if you hearken to my voice and keep my covenant, you shall be my special possession, dearer to me than all other people, though all the earth is mine. You shall be to me a kingdom of priests, a holy nation. That is what you must tell the Israelites." So Moses went and summoned the elders of the people. When he set before them all that the LORD had ordered him to tell them, the people all answered together, "Everything the LORD has said, we will do."

On the morning of the third day there were peals of thunder and lightning, and a heavy cloud over the mountain, and a very loud trumpet blast, so that all the people in the camp trembled. But Moses led the people out of the camp to meet God, and they stationed themselves at the foot of the mountain. Mount Sinai was all wrapped in smoke, for the LORD came down upon it in fire. The smoke rose from it as though from a furnace, and the whole mountain trembled violently. The trumpet blast grew louder and louder, while Moses was speaking, and God answering him with thunder.

When the LORD came down to the top of Mount Sinai, he summoned Moses to the top of the mountain.

**OR:**                                                    *Ezekiel 37:1—14*

The hand of the LORD came upon me, and he led me out in the spirit of the LORD and set me in the center of the plain, which was now filled with bones. He made me walk among the bones in every direction so that I saw how many they were on the surface of the plain. How dry they were! He asked me: Son of man, can these bones come to life? I answered, "Lord GOD, you alone know that." Then he said to me: Prophesy over these bones, and say to them: Dry bones, hear the word of the LORD! Thus says the Lord GOD to these bones: See! I will bring spirit into you, that you may come to life. I will put sinews upon you, make flesh grow over you, cover you with skin, and put spirit in you so that you may come to life and know that I am the LORD. I, Ezekiel, prophesied as I had been told, and even as I was prophesying I heard a noise; it was a rattling as the bones came together, bone joining bone. I saw the sinews and the flesh come upon them, and the skin cover them, but there was no spirit in them. Then the LORD said to me: Prophesy to the spirit, prophesy, son of man, and say to the spirit: Thus says the Lord GOD: From the four winds come, O spirit, and breathe into these slain that they may come to life. I prophesied as he told me, and the spirit came into them; they came alive and stood upright, a vast army. Then he said to me: Son of man, these bones are the whole house of Israel. They have been saying, "Our bones are dried up, our hope is lost, and we are cut off." Therefore, prophesy and say to them: Thus says the Lord GOD: O my people, I will open your graves and have you rise from them, and bring you back to the land of

Israel. Then you shall know that I am the LORD, when I open your graves and have you rise from them, O my people! I will put my spirit in you that you may live, and I will settle you upon your land; thus you shall know that I am the LORD. I have promised, and I will do it, says the LORD.

**OR:**                                                                    *Joel 3:1—5*

Thus says the LORD: I will pour out my spirit upon all flesh. Your sons and daughters shall prophesy, your old men shall dream dreams, your young men shall see visions; even upon the servants and the handmaids, in those days, I will pour out my spirit. And I will work wonders in the heavens and on the earth, blood, fire, and columns of smoke; the sun will be turned to darkness, and the moon to blood, at the coming of the day of the LORD, the great and terrible day. Then everyone shall be rescued who calls on the name of the LORD; for on Mount Zion there shall be a remnant, as the LORD has said, and in Jerusalem survivors whom the Lord shall call.

**PSALM**                              *Psalm 104:1—2, 24, 35, 27—28, 29, 30*

**R. Lord, send out your Spirit, and renew the face of the earth. or R. Alleluia.**

Bless the LORD, O my soul! **/** O LORD, my God, you are great indeed! **/** You are clothed with majesty and glory, **/** robed in light as with a cloak. **R.**
How manifold are your works, O LORD! **/** In wisdom you have wrought them all— **/** the earth is full of your creatures; **/** bless the LORD, O my soul! Alleluia. **R.**
Creatures all look to you **/** to give them food in due time. **/** When you give it to them, they gather it; **/** when you open your hand, they are filled with good things. **R.**
If you take away their breath, they perish **/** and return to their dust. **/** When you send forth your spirit, they are created, **/** and you renew the face of the earth. **R.**

**SECOND READING**                                            *Romans 8:22—27*

Brothers and sisters: We know that all creation is groaning in labor pains even until now; and not only that, but we ourselves, who have the firstfruits of the Spirit, we also groan within ourselves as we wait for adoption, the redemption of our bodies. For in hope we were saved. Now hope that sees is not hope. For who hopes for what one sees? But if we hope for what we do not see, we wait with endurance.

In the same way, the Spirit too comes to the aid of our weakness; for we do not know how to pray as we ought, but the Spirit himself intercedes with inexpressible groanings. And the one who searches hearts knows what is the intention of the Spirit, because he intercedes for the holy ones according to God's will.

**ALLELUIA**                                                                      *Luke 3:4, 6*

**R. Alleluia, alleluia.** Come, Holy Spirit, fill the hearts of the faithful and kindle in them the fire of your love. **R.**


**GOSPEL**                                                                        *John 7:37—39*

On the last and greatest day of the feast, Jesus stood up and exclaimed, "Let anyone who thirsts come to me and drink. As Scripture says: *Rivers of living water will flow from within him who believes in me."*

He said this in reference to the Spirit that those who came to believe in him were to receive. There was, of course, no Spirit yet, because Jesus had not yet been glorified.


**PRAYER OVER THE OFFERINGS**

Pour out upon these gifts the blessing of your Spirit, we pray, O Lord, so that through them your Church may be imbued with such love that the truth of your saving mystery may shine forth for the whole world. Through Christ our Lord.

**COMMUNION ANTIPHON**                                                            **Jn 7: 37**

On the last day of the festival, Jesus stood and cried out: If anyone is thirsty, let him come to me and drink, alleluia.

**PRAYER AFTER COMMUNION**

May these gifts we have consumed benefit us, O Lord, that we may always be aflame with the same Spirit, whom you wondrously poured out on your Apostles. Through Christ our Lord.


## MASS OF THE DAY

**ENTRANCE ANTIPHON**                                                             **Wis 1: 7**

The Spirit of the Lord has filled the whole world and that which contains all things understands what is said, alleluia.

**OR**                                                 **Rm 5: 5; cf. 8: 11**

The love of God has been poured into our hearts through the Spirit of God dwelling within us, alleluia.

**COLLECT**

O God, who by the mystery of today's great feast sanctify your whole Church in every people and nation, pour out, we pray, the gifts of the Holy Spirit across the face of the earth and, with the divine grace that was at work when the Gospel was first proclaimed, fill now once more the hearts of believers. Through our Lord Jesus Christ, your Son, who lives and reigns with you in the unity of the Holy Spirit, one God, for ever and ever.

**FIRST READING**                                    *Acts 2:1—11*

When the time for Pentecost was fulfilled, they were all in one place together. And suddenly there came from the sky a noise like a strong driving wind, and it filled the entire house in which they were. Then there appeared to them tongues as of fire, which parted and came to rest on each one of them. And they were all filled with the Holy Spirit and began to speak in different tongues, as the Spirit enabled them to proclaim.

Now there were devout Jews from every nation under heaven staying in Jerusalem. At this sound, they gathered in a large crowd, but they were confused because each one heard them speaking in his own language. They were astounded, and in amazement they asked, "Are not all these people who are speaking Galileans? Then how does each of us hear them in his native language? We are Parthians, Medes, and Elamites, inhabitants of Mesopotamia, Judea and Cappadocia, Pontus and Asia, Phrygia and Pamphylia, Egypt and the districts of Libya near Cyrene, as well as travelers from Rome, both Jews and converts to Judaism, Cretans and Arabs, yet we hear them speaking in our own tongues of the mighty acts of God."

**PSALM**                              *Psalm 104:1, 24, 29—30, 31, 34*

**R. Lord, send out your Spirit, and renew the face of the earth. or R. Alleluia.**

Bless the LORD, O my soul! / O LORD, my God, you are great indeed! / How manifold are your works, O LORD! / The earth is full of your creatures. **R.**

If you take away their breath, they perish **/** and return to their dust. **/** When you send forth your spirit, they are created, **/** and you renew the face of the earth. **R.**

May the glory of the LORD endure forever; **/** may the LORD be glad in his works! **/** Pleasing to him be my theme; **/** I will be glad in the LORD. **R.**

## SECOND READING                    *1 Corinthians 12:3b—7, 12—13*

Brothers and sisters: No one can say, "Jesus is Lord," except by the Holy Spirit. There are different kinds of spiritual gifts but the same Spirit; there are different forms of service but the same Lord; there are different workings but the same God who produces all of them in everyone. To each individual the manifestation of the Spirit is given for some benefit.

As a body is one though it has many parts, and all the parts of the body, though many, are one body, so also Christ. For in one Spirit we were all baptized into one body, whether Jews or Greeks, slaves or free persons, and we were all given to drink of one Spirit.

## OR:                                      *Galatians 5:16—25*

Brothers and sisters, live by the Spirit and you will certainly not gratify the desire of the flesh. For the flesh has desires against the Spirit, and the Spirit against the flesh; these are opposed to each other, so that you may not do what you want. But if you are guided by the Spirit, you are not under the law. Now the works of the flesh are obvious: immorality, impurity, lust, idolatry, sorcery, hatreds, rivalry, jealousy, outbursts of fury, acts of selfishness, dissensions, factions, occasions of envy, drinking bouts, orgies, and the like. I warn you, as I warned you before, that those who do such things will not inherit the kingdom of God. In contrast, the fruit of the Spirit is love, joy, peace, patience, kindness, generosity, faithfulness, gentleness, self—control. Against such there is no law. Now those who belong to Christ Jesus have crucified their flesh with its passions and desires. If we live in the Spirit, let us also follow the Spirit.

## SEQUENCE
### *VENI, SANCTE SPIRITUS*

**Come, Holy Spirit, come!** **/** And from your celestial home **/** Shed a ray of light divine!

**Come, Father of the poor!** **/** Come, source of all our store! **/** Come, within our bosoms shine.

**You, of comforters the best**; / You, the soul's most welcome guest; / Sweet refreshment here below;

**In our labor, rest most sweet**; / Grateful coolness in the heat; / Solace in the midst of woe.

**O most blessed Light divine,** / Shine within these hearts of yours, / And our inmost being fill!

**Where you are not, we have naught,** / Nothing good in deed or thought, / Nothing free from taint of ill.

**Heal our wounds, our strength renew;** / On our dryness pour your dew; / Wash the stains of guilt away:

**Bend the stubborn heart and will;** / Melt the frozen, warm the chill; / Guide the steps that go astray.

**On the faithful, who adore** / And confess you, evermore / In your sevenfold gift descend;

**Give them virtue's sure reward**; / Give them your salvation, Lord; / Give them joys that never end. Amen. Alleluia.

## ALLELUIA

**R. Alleluia, alleluia.** Come, Holy Spirit, fill the hearts of your faithful and kindle in them the fire of your love. **R**

## GOSPEL                                                        *John 20:19—23*

On the evening of that first day of the week, when the doors were locked, where the disciples were, for fear of the Jews, Jesus came and stood in their midst and said to them, "Peace be with you." When he had said this, he showed them his hands and his side. The disciples rejoiced when they saw the Lord. Jesus said to them again, "Peace be with you." As the Father has sent me, so I send you." And when he had said this, he breathed on them and said to them, "Receive the Holy Spirit." Whose sins you forgive are forgiven them, and whose sins you retain are retained."

**OR:**                                                  *John 15:26—27; 16:12—15*

Jesus said to his disciples: "When the Advocate comes whom I will send you from the Father, the Spirit of truth that proceeds from the Father, he will testify to me. And you also testify, because you have been with me from the beginning.

"I have much more to tell you, but you cannot bear it now. But when he comes, the Spirit of truth, he will guide you to all truth. He will not speak on his own, but he will speak what he hears, and will declare to you the things that are coming. He will glorify me, because he will take from what is mine and declare it to you. Everything that the Father has is mine; for this reason I told you that he will take from what is mine and declare it to you."

## PRAYER OVER THE OFFERINGS

Grant, we pray, O Lord, that, as promised by your Son, the Holy Spirit may reveal to us more abundantly the hidden mystery of this sacrifice and graciously lead us into all truth. Through Christ our Lord.

## COMMUNION ANTIPHON                    Acts 2: 4, 11

They were all filled with the Holy Spirit and spoke of the marvels of God, alleluia.

## PRAYER AFTER COMMUNION

O God, who bestow heavenly gifts upon your Church, safeguard, we pray, the grace you have given, that the gift of the Holy Spirit poured out upon her may retain all its force and that this spiritual food may gain her abundance of eternal redemption. Through Christ our Lord.

## LESSONS LEARNT FROM THE READINGS / HOMILY

1 _____ 2 _____
3 _____ 4 _____
5 _____ 6 _____

## ACTION POINTS FOR THE WEEK

1 _____ 2 _____
3 _____ 4 _____
5 _____ 6 _____

## PRAYER POINTS FOR THE WEEK

1 _____ 2 _____
3 _____ 4 _____
5 _____ 6 _____

## THIS WEEK, I AM GRATEFUL FOR

1 _____ 2 _____
3 _____ 4 _____

# 30 MAY 2021, SOLEMNITY OF THE MOST HOLY TRINITY

**ENTRANCE ANTIPHON**

Blest be God the Father, and the Only Begotten Son of God, and also the Holy Spirit, for he has shown us his merciful love.

**COLLECT**

God our Father, who by sending into the world the Word of truth and the Spirit of sanctification made known to the human race your wondrous mystery, grant us, we pray, that in professing the true faith, we may acknowledge the Trinity of eternal glory and adore your Unity, powerful in majesty. Through our Lord Jesus Christ, your Son, who lives and reigns with you in the unity of the Holy Spirit, one God, for ever and ever.

**FIRST READING**                    *Deuteronomy 4:32—34, 39—40*

Moses said to the people: "Ask now of the days of old, before your time, ever since God created man upon the earth; ask from one end of the sky to the other: Did anything so great ever happen before? Was it ever heard of? Did a people ever hear the voice of God speaking from the midst of fire, as you did, and live? Or did any god venture to go and take a nation for himself from the midst of another nation, by testings, by signs and wonders, by war, with strong hand and outstretched arm, and by great terrors, all of which the LORD, your God, did for you in Egypt before your very eyes? This is why you must now know, and fix in your heart, that the LORD is God in the heavens above and on earth below, and that there is no other. You must keep his statutes and commandments that I enjoin on you today, that you and your children after you may prosper, and that you may have long life on the land which the LORD, your God, is giving you forever."

**PSALM:**                    *Psalm 33:4—5, 6, 9, 18—19, 20, 22 (12b)*

**R. Blessed the people the LORD has chosen to be his own.**

Upright is the word of the Lord, / and all his works are trustworthy. / He loves justice and right; / of the kindness of the LORD the earth is full. **R.**

By the word of the LORD the heavens were made; / by the breath of his mouth all their host. / For he spoke, and it was made;/he commanded, and it stood forth.**R**

See, the eyes of the LORD are upon those who fear him, **/** upon those who hope for his kindness, **/** to deliver them from death **/** and preserve them in spite of famine. **R.**

Our soul waits for the LORD, **/** who is our help and our shield. **/** May your kindness, O LORD, be upon us **/** who have put our hope in you. **R.**

**SECOND READING**                                       *Romans 8:14—17*

Brothers and sisters: Those who are led by the Spirit of God are sons of God. For you did not receive a spirit of slavery to fall back into fear, but you received a Spirit of adoption, through whom we cry, "Abba, Father!" The Spirit himself bears witness with our spirit that we are children of God, and if children, then heirs, heirs of God and joint heirs with Christ, if only we suffer with him so that we may also be glorified with him.

**ALLELUIA**                                               *Revelation 1:8*

**R. Alleluia, alleluia.** Glory to the Father, the Son, and the Holy Spirit; to God who is, who was, and who is to come. **R.**

**GOSPEL**                                               *Matthew 28:16—20*

The eleven disciples went to Galilee, to the mountain to which Jesus had ordered them. When they all saw him, they worshiped, but they doubted. Then Jesus approached and said to them, "All power in heaven and on earth has been given to me. Go, therefore, and make disciples of all nations, baptizing them in the name of the Father, and of the Son, and of the Holy Spirit, teaching them to observe all that I have commanded you. And behold, I am with you always, until the end of the age."

**PRAYER OVER THE OFFERINGS**

Sanctify by the invocation of your name, we pray, O Lord our God, this oblation of our service, and by it make of us an eternal offering to you. Through Christ our Lord.

**COMMUNION ANTIPHON**                                       **Gal 4: 6**

Since you are children of God, God has sent into your hearts the Spirit of his Son, the Spirit who cries out: Abba, Father.

**PRAYER AFTER COMMUNION**

May receiving this Sacrament, O Lord our God, bring us health of body and soul, as we confess your eternal holy Trinity and undivided Unity. Through Christ our Lord.

## LESSONS LEARNT FROM THE READINGS / HOMILY

| 1 | 2 |
|---|---|
| 3 | 4 |
| 5 | 6 |

## ACTION POINTS FOR THE WEEK

| 1 | 2 |
|---|---|
| 3 | 4 |
| 5 | 6 |

## PRAYER POINTS FOR THE WEEK

| 1 | 2 |
|---|---|
| 3 | 4 |
| 5 | 6 |

## THIS WEEK, I AM GRATEFUL FOR

| 1 | 2 |
|---|---|
| 3 | 4 |
| 5 | 6 |

*11*                                          *JUNE*

## 06 JUNE 2021, SOLEMNITY OF THE
## MOST HOLY BODY AND BLOOD OF CHRIST

**ENTRANCE ANTIPHON**                              **Cf. Ps 80: 17**

He fed them with the finest wheat and satisfied them with honey from the rock.

**COLLECT**

O God, who in this wonderful Sacrament have left us a memorial of your Passion, grant us, we pray, so to revere the sacred mysteries of your Body and Blood that we may always experience in ourselves the fruits of your redemption. Who live and reign with God the Father in the unity of the Holy Spirit, one God, for ever and ever.

**FIRST READING**                              *Exodus 24:3—8*

When Moses came to the people and related all the words and ordinances of the LORD, they all answered with one voice, "We will do everything that the LORD has told us." Moses then wrote down all the words of the LORD and, rising early the next day, he erected at the foot of the mountain an altar and twelve pillars for the twelve tribes of Israel. Then, having sent certain young men of the Israelites to offer holocausts and sacrifice young bulls as peace offerings to the LORD, Moses took half of the blood and put it in large bowls; the other half he splashed on the altar. Taking the book of the covenant, he read it aloud to the people, who answered, "All that the LORD has said, we will heed and do." Then he took the blood and sprinkled it on the people, saying, "This is the blood of the covenant that the LORD has made with you in accordance with all these words of his."

**PSALM:** *Psalm 116:12—13, 15—16, 17—18 (13)*
**R. I will take the cup of salvation, and call on the name of the Lord. or R. Alleluia.**
How shall I make a return to the LORD / for all the good he has done for me? / The cup of salvation I will take up, / and I will call upon the name of the LORD. **R**
Precious in the eyes of the LORD / is the death of his faithful ones. / I am your servant, the son of your handmaid; / you have loosed my bonds. **R.**
To you will I offer sacrifice of thanksgiving, / and I will call upon the name of the LORD. / My vows to the LORD I will pay / in the presence of all his people. **R.**

**SECOND READING** *Hebrews 9:11—15*
Brothers and sisters: When Christ came as high priest of the good things that have come to be, passing through the greater and more perfect tabernacle not made by hands, that is, not belonging to this creation, he entered once for all into the sanctuary, not with the blood of goats and calves but with his own blood, thus obtaining eternal redemption. For if the blood of goats and bulls and the sprinkling of a heifer's ashes can sanctify those who are defiled so that their flesh is cleansed, how much more will the blood of Christ, who through the eternal Spirit offered himself unblemished to God, cleanse our consciences from dead works to worship the living God.

For this reason he is mediator of a new covenant: since a death has taken place for deliverance from transgressions under the first covenant, those who are called may receive the promised eternal inheritance.

## LONG SEQUENCE - LAUDA SION

**Laud, O Zion, your salvation,** / Laud with hymns of exultation, / Christ, your king and shepherd true:

**Bring him all the praise you know**, / He is more than you bestow. / Never can you reach his due.

**Special theme for glad thanksgiving** / Is the quick'ning and the living / Bread today before you set:

**From his hands of old partaken**, / As we know, by faith unshaken, / Where the Twelve at supper met.

**Full and clear ring out your chanting,** / Joy nor sweetest grace be wanting, / From your heart let praises burst:

**For today the feast is holden**, / When the institution olden / Of that supper was rehearsed.

**Here the new law's new oblation**, / By the new king's revelation, / Ends the form of ancient rite:

**Now the new the old effaces**, / Truth away the shadow chases, / Light dispels the gloom of night.

**What he did at supper seated**, / Christ ordained to be repeated, / His memorial ne'er to cease:

**And his rule for guidance taking,** / Bread and wine we hallow, making / Thus our sacrifice of peace.

**This the truth each Christian learns,** / Bread into his flesh he turns, / To his precious blood the wine:

**Sight has fail'd, nor thought conceives**, / But a dauntless faith believes, / Resting on a pow'r divine.

**Here beneath these signs are hidden** / Priceless things to sense forbidden; / Signs, not things are all we see:

**Blood is poured and flesh is broken**, / Yet in either wondrous token / Christ entire we know to be.

**Whoso of this food partakes,** / Does not rend the Lord nor breaks; / Christ is whole to all that taste:

**Thousands are, as one, receivers,** / One, as thousands of believers, / Eats of him who cannot waste.

**Bad and good the feast are sharing,** / Of what divers dooms preparing, / Endless death, or endless life.

**Life to these, to those damnation,** / See how like participation / Is with unlike issues rife.

**When the sacrament is broken, /** Doubt not, but believe 'tis spoken, **/** That each sever'd outward token **/** doth the very whole contain.
**Nought the precious gift divides, /** Breaking but the sign betides **/** Jesus still the same abides, **/** still unbroken does remain.

### THE SHORT FORM OF THE SEQUENCE

**Lo! the angel's food is given /** To the pilgrim who has striven; **/** see the children's bread from heaven, **/** which on dogs may not be spent.
**Truth the ancient types fulfilling, /** Isaac bound, a victim willing, **/** Paschal lamb, its lifeblood spilling, **/** manna to the fathers sent.
Very bread, good shepherd, tend us, **/** Jesu, of your love befriend us, **/** You refresh us, you defend us, **/** Your eternal goodness send us **/** In the land of life to see.
**You who all things can and know, /** Who on earth such food bestow, **/** Grant us with your saints, though lowest, **/** Where the heav'nly feast you show, **/** Fellow heirs and guests to be. Amen. Alleluia.

**ALLELUIA**                                                              *John 6:51*
**R. Alleluia, alleluia.** I am the living bread that came down from heaven, says the Lord; whoever eats this bread will live forever. **R.**

**GOSPEL**                                              *Mark 14:12—16, 22—26*
On the first day of the Feast of Unleavened Bread, when they sacrificed the Passover lamb, Jesus' disciples said to him, "Where do you want us to go and prepare for you to eat the Passover?" He sent two of his disciples and said to them, "Go into the city and a man will meet you, carrying a jar of water. Follow him. Wherever he enters, say to the master of the house, 'The Teacher says, "Where is my guest room where I may eat the Passover with my disciples?"' Then he will show you a large upper room furnished and ready. Make the preparations for us there." The disciples then went off, entered the city, and found it just as he had told them; and they prepared the Passover.

While they were eating, he took bread, said the blessing, broke it, gave it to them, and said, "Take it; this is my body." Then he took a cup, gave thanks, and gave it to them, and they all drank from it. He said to them, "This is my blood of the covenant, which will be shed for many. Amen, I say to you, I shall not drink again the fruit of the vine until the day when I drink it new in the kingdom of God." Then, after singing a hymn, they went out to the Mount of Olives.

## PRAYER OVER THE OFFERINGS

Grant your Church, O Lord, we pray, the gifts of unity and peace, whose signs are to be seen in mystery in the offerings we here present. Through Christ our Lord.

## COMMUNION ANTIPHON                                    Jn 6: 57

Whoever eats my flesh and drinks my blood remains in me and I in him, says the Lord.

## PRAYER AFTER COMMUNION

Grant, O Lord, we pray, that we may delight for all eternity in that share in your divine life, which is foreshadowed in the present age by our reception of your precious Body and Blood. Who live and reign for ever and ever.

## LESSONS LEARNT FROM THE READINGS / HOMILY

1 _____  2 _____
3 _____  4 _____
5 _____  6 _____

## ACTION POINTS FOR THE WEEK

1 _____  2 _____
3 _____  4 _____
5 _____  6 _____

## PRAYER POINTS FOR THE WEEK

1 _____  2 _____
3 _____  4 _____
5 _____  6 _____

## THIS WEEK, I AM GRATEFUL FOR

1 _____  2 _____
3 _____  4 _____
5 _____  6 _____

## SOLEMNITY OF THE MOST SACRED HEART OF JESUS

**ENTRANCE ANTIPHON**                            **Ps 32: 11, 19**

The designs of his Heart are from age to age, to rescue their souls from death, and to keep them alive in famine.

**COLLECT**

Grant, we pray, almighty God, that we, who glory in the Heart of your beloved Son and recall the wonders of his love for us, may be made worthy to receive an overflowing measure of grace from that fount of heavenly gifts. Through our Lord Jesus Christ, your Son, who lives and reigns with you in the unity of the Holy Spirit, one God, for ever and ever.

**OR**

O God, who in the Heart of your Son, wounded by our sins, bestow on us in mercy the boundless treasures of your love, grant, we pray, that, in paying him the homage of our devotion, we may also offer worthy reparation. Through our Lord Jesus Christ, your Son, who lives and reigns with you in the unity of the Holy Spirit, one God, for ever and ever.

**FIRST READING**                                *Hosea 11:1, 3—4, 8c—9*

Thus says the LORD: When Israel was a child I loved him, out of Egypt I called my son. Yet it was I who taught Ephraim to walk, who took them in my arms; I drew them with human cords, with bands of love; I fostered them like one who raises an infant to his cheeks; yet, though I stooped to feed my child, they did not know that I was their healer.

My heart is overwhelmed, my pity is stirred. I will not give vent to my blazing anger, I will not destroy Ephraim again; for I am God and not a man, the Holy One present among you; I will not let the flames consume you.

**CANTICLE**                                       *Isaiah 12:2—3, 4, 5—6*

**R. You will draw water joyfully from the springs of salvation.**

God indeed is my savior; / I am confident and unafraid. / My strength and my courage is the LORD, / and he has been my savior. / With joy you will draw water at the fountain of salvation. **R.**

Give thanks to the LORD, acclaim his name; / among the nations make known his deeds, / proclaim how exalted is his name. **R.**

Sing praise to the Lord for his glorious achievement; / let this be known throughout all the earth. / Shout with exultation, O city of Zion, / for great in your midst / is the Holy One of Israel! **R.**

**SECOND READING**                                     *Ephesians 3:8—12, 14—19*
Brothers and sisters: To me, the very least of all the holy ones, this grace was given, to preach to the Gentiles the inscrutable riches of Christ, and to bring to light for all what is the plan of the mystery hidden from ages past in God who created all things, so that the manifold wisdom of God might now be made known through the church to the principalities and authorities in the heavens. This was according to the eternal purpose that he accomplished in Christ Jesus our Lord, in whom we have boldness of speech and confidence of access through faith in him.

For this reason I kneel before the Father, from whom every family in heaven and on earth is named, that he may grant you in accord with the riches of his glory to be strengthened with power through his Spirit in the inner self, and that Christ may dwell in your hearts through faith; that you, rooted and grounded in love, may have strength to comprehend with all the holy ones what is the breadth and length and height and depth, and to know the love of Christ which surpasses knowledge, so that you may be filled with all the fullness of God.

**ALLELUIA**                                          *Matthew 11:29ab*
**R. Alleluia, alleluia.** Take my yoke upon you, says the Lord; and learn from me, for I am meek and humble of heart. **R.**

**GOSPEL**                                              *John 19:31—37*
Since it was preparation day, in order that the bodies might not remain on the cross on the sabbath, for the sabbath day of that week was a solemn one, the Jews asked Pilate that their legs be broken and they be taken down. So the soldiers came and broke the legs of the first and then of the other one who was crucified with Jesus. But when they came to Jesus and saw that he was already dead, they did not break his legs, but one soldier thrust his lance into his side, and immediately blood and water flowed out. An eyewitness has testified, and his testimony is true; he knows that he is speaking the truth, so that you also may come to believe. For this happened so that the Scripture passage might be fulfilled: *Not a bone of it will be broken.* And again another passage says: *They will look upon him whom they have pierced.*

**PRAYER OVER THE OFFERINGS**

Look, O Lord, we pray, on the surpassing charity in the Heart of your beloved Son, that what we offer may be a gift acceptable to you and an expiation of our offences. Through Christ our Lord.

**COMMUNION ANTIPHON    Cf. Jn 7: 37 – 38**

Thus says the Lord: Let whoever is thirsty come to me and drink. Streams of living water will flow from within the one who believes in me.

 **OR**

One of the soldiers opened his side with a lance, and at once there came forth blood and water.

**PRAYER AFTER COMMUNION**

May this sacrament of charity, O Lord, make us fervent with the fire of holy love, so that, drawn always to your Son, we may learn to see him in our neighbour.Through Christ our Lord.

**LESSONS LEARNT FROM THE READINGS / HOMILY**

1 _____ 2 _____
3 _____ 4 _____
5 _____ 6 _____

**ACTION POINTS FOR THE WEEK**

1 _____ 2 _____
3 _____ 4 _____
5 _____ 6 _____

**PRAYER POINTS FOR THE WEEK**

1 _____ 2 _____
3 _____ 4 _____
5 _____ 6 _____

**THIS WEEK, I AM GRATEFUL FOR**

1 _____ 2 _____
3 _____ 4 _____
5 _____ 6 _____

# 13 JUNE 2021, 11TH SUNDAY IN ORDINARY TIME

**ENTRANCE ANTIPHON** Cf. Ps 26: 7, 9

O Lord, hear my voice, for I have called to you; be my help. Do not abandon or forsake me, O God, my Saviour!

**COLLECT**

O God, strength of those who hope in you, graciously hear our pleas, and, since without you mortal frailty can do nothing, grant us always the help of your grace, that in following your commands we may please you by our resolve and our deeds. Through our Lord Jesus Christ, your Son, who lives and reigns with you in the unity of the Holy Spirit, one God, for ever and ever.

**FIRST READING** *Ezekiel 17:22—24*

Thus says the Lord GOD: I, too, will take from the crest of the cedar, from its topmost branches tear off a tender shoot, and plant it on a high and lofty mountain; on the mountain heights of Israel I will plant it. It shall put forth branches and bear fruit, and become a majestic cedar. Birds of every kind shall dwell beneath it, every winged thing in the shade of its boughs. And all the trees of the field shall know that I, the LORD, bring low the high tree, lift high the lowly tree, wither up the green tree, and make the withered tree bloom. As I, the LORD, have spoken, so will I do.

**PSALM** *Psalm 92:2—3, 13—14, 15—16*

**R. Lord, it is good to give thanks to you.**

It is good to give thanks to the LORD, **/** to sing praise to your name, Most High, **/** to proclaim your kindness at dawn**/**and your faithfulness throughout the night. **R.**

The just one shall flourish like the palm tree, **/** like a cedar of Lebanon shall he grow. **/** They that are planted in the house of the LORD **/** shall flourish in the courts of our God. **R.**

They shall bear fruit even in old age; **/** vigorous and sturdy shall they be, **/** declaring how just is the LORD,**/**my rock, in whom there is no wrong.**R**

**SECOND READING** *2 Corinthians 5:6—10*

Brothers and sisters: We are always courageous, although we know that while we are at home in the body we are away from the Lord, for we walk by faith, not by sight. Yet we are courageous, and we would rather leave the body and go home to the Lord. Therefore, we aspire to please him, whether we are at home or away. For we must all appear before the judgment seat of Christ, so that each may receive recompense, according to what he did in the body, whether good or evil.

**ALLELUIA** **Jn 15:15**

**R. Alleluia, alleluia.** The seed is the word of God, Christ is the sower. All who come to him will live for ever. **R.**


**GOSPEL** *Mark 4:26—34*

Jesus said to the crowds: "This is how it is with the kingdom of God; it is as if a man were to scatter seed on the land and would sleep and rise night and day and through it all the seed would sprout and grow, he knows not how. Of its own accord the land yields fruit, first the blade, then the ear, then the full grain in the ear. And when the grain is ripe, he wields the sickle at once, for the harvest has come."

He said, "To what shall we compare the kingdom of God, or what parable can we use for it? It is like a mustard seed that, when it is sown in the ground, is the smallest of all the seeds on the earth. But once it is sown, it springs up and becomes the largest of plants and puts forth large branches, so that the birds of the sky can dwell in its shade." With many such parables he spoke the word to them as they were able to understand it. Without parables he did not speak to them, but to his own disciples he explained everything in private.


**PRAYER OVER THE OFFERINGS**

O God, who in the offerings presented here provide for the twofold needs of human nature, nourishing us with food and renewing us with your Sacrament, grant, we pray, that the sustenance they provide may not fail us in body or in spirit. Through Christ our Lord.

**COMMUNION ANTIPHON** **Ps 26: 4**

There is one thing I ask of the Lord, only this do I seek: to live in the house of the Lord all the days of my life.

**OR**

Holy Father, keep in your name those you have given me, that they may be one as we are one, says the Lord.

**PRAYER AFTER COMMUNION**

As this reception of your Holy Communion, O Lord, foreshadows the union of the faithful in you, so may it bring about unity in your Church. Through Christ our Lord.

## LESSONS LEARNT FROM THE READINGS / HOMILY

1 _____ 2 _____
3 _____ 4 _____
5 _____ 6 _____

## ACTION POINTS FOR THE WEEK

1 _____ 2 _____
3 _____ 4 _____
5 _____ 6 _____

## PRAYER POINTS FOR THE WEEK

1 _____ 2 _____
3 _____ 4 _____
5 _____ 6 _____

## THIS WEEK, I AM GRATEFUL FOR

1 _____ 2 _____
3 _____ 4 _____
5 _____ 6 _____

## 20 JUNE 2021, 12TH SUNDAY IN ORDINARY TIME

**ENTRANCE ANTIPHON**                                    Cf. Ps 27: 8 – 9

The Lord is the strength of his people, a saving refuge for the one he has anointed. Save your people, Lord, and bless your heritage, and govern them for ever.

**COLLECT**

Grant, O Lord, that we may always revere and love your holy name, for you never deprive of your guidance those you set firm on the foundation of your love. Through our Lord Jesus Christ, your Son, who lives and reigns with you in the unity of the Holy Spirit, one God, for ever and ever.

**FIRST READING**                                        *Job 38:1, 8—11*

The Lord addressed Job out of the storm and said: Who shut within doors the sea, when it burst forth from the womb; when I made the clouds its garment and thick darkness its swaddling bands? When I set limits for it and fastened the bar of its door, and said: Thus far shall you come but no farther, and here shall your proud waves be stilled!

**PSALM** *Psalm 107:23—24, 25—26, 28—29, 30—31 (1b)*
**R. Give thanks to the Lord, his love is everlasting. or R. Alleluia.**
They who sailed the sea in ships, / trading on the deep waters, / these saw the works of the LORD/and his wonders in the abyss.**R**
His command raised up a storm wind / which tossed its waves on high. / They mounted up to heaven; they sank to the depths; / their hearts melted away in their plight. **R.**
They cried to the LORD in their distress; / from their straits he rescued them. / He hushed the storm to a gentle breeze, / and the billows of the sea were stilled. **R.**
They rejoiced that they were calmed, / and he brought them to their desired haven. / Let them give thanks to the LORD for his kindness / and his wondrous deeds to the children of men. **R.**

**SECOND READING** *2 Corinthians 5:14—17*
Brothers and sisters: The love of Christ impels us, once we have come to the conviction that one died for all; therefore, all have died. He indeed died for all, so that those who live might no longer live for themselves but for him who for their sake died and was raised.

Consequently, from now on we regard no one according to the flesh; even if we once knew Christ according to the flesh, yet now we know him so no longer. So whoever is in Christ is a new creation: the old things have passed away; behold, new things have come.

**ALLELUIA** *Luke 7:16*
**R. Alleluia, alleluia.** A great prophet has risen in our midst, God has visited his people. **R.**

**GOSPEL** *Mark 4:35—41*
On that day, as evening drew on, Jesus said to his disciples: "Let us cross to the other side." Leaving the crowd, they took Jesus with them in the boat just as he was. And other boats were with him. A violent squall came up and waves were breaking over the boat, so that it was already filling up. Jesus was in the stern, asleep on a cushion. They woke him and said to him, "Teacher, do you not care that we are perishing?" He woke up, rebuked the wind, and said to the sea, "Quiet! Be still!" The wind ceased

and there was great calm. Then he asked them, "Why are you terrified? Do you not yet have faith?" They were filled with great awe and said to one another, "Who then is this whom even wind and sea obey?"

## PRAYER OVER THE OFFERINGS

Receive, O Lord, the sacrifice of conciliation and praise and grant that, cleansed by its action, we may make offering of a heart pleasing to you. Through Christ our Lord.

## COMMUNION ANTIPHON                                    Ps 144: 15

The eyes of all look to you, Lord, and you give them their food in due season.

## OR                                                    Jn 10: 11, 15

I am the Good Shepherd, and I lay down my life for my sheep, says the Lord.

## PRAYER AFTER COMMUNION

Renewed and nourished by the Sacred Body and Precious Blood of your Son, we ask of your mercy, O Lord, that what we celebrate with constant devotion may be our sure pledge of redemption. Through Christ our Lord.

## LESSONS LEARNT FROM THE READINGS / HOMILY

1 _____ 2 _____
3 _____ 4 _____
5 _____ 6 _____

## ACTION POINTS FOR THE WEEK

1 _____ 2 _____
3 _____ 4 _____
5 _____ 6 _____

## PRAYER POINTS FOR THE WEEK

1 _____ 2 _____
3 _____ 4 _____
5 _____ 6 _____

## THIS WEEK, I AM GRATEFUL FOR

1 _____ 2 _____
3 _____ 4 _____
5 _____ 6 _____

## ENTRANCE ANTIPHON                     Lk 1: 15, 14

He will be great in the sight of the Lord and will be filled with the Holy Spirit, even from his mother's womb; and many will rejoice at his birth.

## COLLECT

Grant, we pray, almighty God, that your family may walk in the way of salvation and, attentive to what Saint John the Precursor urged, may come safely to the One he foretold, our Lord Jesus Christ. Who lives and reigns with you in the unity of the Holy Spirit, one God, for ever and ever.

## FIRST READING                        *Jeremiah 1:4—10*

In the days of King Josiah, the word of the LORD came to me, saying: Before I formed you in the womb I knew you, before you were born I dedicated you, a prophet to the nations I appointed you.

"Ah, Lord GOD!" I said, "I know not how to speak; I am too young." But the LORD answered me, Say not, "I am too young." To whomever I send you, you shall go; whatever I command you, you shall speak. Have no fear before them, because I am with you to deliver you, says the LORD.

Then the LORD extended his hand and touched my mouth, saying,

See, I place my words in your mouth! This day I set you over nations and over kingdoms, to root up and to tear down, to destroy and to demolish, to build and to plant.

## PSALM:                    *Psalm 71:1—2, 3—4a, 5—6ab, 15ab, 17 (6)*
**R. Since my mother's womb, you have been my strength.**

In you, O LORD, I take refuge; **/** let me never be put to shame. **/** In your justice rescue me, and deliver me;/incline your ear to me, and save me. **R.**
Be my rock of refuge, **/** a stronghold to give me safety, **/** for you are my rock and my fortress. **/** O my God, rescue me from the hand of the wicked.**R**
For you are my hope, O LORD; **/** my trust, O LORD, from my youth. **/** On you I depend from birth;/from my mother's womb you are my strength.**R.**
My mouth shall declare your justice, **/** day by day your salvation. **/** O God, you have taught me from my youth, **/** and till the present I proclaim your wondrous deeds. **R.**

**SECOND READING**                                              *1 Peter 1:8—12*

Beloved: Although you have not seen Jesus Christ you love him; even though you do not see him now yet believe in him, you rejoice with an indescribable and glorious joy, as you attain the goal of your faith, the salvation of your souls.

Concerning this salvation, prophets who prophesied about the grace that was to be yours searched and investigated it, investigating the time and circumstances that the Spirit of Christ within them indicated when he testified in advance to the sufferings destined for Christ and the glories to follow them. It was revealed to them that they were serving not themselves but you with regard to the things that have now been announced to you by those who preached the Good News to you through the Holy Spirit sent from heaven, things into which angels longed to look.

**ALLELUIA**                                        *see John 1:7; Luke 1:17*

**R. Alleluia, alleluia.** He came to testify to the light, to prepare a people fit for the Lord. **R.**

**GOSPEL**                                                      *Luke 1:5—17*

In the days of Herod, King of Judea, there was a priest named Zechariah of the priestly division of Abijah; his wife was from the daughters of Aaron, and her name was Elizabeth. Both were righteous in the eyes of God, observing all the commandments and ordinances of the Lord blamelessly. But they had no child, because Elizabeth was barren and both were advanced in years. Once when he was serving as priest in his division's turn before God, according to the practice of the priestly service, he was chosen by lot to enter the sanctuary of the Lord to burn incense. Then, when the whole assembly of the people was praying outside at the hour of the incense offering, the angel of the Lord appeared to him, standing at the right of the altar of incense. Zechariah was troubled by what he saw, and fear came upon him. But the angel said to him, "Do not be afraid, Zechariah, because your prayer has been heard. Your wife Elizabeth will bear you a son, and you shall name him John. And you will have joy and gladness, and many will rejoice at his birth, for he will be great in the sight of the Lord. John will drink neither wine nor strong drink. He will be filled with the Holy Spirit even from his mother's womb, and he will turn many of the children of Israel to the Lord their God. He will go before him in the spirit and power of Elijah to turn their hearts toward their children and the disobedient to the understanding of the righteous, to prepare a people fit for the Lord."

## PRAYER OVER THE OFFERINGS
Look with favour, O Lord, upon the offerings made by your people on the Solemnity of Saint John the Baptist, and grant that what we celebrate in mystery we may follow with deeds of devoted service. Through Christ our Lord.

## COMMUNION ANTIPHON                                             Lk 1: 68
Blessed be the Lord, the God of Israel! He has visited his people and redeemed them.

## PRAYER AFTER COMMUNION
May the marvellous prayer of Saint John the Baptist accompany us who have eaten our fill at this sacrificial feast, O Lord, and, since Saint John proclaimed your Son to be the Lamb who would take away our sins, may he implore now for us your favour. Through Christ our Lord.

# MASS OF THE DAY

## ENTRANCE ANTIPHON                                    Jn 1, 6 – 7; Lk 1, 17
A man was sent from God, whose name was John. He came to testify to the light, to prepare a people fit for the Lord.

## COLLECT
O God, who raised up Saint John the Baptist to make ready a nation fit for Christ the Lord, give your people, we pray, the grace of spiritual joys and direct the hearts of all the faithful into the way of salvation and peace. Through our Lord Jesus Christ, your Son, who lives and reigns with you in the unity of the Holy Spirit, one God, for ever and ever.

## FIRST READING                                            *Isaiah 49:1—6*
Hear me, O coastlands, listen, O distant peoples. The LORD called me from birth, from my mother's womb he gave me my name. He made of me a sharp–edged sword and concealed me in the shadow of his arm. He made me a polished arrow, in his quiver he hid me. You are my servant, he said to me, Israel, through whom I show my glory.

Though I thought I had toiled in vain, and for nothing, uselessly, spent my strength, yet my reward is with the LORD, my recompense is with my God. For now the LORD has spoken who formed me as his servant from the womb, that Jacob may be brought back to him and Israel gathered to him; and I am made glorious in the sight of the LORD, and my God is now my strength! It is too little, he says, for you to be my servant, to raise up the tribes of Jacob, and restore the survivors of Israel; I will make you a light to the nations, that my salvation may reach to the ends of the earth.

**PSALM:**                    *Psalm 139:1b—3, 13—14ab, 14c—15 (14)*
**R. I praise you, for I am wonderfully made.**
O LORD, you have probed me, you know me: **/** you know when I sit and when I stand; **/** you understand my thoughts from afar. **/** My journeys and my rest you scrutinize, **/** with all my ways you are familiar. **R.**
Truly you have formed my inmost being; **/** you knit me in my mother's womb. **/** I give you thanks that I am fearfully, wonderfully made; **/** wonderful are your works. **R.**
My soul also you knew full well; **/** nor was my frame unknown to you **/** When I was made in secret, **/** when I was fashioned in the depths of the earth. **R.**

**SECOND READING**                                    *Acts 13:22—26*
In those days, Paul said: "God raised up David as king; of him God testified, *I have found David, son of Jesse, a man after my own heart; he will carry out my every wish.* From this man's descendants God, according to his promise, has brought to Israel a savior, Jesus. John heralded his coming by proclaiming a baptism of repentance to all the people of Israel; and as John was completing his course, he would say, 'What do you suppose that I am? I am not he. Behold, one is coming after me; I am not worthy to unfasten the sandals of his feet.'

"My brothers, sons of the family of Abraham, and those others among you who are God—fearing, to us this word of salvation has been sent."

**ALLELUIA**                                    *see Luke 1:76*
**R. Alleluia, alleluia.** You, child, will be called prophet of the Most High, for you will go before the Lord to prepare his way. **R.**

**GOSPEL**                                    *Luke 1:57—66, 80*
When the time arrived for Elizabeth to have her child she gave birth to a son. Her neighbors and relatives heard that the Lord had shown his great

mercy toward her, and they rejoiced with her. When they came on the eighth day to circumcise the child, they were going to call him Zechariah after his father, but his mother said in reply, "No. He will be called John." But they answered her, "There is no one among your relatives who has this name." So they made signs, asking his father what he wished him to be called. He asked for a tablet and wrote, "John is his name," and all were amazed. Immediately his mouth was opened, his tongue freed, and he spoke blessing God. Then fear came upon all their neighbors, and all these matters were discussed throughout the hill country of Judea. All who heard these things took them to heart, saying, "What, then, will this child be?" For surely the hand of the Lord was with him. The child grew and became strong in spirit, and he was in the desert until the day of his manifestation to Israel.

**PRAYER OVER THE OFFERINGS**
We place these offerings on your altar, O Lord, to celebrate with fitting honour the nativity of him who both foretold the coming of the world's Saviour and pointed him out when he came. Who lives and reigns for ever and ever.

**COMMUNION ANTIPHON**      **Cf. Lk 1: 78**
Through the tender mercy of our God, the Dawn from on high will visit us.

**PRAYER AFTER COMMUNION**
Having feasted at the banquet of the heavenly Lamb, we pray, O Lord, that, finding joy in the nativity of Saint John the Baptist, your Church may know as the author of her rebirth the Christ whose coming John foretold. Who lives and reigns for ever and ever.

**LESSONS LEARNT FROM THE READINGS / HOMILY**

| 1 | 2 |
|---|---|
| 3 | 4 |
| 5 | 6 |

**ACTION POINTS FOR THE WEEK**

| 1 | 2 |
|---|---|
| 3 | 4 |
| 5 | 6 |

## 27 JUNE 2021, 13TH SUNDAY IN ORDINARY TIME

**ENTRANCE**                                    **ANTIPHON Ps 46: 2**

All peoples, clap your hands. Cry to God with shouts of joy!

**COLLECT**

O God, who through the grace of adoption chose us to be children of light, grant, we pray, that we may not be wrapped in the darkness of error but always be seen to stand in the bright light of truth. Through our Lord Jesus Christ, your Son, who lives and reigns with you in the unity of the Holy Spirit, one God, for ever and ever.

**FIRST READING**                              *Wisdom 1:13—15; 2:23—24*

God did not make death, nor does he rejoice in the destruction of the living. For he fashioned all things that they might have being; and the creatures of the world are wholesome, and there is not a destructive drug among them nor any domain of the netherworld on earth, for justice is undying. For God formed man to be imperishable; the image of his own nature he made him. But by the envy of the devil, death entered the world, and they who belong to his company experience it.

**PSALM**                            *Psalm 30:2, 4, 5—6, 11, 12, 13 (2a)*

**R. I will praise you, Lord, for you have rescued me.**

I will extol you, O LORD, for you drew me clear **/** and did not let my enemies rejoice over me. **/** O LORD, you brought me up from the netherworld; **/** you preserved me from among those going down into the pit. **R.**

Sing praise to the LORD, you his faithful ones, **/** and give thanks to his holy name. **/** For his anger lasts but a moment; **/** a lifetime, his good will. **/** At nightfall, weeping enters in, **/** but with the dawn, rejoicing. **R.**

Hear, O LORD, and have pity on me; **/** O LORD, be my helper. **/** You changed my mourning into dancing; **/** O LORD, my God, forever will I give you thanks. **R.**

**SECOND READING**                     *2 Corinthians 8:7, 9, 13—15*

Brothers and sisters: As you excel in every respect, in faith, discourse, knowledge, all earnestness, and in the love we have for you, may you excel in this gracious act also.

For you know the gracious act of our Lord Jesus Christ, that though he was rich, for your sake he became poor, so that by his poverty you might become rich. Not that others should have relief while you are burdened, but that as a matter of equality your abundance at the present time should supply their needs, so that their abundance may also supply your needs, that there may be equality. As it is written: Whoever had much did not have more, and whoever had little did not have less.

**ALLELUIA**                              *see 2 Timothy 1:10*

**R. Alleluia, alleluia.** Our Savior Jesus Christ destroyed death and brought life to light through the Gospel. **R.**

**GOSPEL**                              *Long Form Mark 5:21—43*

When Jesus had crossed again in the boat to the other side, a large crowd gathered around him, and he stayed close to the sea. One of the synagogue officials, named Jairus, came forward. Seeing him he fell at his feet and pleaded earnestly with him, saying, "My daughter is at the point of death. Please, come lay your hands on her that she may get well and live." He went off with him, and a large crowd followed him and pressed upon him.

There was a woman afflicted with hemorrhages for twelve years. She had suffered greatly at the hands of many doctors and had spent all that she had. Yet she was not helped but only grew worse. She had heard about Jesus and came up behind him in the crowd and touched his cloak. She said, "If I but touch his clothes, I shall be cured." Immediately her flow of blood dried up. She felt in her body that she was healed of her affliction. Jesus, aware at once that power had gone out from him, turned around in the crowd and asked, "Who has touched my clothes?" But his disciples said to Jesus, "You see how the crowd is pressing upon you, and yet you ask, 'Who touched me?'" And he looked around to see who had done it. The woman, realizing what had happened to her, approached in fear and trembling. She fell down before Jesus and told him the whole truth. He said to her, "Daughter, your faith has saved you. Go in peace and be cured of your affliction."

While he was still speaking, people from the synagogue official's house arrived and said, "Your daughter has died; why trouble the teacher any longer?" Disregarding the message that was reported, Jesus said to the synagogue official, "Do not be afraid; just have faith." He did not allow anyone to accompany him inside except Peter, James, and John, the brother of James. When they arrived at the house of the synagogue official, he caught sight of a commotion, people weeping and wailing loudly. So he went in and said to them, "Why this commotion and weeping? The child is not dead but asleep." And they ridiculed him. Then he put them all out. He took along the child's father and mother and those who were with him and entered the room where the child was. He took the child by the hand and said to her, "Talitha koum," which means, "Little girl, I say to you, arise!" The girl, a child of twelve, arose immediately and walked around. At that they were utterly astounded. He gave strict orders that no one should know this and said that she should be given something to eat.

### OR: *Short Form*                    *Mark 5:21—24, 35b—43*

When Jesus had crossed again in the boat to the other side, a large crowd gathered around him, and he stayed close to the sea. One of the synagogue officials, named Jairus, came forward. Seeing him he fell at his feet and pleaded earnestly with him, saying, "My daughter is at the point of death. Please, come lay your hands on her that she may get well and live." He went off with him, and a large crowd followed him and pressed upon him.

While he was still speaking, people from the synagogue official's house arrived and said, "Your daughter has died; why trouble the teacher any longer?" Disregarding the message that was reported, Jesus said to the synagogue official, "Do not be afraid; just have faith." He did not allow anyone to accompany him inside except Peter, James, and John, the brother of James. When they arrived at the house of the synagogue official, he caught sight of a commotion, people weeping and wailing loudly. So he went in and said to them, "Why this commotion and weeping? The child is not dead but asleep." And they ridiculed him. Then he put them all out. He took along the child's father and mother and those who were with him and entered the room where the child was. He took the child by the hand and said to her, "Talitha koum," which means, "Little girl, I say to you, arise!" The girl, a child of twelve, arose immediately and walked around. At that they were utterly astounded. He gave strict orders that no one should know this and said that she should be given something to eat.

## PRAYER OVER THE OFFERINGS
O God, who graciously accomplish the effects of your mysteries, grant, we pray, that the deeds by which we serve you may be worthy of these sacred gifts. Through Christ our Lord.

## COMMUNION ANTIPHON Cf. Ps 102: 1
Bless the Lord, O my soul, and all within me, his holy name.

## OR                                                                 Jn 17: 20 – 21
O Father, I pray for them, that they may be one in us, that the world may believe that you have sent me, says the Lord.

## PRAYER AFTER COMMUNION
May this divine sacrifice we have offered and received fill us with life, O Lord, we pray, so that, bound to you in lasting charity, we may bear fruit that lasts for ever. Through Christ our Lord.

## LESSONS LEARNT FROM THE READINGS / HOMILY

| 1 | 2 |
|---|---|
| 3 | 4 |
| 5 | 6 |

### ACTION POINTS FOR THE WEEK

| 1 | 2 |
|---|---|
| 3 | 4 |
| 5 | 6 |

### PRAYER POINTS FOR THE WEEK

| 1 | 2 |
|---|---|
| 3 | 4 |

| 5 | 6 |
|---|---|

## THIS WEEK, I AM GRATEFUL FOR

| 1 | 2 |
|---|---|
| 3 | 4 |
| 5 | 6 |

## 29 JUNE 2021
## SOLEMNITY OF STS. PETER AND PAUL, APOSTLES - VIGIL MASS

**ENTRANCE ANTIPHON**

Peter the Apostle, and Paul the teacher of the Gentiles, these have taught us your law, O Lord.

**COLLECT**

Grant, we pray, O Lord our God, that we may be sustained by the intercession of the blessed Apostles Peter and Paul, that, as through them you gave your Church the foundations of her heavenly office, so through them you may help her to eternal salvation. Through our Lord Jesus Christ, your Son, who lives and reigns with you in the unity of the Holy Spirit, one God, for ever and ever.

**FIRST READING**                                        *Acts 3:1—10*

Peter and John were going up to the temple area for the three o'clock hour of prayer. And a man crippled from birth was carried and placed at the gate of the temple called "the Beautiful Gate" every day to beg for alms from the people who entered the temple. When he saw Peter and John about to go into the temple, he asked for alms. But Peter looked intently at him, as did John, and said, "Look at us." He paid attention to them, expecting to receive something from them. Peter said, "I have neither silver nor gold, but what I do have I give you: in the name of Jesus Christ the Nazorean, rise and walk." Then Peter took him by the right hand and raised him up, and immediately his feet and ankles grew strong. He leaped up, stood, and walked around, and went into the temple with them, walking and jumping and praising God. When all the people saw the man walking and praising God, they recognized him as the one who used to sit begging at the Beautiful Gate of the temple, and they were filled with amazement and astonishment at what had happened to him.

**RESPONSORIAL PSALM**                    *Psalm 19:2—3, 4—5*

**R. Their message goes out through all the earth.**

The heavens declare the glory of God; **/** and the firmament proclaims his handiwork. **/** Day pours out the word to day; **/** and night to night imparts knowledge. **R.**

Not a word nor a discourse **/** whose voice is not heard; **/** through all the earth their voice resounds, **/** and to the ends of the world, their message. **R**


**SECOND READING**                         *Galatians 1:11—20*

I want you to know, brothers and sisters, that the Gospel preached by me is not of human origin. For I did not receive it from a human being, nor was I taught it, but it came through a revelation of Jesus Christ.

For you heard of my former way of life in Judaism, how I persecuted the Church of God beyond measure and tried to destroy it, and progressed in Judaism beyond many of my contemporaries among my race, since I was even more a zealot for my ancestral traditions. But when God, who from my mother's womb had set me apart and called me through his grace, was pleased to reveal his Son to me, so that I might proclaim him to the Gentiles, I did not immediately consult flesh and blood, nor did I go up to Jerusalem to those who were apostles before me; rather, I went into Arabia and then returned to Damascus.

Then after three years I went up to Jerusalem to confer with Cephas and remained with him for fifteen days. But I did not see any other of the Apostles, only James the brother of the Lord. —As to what I am writing to you, behold, before God, I am not lying.

**ALLELUIA**                                 *John 21:17*

**R. Alleluia, alleluia.** Lord, you know everything; you know that I love you. **R.**


**GOSPEL**                                   *John 21:15—19*

After Jesus had revealed himself to his disciples and eaten breakfast with them, he said to Simon Peter, "Simon, son of John, do you love me more than these?" Simon Peter answered him, "Yes, Lord, you know that I love you." Jesus said to him, "Feed my lambs." He then said to Simon Peter a second time, "Simon, son of John, do you love me?" Simon Peter answered him, "Yes, Lord, you know that I love you." He said to him, "Tend my sheep." He said to him the third time, "Simon, son of John, do you love me?" Peter was distressed that Jesus had said to him a third time, "Do you love me?" and he said to him, "Lord, you know everything; you know that I love you." Jesus said to him, "Feed my sheep. Amen, amen, I say to you, when you were younger, you used to dress yourself and go where you wanted; but when you grow old, you will stretch out your hands, and someone else will dress you and lead you where you do not want to go." He said this signifying by what kind of death he would glorify God. And when he had said this, he said to him, "Follow me."

## PRAYER OVER THE OFFERINGS
We bring offerings to your altar, O Lord, as we glory in the solemn feast of the blessed Apostles Peter and Paul, so that the more we doubt our own merits, the more we may rejoice that we are to be saved by your loving kindness. Through Christ our Lord.

## COMMUNION ANTIPHON                                    Cf. 21: 15, 17
Simon, Son of John, do you love me more than these? Lord, you know everything; you know that I love you.

## PRAYER AFTER COMMUNION
By this heavenly Sacrament, O Lord, we pray, strengthen your faithful, whom you have enlightened with the teaching of the Apostles. Through Christ our Lord.

# MASS OF THE DAY

## ENTRANCE ANTIPHON
These are the ones who, living in the flesh, planted the Church with their blood; they drank the chalice of the Lord and became the friends of God.

## COLLECT
O God, who on the Solemnity of the Apostles Peter and Paul give us the noble and holy joy of this day, grant, we pray, that your Church may in all things follow the teaching of those through whom she received the beginnings of right religion. Through our Lord Jesus Christ, your Son, who lives and reigns with you in the unity of the Holy Spirit, one God, for ever and ever.

## FIRST READING                                         Acts 12:1—11
In those days, King Herod laid hands upon some members of the Church to harm them. He had James, the brother of John, killed by the sword, and when he saw that this was pleasing to the Jews he proceeded to

arrest Peter also. —It was the feast of Unleavened Bread.— He had him taken into custody and put in prison under the guard of four squads of four soldiers each. He intended to bring him before the people after Passover. Peter thus was being kept in prison, but prayer by the Church was fervently being made to God on his behalf.

On the very night before Herod was to bring him to trial, Peter, secured by double chains, was sleeping between two soldiers, while outside the door guards kept watch on the prison. Suddenly the angel of the Lord stood by him, and a light shone in the cell. He tapped Peter on the side and awakened him, saying, "Get up quickly." The chains fell from his wrists. The angel said to him, "Put on your belt and your sandals." He did so. Then he said to him, "Put on your cloak and follow me." So he followed him out, not realizing that what was happening through the angel was real; he thought he was seeing a vision. They passed the first guard, then the second, and came to the iron gate leading out to the city, which opened for them by itself. They emerged and made their way down an alley, and suddenly the angel left him.

Then Peter recovered his senses and said, "Now I know for certain that the Lord sent his angel and rescued me from the hand of Herod and from all that the Jewish people had been expecting."

## PSALM                              Psalm 34:2—3, 4—5, 6—7, 8—9

**R. The angel of the Lord will rescue those who fear him.**
I will bless the LORD at all times; / his praise shall be ever in my mouth. / Let my soul glory in the LORD; / the lowly will hear me and be glad. **R.**
Glorify the LORD with me, / let us together extol his name. / I sought the LORD, and he answered me / and delivered me from all my fears. **R.**
Look to him that you may be radiant with joy, / and your faces may not blush with shame. / When the poor one called out, the LORD heard, / and from all his distress he saved him. **R.**
The angel of the LORD encamps / around those who fear him, and delivers them. / Taste and see how good the LORD is; / blessed the man who takes refuge in him. **R.**

## SECOND READING                        2 Timothy 4:6—8, 17—18

I, Paul, am already being poured out like a libation, and the time of my departure is at hand. I have competed well; I have finished the race; I have kept the faith. From now on the crown of righteousness awaits me, which the Lord, the just judge, will award to me on that day, and not only to me, but to all who have longed for his appearance.

The Lord stood by me and gave me strength, so that through me the proclamation might be completed and all the Gentiles might hear it. And I was rescued from the lion's mouth. The Lord will rescue me from every evil threat and will bring me safe to his heavenly kingdom. To him be glory forever and ever. Amen.

**ALLELUIA** *Matthew 16:18*

**R. Alleluia, alleluia.** You are Peter and upon this rock I will build my Church, and the gates of the netherworld shall not prevail against it. **R.**


**GOSPEL** *Matthew 16:13—19*

When Jesus went into the region of Caesarea Philippi he asked his disciples, "Who do people say that the Son of Man is?" They replied, "Some say John the Baptist, others Elijah, still others Jeremiah or one of the prophets." He said to them, "But who do you say that I am?" Simon Peter said in reply, "You are the Christ, the Son of the living God." Jesus said to him in reply, "Blessed are you, Simon son of Jonah. For flesh and blood has not revealed this to you, but my heavenly Father. And so I say to you, you are Peter, and upon this rock I will build my Church, and the gates of the netherworld shall not prevail against it. I will give you the keys to the Kingdom of heaven. Whatever you bind on earth shall be bound in heaven; and whatever you loose on earth shall be loosed in heaven."


**PRAYER OVER THE OFFERINGS**

May the prayer of the Apostles, O Lord, accompany the sacrificial gift that we present to your name for consecration, and may their intercession make us devoted to you in celebration of the sacrifice. Through Christ our Lord.

**COMMUNION ANTIPHON** **Cf. Mt 16: 16, 18**

Peter said to Jesus: You are the Christ, the Son of the living God. And Jesus replied: You are Peter, and upon this rock I will build my Church.

**PRAYER AFTER COMMUNION**

Grant us, O Lord, who have been renewed by this Sacrament, so to live in the Church, that, persevering in the breaking of the Bread and in the teaching of the Apostles, we may be one heart and one soul, made steadfast in your love. Through Christ our Lord.

## LESSONS LEARNT FROM THE READINGS / HOMILY

1 _____ 2 _____
3 _____ 4 _____
5 _____ 6 _____

## ACTION POINTS FOR THE WEEK

1 _____ 2 _____
3 _____ 4 _____
5 _____ 6 _____

## PRAYER POINTS FOR THE WEEK

1 _____ 2 _____
3 _____ 4 _____
5 _____ 6 _____

## THIS WEEK, I AM GRATEFUL FOR

1 _____ 2 _____
3 _____ 4 _____
5 _____ 6 _____

*12*        *JULY*

## 04 JULY 2021, 14TH SUNDAY IN ORDINARY TIME

**ENTRANCE ANTIPHON**      Cf. Ps 47: 10 – 11

Your merciful love, O God, we have received in the midst of your temple. Your praise, O God, like your name, reaches the ends of the earth; your right hand is filled with saving justice.

**COLLECT**

O God, who in the abasement of your Son have raised up a fallen world, fill your faithful with holy joy, for on those you have rescued from slavery to sin you bestow eternal gladness. Through our Lord Jesus Christ, your Son, who lives and reigns with you in the unity of the Holy Spirit, one God, for ever and ever.

**FIRST READING**      *Ezekiel 2:2—5*

As the LORD spoke to me, the spirit entered into me and set me on my feet, and I heard the one who was speaking say to me: Son of man, I am sending you to the Israelites, rebels who have rebelled against me; they and their ancestors have revolted against me to this very day. Hard of face and obstinate of heart are they to whom I am sending you. But you shall say to them: Thus says the LORD God! And whether they heed or resist—for they are a rebellious house— they shall know that a prophet has been among them.

**RESPONSORIAL PSALM**                                    *Psalm 123:1—2, 2,3—4*
**R. Our eyes are fixed on the Lord, pleading for his mercy.**
To you I lift up my eyes **/** who are enthroned in heaven— **/** as the eyes of servants **/** are on the hands of their masters. **R.**
As the eyes of a maid **/** are on the hands of her mistress, **/** so are our eyes on the LORD, our God, **/** till he have pity on us. **R.**
Have pity on us, O LORD, have pity on us, **/** for we are more than sated with contempt; **/** our souls are more than sated **/** with the mockery of the arrogant, **/** with the contempt of the proud. **R.**

**SECOND READING**                                    *2 Corinthians 12:7—10*
Brothers and sisters: That I, Paul, might not become too elated, because of the abundance of the revelations, a thorn in the flesh was given to me, an angel of Satan, to beat me, to keep me from being too elated. Three times I begged the Lord about this, that it might leave me, but he said to me, "My grace is sufficient for you, for power is made perfect in weakness." I will rather boast most gladly of my weaknesses, in order that the power of Christ may dwell with me. Therefore, I am content with weaknesses, insults, hardships, persecutions and constraints, for the sake of Christ; for when I am weak, then I am strong.
**ALLELUIA**                                    *see Luke 4:18*
**R. Alleluia, alleluia.** The Spirit of the Lord is upon me, for he sent me to bring glad tidings to the poor. **R.**

**GOSPEL**                                    *Mark 6:1—6*
Jesus departed from there and came to his native place, accompanied by his disciples. When the sabbath came he began to teach in the synagogue, and many who heard him were astonished. They said, "Where did this man get all this? What kind of wisdom has been given him? What mighty deeds are wrought by his hands! Is he not the carpenter, the son of Mary, and the brother of James and Joses and Judas and Simon? And are not his

sisters here with us?" And they took offense at him. Jesus said to them, "A prophet is not without honor except in his native place and among his own kin and in his own house." So he was not able to perform any mighty deed there, apart from curing a few sick people by laying his hands on them. He was amazed at their lack of faith.

## PRAYER OVER THE OFFERINGS
May this oblation dedicated to your name purify us, O Lord, and day by day bring our conduct closer to the life of heaven. Through Christ our Lord.

## COMMUNION ANTIPHON                                      Ps 33: 9
Taste and see that the Lord is good; blessed the man who seeks refuge in him.

## OR                                                      Mt 11: 28
Come to me, all who labour and are burdened, and I will refresh you, says the Lord.

## PRAYER AFTER COMMUNION
Grant, we pray, O Lord, that, having been replenished by such great gifts, we may gain the prize of salvation and never cease to praise you. Through Christ our Lord.

## LESSONS LEARNT FROM THE READINGS / HOMILY
1 _____ 2 _____
3 _____ 4 _____
5 _____ 6 _____

## ACTION POINTS FOR THE WEEK
1 _____ 2 _____
3 _____ 4 _____
5 _____ 6 _____

## PRAYER POINTS FOR THE WEEK
1 _____ 2 _____
3 _____ 4 _____
5 _____ 6 _____

## THIS WEEK, I AM GRATEFUL FOR

| 1 | 2 |
|---|---|
| 3 | 4 |
| 5 | 6 |

## 11 JULY 2021, 15TH SUNDAY IN ORDINARY TIME

**ENTRANCE ANTIPHON**                                              Cf. Ps 16: 15

As for me, in justice I shall behold your face; I shall be filled with the vision of your glory.

**COLLECT**

O God, who show the light of your truth to those who go astray, so that they may return to the right path, give all who for the faith they profess are accounted Christians the grace to reject whatever is contrary to the name of Christ and to strive after all that does it honour. Through our Lord Jesus Christ, your Son, who lives and reigns with you in the unity of the Holy Spirit, one God, for ever and ever.

**FIRST READING**                                              *Amos 7:12—15*

Amaziah, priest of Bethel, said to Amos, "Off with you, visionary, flee to the land of Judah! There earn your bread by prophesying, but never again prophesy in Bethel; for it is the king's sanctuary and a royal temple." Amos answered Amaziah, "I was no prophet, nor have I belonged to a company of prophets; I was a shepherd and a dresser of sycamores. The LORD took me from following the flock, and said to me, Go, prophesy to my people Israel."

**PSALM**                                              *Psalm 85:9—10, 11—12, 13—14 (8)*

**R. Lord, let us see your kindness, and grant us your salvation.**

I will hear what God proclaims; / the LORD—for he proclaims peace. / Near indeed is his salvation to those who fear him, / glory dwelling in our land. **R.**

Kindness and truth shall meet; / justice and peace shall kiss. / Truth shall spring out of the earth, / and justice shall look down from heaven. **R.**

The LORD himself will give his benefits; / our land shall yield its increase. / Justice shall walk before him, / and prepare the way of his steps. **R.**

**SECOND READING EITEHR:**                                              *Ephesians 1:3—14*

Blessed be the God and Father of our Lord Jesus Christ, who has blessed us in Christ with every spiritual blessing in the heavens, as he chose us in him, before the foundation of the world, to be holy and without blemish before him. In love he destined us for adoption to himself through Jesus Christ, in accord with the favor of his will, for the praise of the glory of his grace that he granted us in the beloved. In him we have redemption by his blood, the forgiveness of transgressions, in accord with the riches of his grace that he lavished upon us. In all wisdom and insight, he has made known to us the mystery of his will in accord with his favor that he set forth in him as a plan for the fullness of times, to sum up all things in Christ, in heaven and on earth.

In him we were also chosen, destined in accord with the purpose of the One who accomplishes all things according to the intention of his will, so that we might exist for the praise of his glory, we who first hoped in Christ. In him you also, who have heard the word of truth, the gospel of your salvation, and have believed in him, were sealed with the promised Holy Spirit, which is the first installment of our inheritance toward redemption as God's possession, to the praise of his glory.

**OR:** *Ephesians 1:3—10*

Blessed be the God and Father of our Lord Jesus Christ, who has blessed us in Christ with every spiritual blessing in the heavens, as he chose us in him, before the foundation of the world, to be holy and without blemish before him. In love he destined us for adoption to himself through Jesus Christ, in accord with the favor of his will, for the praise of the glory of God's grace that he granted us in the beloved.

In him we have redemption by his blood, the forgiveness of transgressions, in accord with the riches of his grace that he lavished upon us. In all wisdom and insight, he has made known to us the mystery of his will in accord with his favor that he set forth in him as a plan for the fullness of times, to sum up all things in Christ, in heaven and on earth.

**ALLELUIA** *see Ephesians 1:17—18*

**R. Alleluia, alleluia.** May the Father of our Lord Jesus Christ enlighten the eyes of our hearts, that we may know what is the hope that belongs to our call. **R.**

**GOSPEL** *Mark 6:7—13*

Jesus summoned the Twelve and began to send them out two by two and gave them authority over unclean spirits. He instructed them to take nothing for the journey but a walking stick— no food, no sack, no money in their belts. They were, however, to wear sandals but not a second tunic. He said to them, "Wherever you enter a house, stay there until you leave. Whatever place does not welcome you or listen to you, leave there and shake the dust off your feet in testimony against them." So they went off and preached repentance. The Twelve drove out many demons, and they anointed with oil many who were sick and cured them.

## PRAYER OVER THE OFFERINGS
Look upon the offerings of the Church, O Lord, as she makes her prayer to you, and grant that, when consumed by those who believe, they may bring ever greater holiness. Through Christ our Lord.

**COMMUNION ANTIPHON**                                    **Cf. Ps 83: 4 – 5**
The sparrow finds a home, and the swallow a nest for her young: by your altars, O Lord of hosts, my King and my God. Blessed are they who dwell in your house, for ever singing your praise.

**OR**                                                          **Jn 6: 57**
Whoever eats my flesh and drinks my blood remains in me and I in him, says the Lord.

## PRAYER AFTER COMMUNION
Having consumed these gifts, we pray, O Lord, that, by our participation in this mystery, its saving effects upon us may grow. Through Christ our Lord.

**LESSONS LEARNT FROM THE READINGS / HOMILY**

1 _____  2 _____
3 _____  4 _____
5 _____  6 _____

**ACTION POINTS FOR THE WEEK**

1 _____  2 _____
3 _____  4 _____
5 _____  6 _____

**PRAYER POINTS FOR THE WEEK**

1 _____  2 _____
3 _____  4 _____
5 _____  6 _____

| 1 | 2 |
|---|---|
| 3 | 4 |
| 5 | 6 |

## 18 JULY 2021, 16TH SUNDAY IN ORDINARY TIME

**ENTRANCE ANTIPHON**           Ps 53: 6, 8

See, I have God for my help. The Lord sustains my soul. I will sacrifice to you with willing heart, and praise your name, O Lord, for it is good.

**COLLECT**

Show favour, O Lord, to your servants and mercifully increase the gifts of your grace, that, made fervent in hope, faith and charity, they may be ever watchful in keeping your commands. Through our Lord Jesus Christ, your Son, who lives and reigns with you in the unity of the Holy Spirit, one God, for ever and ever.

**FIRST READING**           *Jeremiah 23:1—6*

Woe to the shepherds who mislead and scatter the flock of my pasture, says the LORD. Therefore, thus says the LORD, the God of Israel, against the shepherds who shepherd my people: You have scattered my sheep and driven them away. You have not cared for them, but I will take care to punish your evil deeds. I myself will gather the remnant of my flock from all the lands to which I have driven them and bring them back to their meadow; there they shall increase and multiply. I will appoint shepherds for them who will shepherd them so that they need no longer fear and tremble; and none shall be missing, says the LORD.

      Behold, the days are coming, says the LORD, when I will raise up a righteous shoot to David; as king he shall reign and govern wisely, he shall do what is just and right in the land. In his days Judah shall be saved, Israel shall dwell in security. This is the name they give him: "The LORD our justice."

**RESPONSORIAL PSALM**        *Psalm 23:1—3, 3—4, 5, 6*

**R. The Lord is my shepherd; there is nothing I shall want.**

The LORD is my shepherd; I shall not want. **/** In verdant pastures he gives me repose; **/** beside restful waters he leads me; **/** he refreshes my soul. **R.**

He guides me in right paths / for his name's sake. / Even though I walk in the dark valley / I fear no evil; for you are at my side / with your rod and your staff / that give me courage. **R.**

You spread the table before me / in the sight of my foes; / you anoint my head with oil; / my cup overflows. **R.**

Only goodness and kindness follow me / all the days of my life; / and I shall dwell in the house of the LORD / for years to come. **R.**

**SECOND READING**                                               *Ephesians 2:13—18*

Brothers and sisters: In Christ Jesus you who once were far off have become near by the blood of Christ.

For he is our peace, he who made both one and broke down the dividing wall of enmity, through his flesh, abolishing the law with its commandments and legal claims, that he might create in himself one new person in place of the two, thus establishing peace, and might reconcile both with God, in one body, through the cross, putting that enmity to death by it. He came and preached peace to you who were far off and peace to those who were near, for through him we both have access in one Spirit to the Father.

**ALLELUIA**                                                          *John 10:27*

**R. Alleluia, alleluia.** My sheep hear my voice, says the Lord; I know them, and they follow me. **R**

**GOSPEL**                                                            *Mark 6:30—34*

The apostles gathered together with Jesus and reported all they had done and taught. He said to them, "Come away by yourselves to a deserted place and rest a while." People were coming and going in great numbers, and they had no opportunity even to eat. So they went off in the boat by themselves to a deserted place. People saw them leaving and many came to know about it. They hastened there on foot from all the towns and arrived at the place before them.

When he disembarked and saw the vast crowd, his heart was moved with pity for them, for they were like sheep without a shepherd; and he began to teach them many things.

**PRAYER OVER THE OFFERINGS**

O God, who in the one perfect sacrifice brought to completion varied offerings of the law, accept, we pray, this sacrifice from your faithful servants and make it holy, as you blessed the gifts of Abel, so that what each has offered to the honour of your majesty may benefit the salvation of all. Through Christ our Lord.

## COMMUNION ANTIPHON                                    Ps 110: 4 – 5

The Lord, the gracious, the merciful, has made a memorial of his wonders; he gives food to those who fear him.

## OR                                                         Rv 3: 20

Behold, I stand at the door and knock, says the Lord. If anyone hears my voice and opens the door to me, I will enter his house and dine with him, and he with me.

## PRAYER AFTER COMMUNION

Graciously be present to your people, we pray, O Lord, and lead those you have imbued with heavenly mysteries to pass from former ways to newness of life. Through Christ our Lord.

## LESSONS LEARNT FROM THE READINGS / HOMILY

| 1 | 2 |
|---|---|
| 3 | 4 |
| 5 | 6 |

## ACTION POINTS FOR THE WEEK

| 1 | 2 |
|---|---|
| 3 | 4 |
| 5 | 6 |

## PRAYER POINTS FOR THE WEEK

| 1 | 2 |
|---|---|
| 3 | 4 |
| 5 | 6 |

## THIS WEEK, I AM GRATEFUL FOR

| 1 | 2 |
|---|---|
| 3 | 4 |
| 5 | 6 |

**ENTRANCE ANTIPHON**　　　　　　　　　　　　**Cf. Ps 67: 6 – 7, 36**

God is in his holy place, God who unites those who dwell in his house; he himself gives might and strength to his people.

**COLLECT**

O God, protector of those who hope in you, without whom nothing has firm foundation, nothing is holy, bestow in abundance your mercy upon us and grant that, with you as our ruler and guide, we may use the good things that pass in such a way as to hold fast even now to those that ever endure. Through our Lord Jesus Christ, your Son, who lives and reigns with you in the unity of the Holy Spirit, one God, for ever and ever.

**FIRST READING**　　　　　　　　　　　　　　*2 Kings 4:42—44*

A man came from Baal–shalishah bringing to Elisha, the man of God, twenty barley loaves made from the firstfruits, and fresh grain in the ear. Elisha said, "Give it to the people to eat." But his servant objected, "How can I set this before a hundred people?" Elisha insisted, "Give it to the people to eat. For thus says the LORD, 'They shall eat and there shall be some left over.'" And when they had eaten, there was some left over, as the LORD had said.

**PSALM:**　　　　　　*Psalm 145:10—11, 15—16, 17—18 (see 16)*
**R. The hand of the Lord feeds us; he answers all our needs.**
Let all your works give you thanks, O LORD, **/** and let your faithful ones bless you. **/** Let them discourse of the glory of your kingdom**/** and speak of your might. **R.**
The eyes of all look hopefully to you, **/** and you give them their food in due season;**/** you open your hand**/**and satisfy the desire of every living thing.**R.**
The LORD is just in all his ways **/** and holy in all his works. **/** The LORD is near to all who call upon him, **/** to all who call upon him in truth. **R.**

**SECOND READING**　　　　　　　　　　　　　*Ephesians 4:1—6*

Brothers and sisters: I, a prisoner for the Lord, urge you to live in a manner worthy of the call you have received, with all humility and gentleness, with patience, bearing with one another through love, striving to preserve the unity of the spirit through the bond of peace: one body and one Spirit, as you were also called to the one hope of your call; one

Lord, one faith, one baptism; one God and Father of all, who is over all and through all and in all.

**ALLELUIA** *Luke 7:16*

R. **Alleluia, alleluia.** A great prophet has risen in our midst. God has visited his people. **R.**

**GOSPEL** *John 6:1—15*

Jesus went across the Sea of Galilee. A large crowd followed him, because they saw the signs he was performing on the sick. Jesus went up on the mountain, and there he sat down with his disciples. The Jewish feast of Passover was near. When Jesus raised his eyes and saw that a large crowd was coming to him, he said to Philip, "Where can we buy enough food for them to eat?" He said this to test him, because he himself knew what he was going to do. Philip answered him, "Two hundred days' wages worth of food would not be enough for each of them to have a little." One of his disciples, Andrew, the brother of Simon Peter, said to him, "There is a boy here who has five barley loaves and two fish; but what good are these for so many?" Jesus said, "Have the people recline." Now there was a great deal of grass in that place. So the men reclined, about five thousand in number. Then Jesus took the loaves, gave thanks, and distributed them to those who were reclining, and also as much of the fish as they wanted. When they had had their fill, he said to his disciples, "Gather the fragments left over, so that nothing will be wasted." So they collected them, and filled twelve wicker baskets with fragments from the five barley loaves that had been more than they could eat. When the people saw the sign he had done, they said, "This is truly the Prophet, the one who is to come into the world." Since Jesus knew that they were going to come and carry him off to make him king, he withdrew again to the mountain alone.

**PRAYER OVER THE OFFERINGS**

Accept, O Lord, we pray, the offerings which we bring from the abundance of your gifts, that through the powerful working of your grace these most sacred mysteries may sanctify our present way of life and lead us to eternal gladness. Through Christ our Lord.

**COMMUNION ANTIPHON** *Ps 102: 2*

Bless the Lord, O my soul, and never forget all his benefits.

**OR**                                                           **Mt 5: 7 – 8**

Blessed are the merciful, for they shall receive mercy. Blessed are the clean of heart, for they shall see God.

**PRAYER AFTER COMMUNION**

We have consumed, O Lord, this divine Sacrament, the perpetual memorial of the Passion of your Son; grant, we pray, that this gift, which he himself gave us with love beyond all telling, may profit us for salvation. Through Christ our Lord.

**LESSONS LEARNT FROM THE READINGS / HOMILY**

1 _____ 2 _____
3 _____ 4 _____
5 _____ 6 _____

**ACTION POINTS FOR THE WEEK**

1 _____ 2 _____
3 _____ 4 _____
5 _____ 6 _____

**PRAYER POINTS FOR THE WEEK**

1 _____ 2 _____
3 _____ 4 _____
5 _____ 6 _____

**THIS WEEK, I AM GRATEFUL FOR**

1 _____ 2 _____
3 _____ 4 _____
5 _____ 6 _____

13                                    *AUGUST*

01 AUGUST 2021, 18TH SUNDAY IN ORDINARY TIME

**ENTRANCE ANTIPHON**                                        **Ps 69: 2, 6**

O God, come to my assistance; O Lord, make haste to help me! You are my rescuer, my help; O Lord, do not delay.

## COLLECT

Draw near to your servants, O Lord, and answer their prayers with unceasing kindness, that, for those who glory in you as their Creator and guide, you may restore what you have created and keep safe what you have restored. Through our Lord Jesus Christ, your Son, who lives and reigns with you in the unity of the Holy Spirit, one God, for ever and ever.

## FIRST READING                                        *Exodus 16:2—4, 12—15*

The whole Israelite community grumbled against Moses and Aaron. The Israelites said to them, "Would that we had died at the LORD's hand in the land of Egypt, as we sat by our fleshpots and ate our fill of bread! But you had to lead us into this desert to make the whole community die of famine!"

Then the LORD said to Moses, "I will now rain down bread from heaven for you. Each day the people are to go out and gather their daily portion; thus will I test them, to see whether they follow my instructions or not.

"I have heard the grumbling of the Israelites. Tell them: In the evening twilight you shall eat flesh, and in the morning you shall have your fill of bread, so that you may know that I, the LORD, am your God."

In the evening quail came up and covered the camp. In the morning a dew lay all about the camp, and when the dew evaporated, there on the surface of the desert were fine flakes like hoarfrost on the ground. On seeing it, the Israelites asked one another, "What is this?" for they did not know what it was. But Moses told them, "This is the bread that the Lord has given you to eat."

## PSALM                                   *Psalm 78:3—4, 23—24, 25, 54 (24b)*
**R. The Lord gave them bread from heaven.**

What we have heard and know, / and what our fathers have declared to us, / we will declare to the generation to come / the glorious deeds of the LORD and his strength / and the wonders that he wrought. **R**

He commanded the skies above / and opened the doors of heaven; / he rained manna upon them for food / and gave them heavenly bread. **R**

Man ate the bread of angels, / food he sent them in abundance. / And he brought them to his holy land,/to the mountains his right hand had won.**R**

## SECOND READING                                    *Ephesians 4:17, 20—24*

Brothers and sisters: I declare and testify in the Lord that you must no longer live as the Gentiles do, in the futility of their minds; that is not how you learned Christ, assuming that you have heard of him and were taught in him, as truth is in Jesus, that you should put away the old self of your former way of life, corrupted through deceitful desires, and be renewed in the spirit of your minds, and put on the new self, created in God's way in righteousness and holiness of truth.

## ALLELUIA                                                    *Matthew 4:4b*

**R. Alleluia, alleluia.** One does not live on bread alone, but by every word that comes forth from the mouth of God. **R.**


## GOSPEL                                                    *John 6:24—35*

When the crowd saw that neither Jesus nor his disciples were there, they themselves got into boats and came to Capernaum looking for Jesus. And when they found him across the sea they said to him, "Rabbi, when did you get here?" Jesus answered them and said, "Amen, amen, I say to you, you are looking for me not because you saw signs but because you ate the loaves and were filled. Do not work for food that perishes but for the food that endures for eternal life, which the Son of Man will give you. For on him the Father, God, has set his seal." So they said to him, "What can we do to accomplish the works of God?" Jesus answered and said to them, "This is the work of God, that you believe in the one he sent." So they said to him, "What sign can you do, that we may see and believe in you? What can you do? Our ancestors ate manna in the desert, as it is written: He gave them bread from heaven to eat." So Jesus said to them, "Amen, amen, I say to you, it was not Moses who gave the bread from heaven; my Father gives you the true bread from heaven. For the bread of God is that which comes down from heaven and gives life to the world." So they said to him, "Sir, give us this bread always." Jesus said to them, "I am the bread of life; whoever comes to me will never hunger, and whoever believes in me will never thirst."


## PRAYER OVER THE OFFERINGS

Graciously sanctify these gifts, O Lord, we pray, and, accepting the oblation of this spiritual sacrifice, make of us an eternal offering to you. Through Christ our Lord.

**COMMUNION ANTIPHON**　　　　　　　　　　　　　　**Wis 16: 20**

You have given us, O Lord, bread from heaven, endowed with all delights and sweetness in every taste.

**OR**　　　　　　　　　　　　　　　　　　　　　　**Jn 6: 35**

I am the bread of life, says the Lord; whoever comes to me will not hunger and whoever believes in me will not thirst.

**PRAYER AFTER COMMUNION**

Accompany with constant protection, O Lord, those you renew with these heavenly gifts and, in your never-failing care for them, make them worthy of eternal redemption. Through Christ our Lord.

## LESSONS LEARNT FROM THE READINGS / HOMILY

1 _____ 2 _____
3 _____ 4 _____
5 _____ 6 _____

## ACTION POINTS FOR THE WEEK

1 _____ 2 _____
3 _____ 4 _____
5 _____ 6 _____

## PRAYER POINTS FOR THE WEEK

1 _____ 2 _____
3 _____ 4 _____
5 _____ 6 _____

## THIS WEEK, I AM GRATEFUL FOR

1 _____ 2 _____
3 _____ 4 _____
5 _____ 6 _____

## 08 AUGUST 2021, 19TH SUNDAY IN ORDINARY TIME

**ENTRANCE ANTIPHON**　　　　　　　　　**Cf. Ps 73: 20, 19, 22, 23**

Look to your covenant, O Lord, and forget not the life of your poor ones for ever. Arise, O God, and defend your cause, and forget not the cries of those who seek you.

## COLLECT

Almighty ever-living God, whom, taught by the Holy Spirit, we dare to call our Father, bring, we pray, to perfection in our hearts the spirit of adoption as your sons and daughters, that we may merit to enter into the inheritance which you have promised. Through our Lord Jesus Christ, your Son, who lives and reigns with you in the unity of the Holy Spirit, one God, for ever and ever.

## FIRST READING                                                    *1 Kings 19:4—8*

Elijah went a day's journey into the desert, until he came to a broom tree and sat beneath it. He prayed for death, saying: "This is enough, O LORD! Take my life, for I am no better than my fathers." He lay down and fell asleep under the broom tree, but then an angel touched him and ordered him to get up and eat. Elijah looked and there at his head was a hearth cake and a jug of water. After he ate and drank, he lay down again, but the angel of the LORD came back a second time, touched him, and ordered, "Get up and eat, else the journey will be too long for you!" He got up, ate, and drank; then strengthened by that food, he walked forty days and forty nights to the mountain of God, Horeb.

## PSALM                                  *Psalm 34:2—3, 4—5, 6—7, 8—9 (9a)*

**R. Taste and see the goodness of the Lord.**

I will bless the LORD at all times; **/** his praise shall be ever in my mouth. **/** Let my soul glory in the LORD; **/** the lowly will hear me and be glad. **R.**
Glorify the LORD with me, **/** let us together extol his name. **/** I sought the LORD, and he answered me **/** and delivered me from all my fears. **R.**
Look to him that you may be radiant with joy, **/** and your faces may not blush with shame. **/** When the afflicted man called out, the LORD heard, **/** and from all his distress he saved him. **R.**
The angel of the LORD encamps **/** around those who fear him and delivers them. **/** Taste and see how good the LORD is; **/** blessed the man who takes refuge in him. **R.**

## SECOND READING                                              *Ephesians 4:30—5:2*

Brothers and sisters: Do not grieve the Holy Spirit of God, with which you were sealed for the day of redemption. All bitterness, fury, anger, shouting, and reviling must be removed from you, along with all malice.

214

And be kind to one another, compassionate, forgiving one another as God has forgiven you in Christ.

So be imitators of God, as beloved children, and live in love, as Christ loved us and handed himself over for us as a sacrificial offering to God for a fragrant aroma.

**ALLELUIA** *John 6:51*

**R. Alleluia, alleluia.** I am the living bread that came down from heaven, says the Lord; whoever eats this bread will live forever. **R.**

**GOSPEL** *John 6:41—51*

The Jews murmured about Jesus because he said, "I am the bread that came down from heaven," and they said, "Is this not Jesus, the son of Joseph? Do we not know his father and mother? Then how can he say, 'I have come down from heaven'?" Jesus answered and said to them, "Stop murmuring among yourselves. No one can come to me unless the Father who sent me draw him, and I will raise him on the last day. It is written in the prophets: They shall all be taught by God. Everyone who listens to my Father and learns from him comes to me. Not that anyone has seen the Father except the one who is from God; he has seen the Father. Amen, amen, I say to you, whoever believes has eternal life. I am the bread of life. Your ancestors ate the manna in the desert, but they died; this is the bread that comes down from heaven so that one may eat it and not die. I am the living bread that came down from heaven; whoever eats this bread will live forever; and the bread that I will give is my flesh for the life of the world."

**PRAYER OVER THE OFFERINGS**

Be pleased, O Lord, to accept the offerings of your Church, for in your mercy you have given them to be offered and by your power you transform them into the mystery of our salvation. Through Christ our Lord.

**COMMUNION ANTIPHON** **Psalm 147: 12, 14**

O Jerusalem, glorify the Lord, who gives you your fill of finest wheat.

 **OR** **Jn 6: 51**

The bread that I will give, says the Lord, is my flesh for the life of the world.

**PRAYER AFTER COMMUNION**

May the communion in your Sacrament that we have consumed, save us, O Lord, and confirm us in the light of your truth. Through Christ our Lord.

**LESSONS LEARNT FROM THE READINGS / HOMILY**

1 _____ 2 _____
3 _____ 4 _____
5 _____ 6 _____

**ACTION POINTS FOR THE WEEK**

1 _____ 2 _____
3 _____ 4 _____
5 _____ 6 _____

**PRAYER POINTS FOR THE WEEK**

1 _____ 2 _____
3 _____ 4 _____
5 _____ 6 _____

**THIS WEEK, I AM GRATEFUL FOR**

1 _____ 2 _____
3 _____ 4 _____
5 _____ 6 _____

# 15 AUGUST 2021, SOLEMNITY OF THE ASSUMPTION OF THE BLESSED VIRGIN MARY, VIGIL MASS

**ENTRANCE ANTIPHON**

Glorious things are spoken of you, O Mary, who today were exalted above the choirs of Angels into eternal triumph with Christ.

**COLLECT**

O God, who, looking on the lowliness of the Blessed Virgin Mary, raised her to this grace, that your Only Begotten Son was born of her according to the flesh and that she was crowned this day with surpassing glory, grant through her prayers, that, saved by the mystery of your redemption, we may merit to be exalted by you on high. Through our

Lord Jesus Christ, your Son, who lives and reigns with you in the unity of the Holy Spirit, one God, for ever and ever.

**FIRST READING**                                  *1 Chronicles 15:3—4, 15—16; 16:1—2*
David assembled all Israel in Jerusalem to bring the ark of the LORD to the place that he had prepared for it. David also called together the sons of Aaron and the Levites.

The Levites bore the ark of God on their shoulders with poles, as Moses had ordained according to the word of the LORD.

David commanded the chiefs of the Levites to appoint their kinsmen as chanters, to play on musical instruments, harps, lyres, and cymbals, to make a loud sound of rejoicing.

They brought in the ark of God and set it within the tent which David had pitched for it. Then they offered up burnt offerings and peace offerings to God. When David had finished offering up the burnt offerings and peace offerings, he blessed the people in the name of the LORD.

**PSALM**                                          *Psalm 132:6—7, 9—10, 13—14 (8)*
**R. Lord, go up to the place of your rest, you and the ark of your holiness.**
Behold, we heard of it in Ephrathah; / we found it in the fields of Jaar. / Let us enter into his dwelling, / let us worship at his footstool. **R.**
May your priests be clothed with justice; / let your faithful ones shout merrily for joy. / For the sake of David your servant, / reject not the plea of your anointed. **R.**
For the Lord has chosen Zion; / he prefers her for his dwelling. / "Zion is my resting place forever; / in her will I dwell, for I prefer her." **R.**

**SECOND READING**                                 *1 Corinthians 15:54b—57*
Brothers and sisters: When that which is mortal clothes itself with immortality, then the word that is written shall come about:

*Death is swallowed up in victory. Where, O death, is your victory? Where, O death, is your sting?*

The sting of death is sin, and the power of sin is the law. But thanks be to God who gives us the victory through our Lord Jesus Christ.
**ALLELUIA**                                        *Luke 11:28*
**R. Alleluia, alleluia.** Blessed are they who hear the word of God and observe it. **R.**

**GOSPEL**                                                      *Luke 11:27—28*

While Jesus was speaking, a woman from the crowd called out and said to him, "Blessed is the womb that carried you and the breasts at which you nursed." He replied, "Rather, blessed are those who hear the word of God and observe it."

**PRAYER OVER THE OFFERINGS**

Receive, we pray, O Lord, the sacrifice of conciliation and praise, which we celebrate on the Assumption of the holy Mother of God, that it may lead us to your pardon and confirm us in perpetual thanksgiving. Through Christ our Lord.

**COMMUNION ANTIPHON**                                          **Cf. Lk 11: 27**

Blessed is the womb of the Virgin Mary, which bore the Son of the eternal Father.

**PRAYER AFTER COMMUNION**

Having partaken of this heavenly table, we beseech your mercy, Lord our God, that we, who honour the Assumption of the Mother of God, may be freed from every threat of harm. Through Christ our Lord.

## MASS OF THE DAY

**ENTRANCE ANTIPHON**                                           **Cf. Rev. 12: 1**

A great sign appeared in heaven: a woman clothed with the sun, and the moon beneath her feet, and on her head a crown of twelve stars.

**OR**

Let us all rejoice in the Lord, as we celebrate the feast day in honour of the Virgin Mary, at whose Assumption the Angels rejoice and praise the Son of God.

**COLLECT**

Almighty ever-living God, who assumed the Immaculate Virgin Mary, the Mother of your Son, body and soul into heavenly glory, grant, we pray, that, always attentive to the things that are above, we may merit to be sharers of her glory. Through our Lord Jesus Christ, your Son, who lives and reigns with you in the unity of the Holy Spirit, one God, for ever and ever.

**FIRST READING**                          *Revelation 11:19a; 12:1—6a, 10ab*

God's temple in heaven was opened, and the ark of his covenant could be seen in the temple.

A great sign appeared in the sky, a woman clothed with the sun, with the moon under her feet, and on her head a crown of twelve stars. She was with child and wailed aloud in pain as she labored to give birth. Then another sign appeared in the sky; it was a huge red dragon, with seven heads and ten horns, and on its heads were seven diadems. Its tail swept away a third of the stars in the sky and hurled them down to the earth. Then the dragon stood before the woman about to give birth, to devour her child when she gave birth. She gave birth to a son, a male child, destined to rule all the nations with an iron rod. Her child was caught up to God and his throne. The woman herself fled into the desert where she had a place prepared by God.

Then I heard a loud voice in heaven say: "Now have salvation and power come, and the kingdom of our God and the authority of his Anointed One."

## PSALM — *Psalm 45:10, 11, 12, 16 (10bc)*
**R. The queen stands at your right hand, arrayed in gold.**
The queen takes her place at your right hand in gold of Ophir. **R.**
Hear, O daughter, and see; turn your ear, **/** forget your people and your father's house. **R.**
So shall the king desire your beauty; **/** for he is your lord. **R.**
They are borne in with gladness and joy; **/** they enter the palace of the king. **R.**

## SECOND READING — *1 Corinthians 15:20—27*
Brothers and sisters: Christ has been raised from the dead, the firstfruits of those who have fallen asleep. For since death came through man, the resurrection of the dead came also through man. For just as in Adam all die, so too in Christ shall all be brought to life, but each one in proper order: Christ the firstfruits; then, at his coming, those who belong to Christ; then comes the end, when he hands over the kingdom to his God and Father, when he has destroyed every sovereignty and every authority and power. For he must reign until he has put all his enemies under his feet. The last enemy to be destroyed is death, for "he subjected everything under his feet."

## ALLELUIA
**R. Alleluia, alleluia.** Mary is taken up to heaven; a chorus of angels exults.
**R.**

## GOSPEL                                    *Luke 1:39—56*

Mary set out and traveled to the hill country in haste to a town of Judah, where she entered the house of Zechariah and greeted Elizabeth. When Elizabeth heard Mary's greeting, the infant leaped in her womb, and Elizabeth, filled with the Holy Spirit, cried out in a loud voice and said, "Blessed are you among women, and blessed is the fruit of your womb. And how does this happen to me, that the mother of my Lord should come to me? For at the moment the sound of your greeting reached my ears, the infant in my womb leaped for joy. Blessed are you who believed that what was spoken to you by the Lord would be fulfilled."

And Mary said:

"My soul proclaims the greatness of the Lord; my spirit rejoices in God my Savior for he has looked with favor on his lowly servant. From this day all generations will call me blessed: the Almighty has done great things for me and holy is his Name. He has mercy on those who fear him in every generation. He has shown the strength of his arm, and has scattered the proud in their conceit. He has cast down the mighty from their thrones, and has lifted up the lowly. He has filled the hungry with good things, and the rich he has sent away empty. He has come to the help of his servant Israel for he has remembered his promise of mercy, the promise he made to our fathers, to Abraham and his children for ever."

Mary remained with her about three months and then returned to her home.

## PRAYER OVER THE OFFERINGS

May this oblation, our tribute of homage, rise up to you, O Lord, and, through the intercession of the Most Blessed Virgin Mary, whom you assumed into heaven, may our hearts, aflame with the fire of love, constantly long for you. Through Christ our Lord.

## COMMUNION ANTIPHON                         **Luke 1: 48 – 49**

All generations will call me blessed, for he who is mighty has done great things for me.

## PRAYER AFTER COMMUNION

Having received the Sacrament of salvation, we ask you to grant, O Lord, that, through the intercession of the Blessed Virgin Mary, whom you assumed into heaven, we may be brought to the glory of the resurrection. Through Christ our Lord.

## LESSONS LEARNT FROM THE READINGS / HOMILY

1_____ 2_____
3_____ 4_____
5_____ 6_____

## ACTION POINTS FOR THE WEEK

1_____ 2_____
3_____ 4_____
5_____ 6_____

## PRAYER POINTS FOR THE WEEK

1_____ 2_____
3_____ 4_____
5_____ 6_____

## THIS WEEK, I AM GRATEFUL FOR

1_____ 2_____
3_____ 4_____
5_____ 6_____

## 22 AUGUST 2021, 21ST SUNDAY IN ORDINARY TIME

**ENTRANCE ANTIPHON**

Turn your ear, O Lord, and answer me; save the servant who trusts in you, my God. Have mercy on me, O Lord, for I cry to you all the day long.

**COLLECT**

O God, who cause the minds of the faithful to unite in a single purpose, grant your people to love what you command and to desire what you promise, that, amid the uncertainties of this world, our hearts may be fixed on that place where true gladness is found. Through our Lord Jesus Christ, your Son, who lives and reigns with you in the unity of the Holy Spirit, one God, for ever and ever.

**FIRST READING**                    *Joshua 24:1—2a, 15—17, 18b*

Joshua gathered together all the tribes of Israel at Shechem, summoning their elders, their leaders, their judges, and their officers. When they stood in ranks before God, Joshua addressed all the people: "If it does not please you to serve the LORD, decide today whom you will serve, the gods your fathers served beyond the River or the gods of the Amorites in whose country you are now dwelling. As for me and my household, we will serve the LORD."

But the people answered, "Far be it from us to forsake the LORD for the service of other gods. For it was the LORD, our God, who brought us and our fathers up out of the land of Egypt, out of a state of slavery. He performed those great miracles before our very eyes and protected us along our entire journey and among the peoples through whom we passed. Therefore we also will serve the LORD, for he is our God."

**PSALM:**                              *Psalm 34:2—3, 16—17, 18—19, 20—21 (9a)*
**R. Taste and see the goodness of the Lord.**
I will bless the LORD at all times; **/** his praise shall be ever in my mouth. **/** Let my soul glory in the LORD; **/** the lowly will hear me and be glad. **R.**
The LORD has eyes for the just, **/** and ears for their cry. **/** The LORD confronts the evildoers, **/** to destroy remembrance of them from the earth. **R.**
When the just cry out, the LORD hears them, **/** and from all their distress he rescues them. **/** The LORD is close to the brokenhearted;**/** and those who are crushed in spirit he saves. **R.**
Many are the troubles of the just one, **/** but out of them all the LORD delivers him; **/** he watches over all his bones; **/** not one of them shall be broken. **R.**

**EITHER SECOND READING**                    *Ephesians 5:21—32*
Brothers and sisters: Be subordinate to one another out of reverence for Christ. Wives should be subordinate to their husbands as to the Lord. For the husband is head of his wife just as Christ is head of the church, he himself the savior of the body. As the church is subordinate to Christ, so wives should be subordinate to their husbands in everything. Husbands, love your wives, even as Christ loved the church and handed himself over for her to sanctify her, cleansing her by the bath of water with the word, that he might present to himself the church in splendor, without spot or wrinkle or any such thing, that she might be holy and without blemish. So also husbands should love their wives as their own bodies. He who loves his wife loves himself. For no one hates his own flesh but rather nourishes and cherishes it, even as Christ does the church, because we are members

of his body. For this reason a man shall leave his father and his mother and be joined to his wife, and the two shall become one flesh. This is a great mystery, but I speak in reference to Christ and the church.

**OR:**                                                    *Ephesians 5:2a, 25—32*

Brothers and sisters: Live in love, as Christ loved us. Husbands, love your wives, even as Christ loved the church and handed himself over for her to sanctify her, cleansing her by the bath of water with the word, that he might present to himself the church in splendor, without spot or wrinkle or any such thing, that she might be holy and without blemish. So also husbands should love their wives as their own bodies. He who loves his wife loves himself. For no one hates his own flesh but rather nourishes and cherishes it, even as Christ does the church, because we are members of his body. *For this reason a man shall leave his father and his mother and be joined to his wife, and the two shall become one flesh.* This is a great mystery, but I speak in reference to Christ and the church.

**ALLELUIA**                                                  *John 6:63c, 68c*

**R. Alleluia, alleluia.** Your words, Lord, are Spirit and life; you have the words of everlasting life. **R.**

**GOSPEL**                                                      *John 6:60—69*

Many of Jesus' disciples who were listening said, "This saying is hard; who can accept it?" Since Jesus knew that his disciples were murmuring about this, he said to them, "Does this shock you? What if you were to see the Son of Man ascending to where he was before? It is the spirit that gives life, while the flesh is of no avail. The words I have spoken to you are Spirit and life. But there are some of you who do not believe." Jesus knew from the beginning the ones who would not believe and the one who would betray him. And he said, "For this reason I have told you that no one can come to me unless it is granted him by my Father."

As a result of this, many of his disciples returned to their former way of life and no longer accompanied him. Jesus then said to the Twelve, "Do you also want to leave?" Simon Peter answered him, "Master, to whom shall we go? You have the words of eternal life. We have come to believe and are convinced that you are the Holy One of God."

## PRAYER OVER THE OFFERINGS

O Lord, who gained for yourself a people by adoption through the one sacrifice offered once for all, bestow graciously on us, we pray, the gifts of unity and peace in your Church. Through Christ our Lord.

## COMMUNION ANTIPHON Cf. Ps 103: 13 – 15

The earth is replete with the fruits of your work, O Lord; you bring forth bread from the earth and wine to cheer the heart.

**OR**                                                                                   *Jn 6: 54*

Whoever eats my flesh and drinks my blood has eternal life, says the Lord, and I will raise him up on the last day.

## PRAYER AFTER COMMUNION

Complete within us, O Lord, we pray, the healing work of your mercy and graciously perfect and sustain us, so that in all things we may please you. Through Christ our Lord.

## LESSONS LEARNT FROM THE READINGS / HOMILY

1 _____ 2 _____
3 _____ 4 _____
5 _____ 6 _____

### ACTION POINTS FOR THE WEEK

1 _____ 2 _____
3 _____ 4 _____
5 _____ 6 _____

### PRAYER POINTS FOR THE WEEK

1 _____ 2 _____
3 _____ 4 _____
5 _____ 6 _____

### THIS WEEK, I AM GRATEFUL FOR

1 _____ 2 _____
3 _____ 4 _____
5 _____ 6 _____

# 29 AUGUST 2021, 22ND SUNDAY IN ORDINARY TIME

**ENTRANCE ANTIPHON**                    Cf. Ps 85: 3, 5

Have mercy on me, O Lord, for I cry to you all the day long. O Lord, you are good and forgiving, full of mercy to all who call to you.

**COLLECT**

God of might, giver of every good gift, put into our hearts the love of your name, so that, by deepening our sense of reverence, you may nurture in us what is good and, by your watchful care, keep safe what you have nurtured. Through our Lord Jesus Christ, your Son, who lives and reigns with you in the unity of the Holy Spirit, one God, for ever and ever.

**FIRST READING**                    *Deuteronomy 4:1—2, 6—8*

Moses said to the people: "Now, Israel, hear the statutes and decrees which I am teaching you to observe, that you may live, and may enter in and take possession of the land which the LORD, the God of your fathers, is giving you. In your observance of the commandments of the LORD, your God, which I enjoin upon you, you shall not add to what I command you nor subtract from it. Observe them carefully, for thus will you give evidence of your wisdom and intelligence to the nations, who will hear of all these statutes and say, 'This great nation is truly a wise and intelligent people.' For what great nation is there that has gods so close to it as the LORD, our God, is to us whenever we call upon him? Or what great nation has statutes and decrees that are as just as this whole law which I am setting before you today?"

**PSALM**                    *Psalm 15:2—3, 3—4, 4—5 (1a)*

**R. The one who does justice will live in the presence of the Lord.**

Whoever walks blamelessly and does justice; / who thinks the truth in his heart / and slanders not with his tongue. **R.**

Who harms not his fellow man, / nor takes up a reproach against his neighbor; / by whom the reprobate is despised, / while he honors those who fear the Lord. **R.**

Who lends not his money at usury / and accepts no bribe against the innocent. / Whoever does these things / shall never be disturbed. **R.**

**SECOND READING**                    *James 1:17—18, 21b—22, 27*

Dearest brothers and sisters: All good giving and every perfect gift is from above, coming down from the Father of lights, with whom there is no alteration or shadow caused by change. He willed to give us birth by the word of truth that we may be a kind of firstfruits of his creatures.

Humbly welcome the word that has been planted in you and is able to save your souls.

Be doers of the word and not hearers only, deluding yourselves.

Religion that is pure and undefiled before God and the Father is this: to care for orphans and widows in their affliction and to keep oneself unstained by the world.

**ALLELUIA** *James 1:18*

**R. Alleluia, alleluia.** The Father willed to give us birth by the word of truth that we may be a kind of firstfruits of his creatures. **R.**

**GOSPEL** *Mark 7:1—8, 14—15, 21—23*

When the Pharisees with some scribes who had come from Jerusalem gathered around Jesus, they observed that some of his disciples ate their meals with unclean, that is, unwashed, hands. —For the Pharisees and, in fact, all Jews, do not eat without carefully washing their hands, keeping the tradition of the elders. And on coming from the marketplace they do not eat without purifying themselves. And there are many other things that they have traditionally observed, the purification of cups and jugs and kettles and beds.— So the Pharisees and scribes questioned him, "Why do your disciples not follow the tradition of the elders but instead eat a meal with unclean hands?" He responded, *"Well did Isaiah prophesy about you hypocrites, as it is written:*

*This people honors me with their lips, but their hearts are far from me; in vain do they worship me, teaching as doctrines human precepts.*

*You disregard God's commandment but cling to human tradition."* He summoned the crowd again and said to them, "Hear me, all of you, and understand. Nothing that enters one from outside can defile that person; but the things that come out from within are what defile.

"From within people, from their hearts, come evil thoughts, unchastity, theft, murder, adultery, greed, malice, deceit, licentiousness, envy, blasphemy, arrogance, folly. All these evils come from within and they defile."

**PRAYER OVER THE OFFERINGS**

May this sacred offering, O Lord, confer on us always the blessing of salvation, that what it celebrates in mystery it may accomplish in power. Through Christ our Lord.

**COMMUNION ANTIPHON**                                        **Psalm 30: 20**
How great is the goodness, Lord, that you keep for those who fear you.
**OR**                                                           **Mt 5: 9 – 20**
Blessed are the peacemakers, for they shall be called children of God.
Blessed are they who are persecuted for the sake of righteousness, for
theirs is the kingdom of heaven.
**PRAYER AFTER COMMUNION**
Renewed by this bread from the heavenly table, we beseech you, Lord,
that, being the food of charity, it may confirm our hearts and stir us to
serve you in our neighbour. Through Christ our Lord.

**LESSONS LEARNT FROM THE READINGS / HOMILY**

| 1 | 2 |
|---|---|
| 3 | 4 |
| 5 | 6 |

**ACTION POINTS FOR THE WEEK**

| 1 | 2 |
|---|---|
| 3 | 4 |
| 5 | 6 |

**PRAYER POINTS FOR THE WEEK**

| 1 | 2 |
|---|---|
| 3 | 4 |
| 5 | 6 |

**THIS WEEK, I AM GRATEFUL FOR**

| 1 | 2 |
|---|---|
| 3 | 4 |
| 5 | 6 |

## *14*      *SEPTEMBER*

### 05 SEPTEMBER 2021, 23RD SUNDAY IN ORDINARY TIME

**ENTRANCE ANTIPHON**                                    **Ps 118: 137, 124**
You are just, O Lord, and your judgement is right; treat your servant in
accord with your merciful love.

## COLLECT

O God, by whom we are redeemed and receive adoption, look graciously upon your beloved sons and daughters, that those who believe in Christ may receive true freedom and an everlasting inheritance. Through our Lord Jesus Christ, your Son, who lives and reigns with you in the unity of the Holy Spirit, one God, for ever and ever.

## FIRST READING                                    *Isaiah 35:4—7a*

Thus says the LORD: Say to those whose hearts are frightened: Be strong, fear not! Here is your God, he comes with vindication; with divine recompense he comes to save you. Then will the eyes of the blind be opened, the ears of the deaf be cleared; then will the lame leap like a stag, then the tongue of the mute will sing. Streams will burst forth in the desert, and rivers in the steppe. The burning sands will become pools, and the thirsty ground, springs of water.

## PSALM                                   *Psalm 146:7, 8—9, 9—10 (1b)*

**R. Praise the Lord, my soul! or R. Alleluia.**

The God of Jacob keeps faith forever, **/** secures justice for the oppressed, **/** gives food to the hungry. **/** The LORD sets captives free. **R.**
The LORD gives sight to the blind; **/** the LORD raises up those who were bowed down. **/** The LORD loves the just; **/** the LORD protects strangers. **R.**
The fatherless and the widow the LORD sustains, **/** but the way of the wicked he thwarts. **/** The LORD shall reign forever; **/** your God, O Zion, through all generations. **R.**

## SECOND READING                                    *James 2:1—5*

My brothers and sisters, show no partiality as you adhere to the faith in our glorious Lord Jesus Christ. For if a man with gold rings and fine clothes comes into your assembly, and a poor person in shabby clothes also comes in, and you pay attention to the one wearing the fine clothes and say, "Sit here, please," while you say to the poor one, "Stand there," or "Sit at my feet," have you not made distinctions among yourselves and become judges with evil designs?

Listen, my beloved brothers and sisters. Did not God choose those who are poor in the world to be rich in faith and heirs of the kingdom that he promised to those who love him?

## ALLELUIA                                    *see Matthew 4:23*

R. **Alleluia, alleluia.** Jesus proclaimed the Gospel of the kingdom and cured every disease among the people. **R.**

**GOSPEL** *Mark 7:31—37*

Again Jesus left the district of Tyre and went by way of Sidon to the Sea of Galilee, into the district of the Decapolis. And people brought to him a deaf man who had a speech impediment and begged him to lay his hand on him. He took him off by himself away from the crowd. He put his finger into the man's ears and, spitting, touched his tongue; then he looked up to heaven and groaned, and said to him, "Ephphatha!"—that is, "Be opened!"— And immediately the man's ears were opened, his speech impediment was removed, and he spoke plainly. He ordered them not to tell anyone. But the more he ordered them not to, the more they proclaimed it. They were exceedingly astonished and they said, "He has done all things well. He makes the deaf hear and the mute speak."

**PRAYER OVER THE OFFERINGS**

O God, who give us the gift of true prayer and of peace, graciously grant that through this offering, we may do fitting homage to your divine majesty and, by partaking of the sacred mystery, we may be faithfully united in mind and heart. Through Christ our Lord.

**COMMUNION ANTIPHON** *Cf. Ps 41: 2 – 3*

Like the deer that yearns for running streams, so my soul is yearning for you, my God; my soul is thirsting for God, the living God.

**OR** *Jn 8: 12*

I am the light of the world, says the Lord; whoever follows me will not walk in darkness, but will have the light of life.

**PRAYER AFTER COMMUNION**

Grant that your faithful, O Lord, whom you nourish and endow with life through the food of your Word and heavenly Sacrament, may so benefit from your beloved Son's great gifts that we may merit an eternal share in his life. Who lives and reigns for ever and ever.

**LESSONS LEARNT FROM THE READINGS / HOMILY**

1 _____  2 _____

3 _____  4 _____

5 _____  6 _____

## ACTION POINTS FOR THE WEEK

1 _____ 2 _____
3 _____ 4 _____
5 _____ 6 _____

## PRAYER POINTS FOR THE WEEK

1 _____ 2 _____
3 _____ 4 _____
5 _____ 6 _____

## THIS WEEK, I AM GRATEFUL FOR

1 _____ 2 _____
3 _____ 4 _____
5 _____ 6 _____

# 12 SEPTEMBER 2021, 24TH SUNDAY IN ORDINARY TIME

**ENTRANCE ANTIPHON**                                  **Cf. Sir 36: 18**

Give peace, O Lord, to those who wait for you, that your prophets be found true. Hear the prayers of your servant, and of your people Israel.

**COLLECT**

Look upon us, O God, Creator and ruler of all things, and, that we may feel the working of your mercy, grant that we may serve you with all our heart. Through our Lord Jesus Christ, your Son, who lives and reigns with you in the unity of the Holy Spirit, one God, for ever and ever.

**FIRST READING**                                  *Isaiah 50:4c—9a*

The Lord GOD opens my ear that I may hear; and I have not rebelled, have not turned back. I gave my back to those who beat me, my cheeks to those who plucked my beard; my face I did not shield from buffets and spitting.

The Lord GOD is my help, therefore I am not disgraced; I have set my face like flint, knowing that I shall not be put to shame. He is near who upholds my right; if anyone wishes to oppose me, let us appear together. Who disputes my right? Let that man confront me. See, the Lord GOD is my help; who will prove me wrong?

**PSALM**                                  *Psalm 116:1—2, 3—4, 5—6, 8—9 (9)*

**R. I will walk before the Lord, in the land of the living. or R. Alleluia.**

I love the LORD because he has heard **/** my voice in supplication, **/** because he has inclined his ear to me **/** the day I called. **R.**

The cords of death encompassed me; **/** the snares of the netherworld seized upon me; **/** I fell into distress and sorrow, **/** and I called upon the name of the LORD, **/** "O LORD, save my life!" **R.**

Gracious is the LORD and just; **/** yes, our God is merciful. **/** The LORD keeps the little ones; **/** I was brought low, and he saved me. **R.**

For he has freed my soul from death, **/** my eyes from tears, my feet from stumbling. **/** I shall walk before the LORD **/** in the land of the living. **R.**

**SECOND READING** *James 2:14—18*

What good is it, my brothers and sisters, if someone says he has faith but does not have works? Can that faith save him? If a brother or sister has nothing to wear and has no food for the day, and one of you says to them, "Go in peace, keep warm, and eat well," but you do not give them the necessities of the body, what good is it? So also faith of itself, if it does not have works, is dead.

Indeed someone might say, "You have faith and I have works." Demonstrate your faith to me without works, and I will demonstrate my faith to you from my works.

**ALLELUIA** *Galatians 6:14*

R. Alleluia, alleluia. May I never boast except in the cross of our Lord through which the world has been crucified to me and I to the world. **R.**

**GOSPEL** *Mark 8:27—35*

Jesus and his disciples set out for the villages of Caesarea Philippi. Along the way he asked his disciples, "Who do people say that I am?" They said in reply, "John the Baptist, others Elijah, still others one of the prophets." And he asked them, "But who do you say that I am?" Peter said to him in reply, "You are the Christ." Then he warned them not to tell anyone about him.

He began to teach them that the Son of Man must suffer greatly and be rejected by the elders, the chief priests, and the scribes, and be killed, and rise after three days. He spoke this openly. Then Peter took him aside and began to rebuke him. At this he turned around and, looking at his disciples, rebuked Peter and said, "Get behind me, Satan. You are thinking not as God does, but as human beings do."

He summoned the crowd with his disciples and said to them, "Whoever wishes to come after me must deny himself, take up his cross, and follow me. For whoever wishes to save his life will lose it, but whoever loses his life for my sake and that of the gospel will save it."

## PRAYER OVER THEOFFERINGS

Look with favour on our supplications, O Lord, and in your kindness accept these, your servants' offerings, that what each has offered to the honour of your name may serve the salvation of all. Through Christ our Lord.

## COMMUNION ANTIPHON                                    Cf. Ps 35: 6

How precious is your mercy, O God! The children of men seek shelter in the shadow of your wings.

## OR                                                    Cf. 1Cor 10: 16

The chalice of blessing that we bless is a communion in the Blood of Christ; and the bread that we break is a sharing in the Body of the Lord.

## PRAYER AFTER COMMUNION

May the working of this heavenly gift, O Lord, we pray, take possession of our minds and bodies, so that its effects, and not our own desires, may always prevail in us. Through Christ our Lord.

## LESSONS LEARNT FROM THE READINGS / HOMILY

| 1 | 2 |
|---|---|
| 3 | 4 |
| 5 | 6 |

### ACTION POINTS FOR THE WEEK

| 1 | 2 |
|---|---|
| 3 | 4 |
| 5 | 6 |

### PRAYER POINTS FOR THE WEEK

| 1 | 2 |
|---|---|
| 3 | 4 |
| 5 | 6 |

### THIS WEEK, I AM GRATEFUL FOR

| 1 | 2 |
|---|---|
| 3 | 4 |

## 19 SEPTEMBER 2021, 25TH SUNDAY IN ORDINARY TIME

**ENTRANCE ANTIPHON**

I am the salvation of the people, says the Lord. Should they cry to me in any distress, I will hear them, and I will be their Lord for ever.

**COLLECT**

O God, who founded all the commands of your sacred Law upon love of you and of our neighbour, grant that, by keeping your precepts, we may merit to attain eternal life. Through our Lord Jesus Christ, your Son, who lives and reigns with you in the unity of the Holy Spirit, one God, for ever and ever.

**FIRST READING**                              *Wisdom 2:12, 17—20*

The wicked say: Let us beset the just one, because he is obnoxious to us; he sets himself against our doings, reproaches us for transgressions of the law and charges us with violations of our training. Let us see whether his words be true; let us find out what will happen to him. For if the just one be the son of God, God will defend him and deliver him from the hand of his foes. With revilement and torture let us put the just one to the test that we may have proof of his gentleness and try his patience. Let us condemn him to a shameful death; for according to his own words, God will take care of him.

**PSALM**                                *Psalm 54:3—4, 5, 6—8 (6b)*

R.     *The Lord upholds my life.*

O God, by your name save me, **/** and by your might defend my cause. **/** O God, hear my prayer; **/** hearken to the words of my mouth. **R.**

For the haughty have risen up against me, **/** the ruthless seek my life; **/** they set not God before their eyes. **R.**

Behold, God is my helper; **/** the Lord sustains my life. **/** Freely will I offer you sacrifice; **/** I will praise your name, O LORD, for its goodness. **R.**

**SECOND READING**                              *James 3:16—4:3*

Beloved: Where jealousy and selfish ambition exist, there is disorder and every foul practice. But the wisdom from above is first of all pure, then peaceable, gentle, compliant, full of mercy and good fruits, without inconstancy or insincerity. And the fruit of righteousness is sown in peace for those who cultivate peace.

Where do the wars and where do the conflicts among you come from? Is it not from your passions that make war within your members? You covet but do not possess. You kill and envy but you cannot obtain; you fight and wage war. You do not possess because you do not ask. You ask but do not receive, because you ask wrongly, to spend it on your passions.

**ALLELUIA** *see 2 Thessalonians 2:14*

**R. Alleluia, alleluia.** God has called us through the Gospel to possess the glory of our Lord Jesus Christ. **R.**

**GOSPEL** *Mark 9:30—37*

Jesus and his disciples left from there and began a journey through Galilee, but he did not wish anyone to know about it. He was teaching his disciples and telling them, "The Son of Man is to be handed over to men and they will kill him, and three days after his death the Son of Man will rise." But they did not understand the saying, and they were afraid to question him.

They came to Capernaum and, once inside the house, he began to ask them, "What were you arguing about on the way?" But they remained silent. They had been discussing among themselves on the way who was the greatest. Then he sat down, called the Twelve, and said to them, "If anyone wishes to be first, he shall be the last of all and the servant of all." Taking a child, he placed it in their midst, and putting his arms around it, he said to them, "Whoever receives one child such as this in my name, receives me; and whoever receives me, receives not me but the One who sent me."

**PRAYER OVER THE OFFERINGS**

Receive with favour, O Lord, we pray, the offerings of your people, that what they profess with devotion and faith may be theirs through these heavenly mysteries. Through Christ our Lord.

**COMMUNION ANTIPHON** Ps 118: 4 – 5

You have laid down your precepts to be carefully kept; may my ways be firm in keeping your statutes.

**OR** Jn 10: 14

I am the Good Shepherd, says the Lord; I know my sheep, and mine know me.

## PRAYER AFTER COMMUNION

Graciously raise up, O Lord, those you renew with this Sacrament, that we may come to possess your redemption both in mystery and in the manner of our life. Through Christ our Lord.

## LESSONS LEARNT FROM THE READINGS / HOMILY

| 1 | 2 |
|---|---|
| 3 | 4 |
| 5 | 6 |

### ACTION POINTS FOR THE WEEK

| 1 | 2 |
|---|---|
| 3 | 4 |
| 5 | 6 |

### PRAYER POINTS FOR THE WEEK

| 1 | 2 |
|---|---|
| 3 | 4 |
| 5 | 6 |

### THIS WEEK, I AM GRATEFUL FOR

| 1 | 2 |
|---|---|
| 3 | 4 |
| 5 | 6 |

## 26 SEPTEMBER 2021, 26TH SUNDAY IN ORDINARY TIME

**ENTRANCE ANTIPHON**                    **Dn 3: 31, 29, 30, 43, 42**

All that you have done to us, O Lord, you have done with true judgement, for we have sinned against you and not obeyed your commandments. But give glory to your name and deal with us according to the bounty of your mercy.

## COLLECT

O God, who manifest your almighty power above all by pardoning and showing mercy, bestow, we pray, your grace abundantly upon us and make those hastening to attain your promises heirs to the treasures of heaven. Through our Lord Jesus Christ, your Son, who lives and reigns with you in the unity of the Holy Spirit, one God, for ever and ever.

## FIRST READING                                    *Numbers 11:25—29*

The LORD came down in the cloud and spoke to Moses. Taking some of the spirit that was on Moses, the LORD bestowed it on the seventy elders; and as the spirit came to rest on them, they prophesied.

Now two men, one named Eldad and the other Medad, were not in the gathering but had been left in the camp. They too had been on the list, but had not gone out to the tent; yet the spirit came to rest on them also, and they prophesied in the camp. So, when a young man quickly told Moses, "Eldad and Medad are prophesying in the camp," Joshua, son of Nun, who from his youth had been Moses' aide, said, "Moses, my lord, stop them." But Moses answered him, "Are you jealous for my sake? Would that all the people of the LORD were prophets! Would that the LORD might bestow his spirit on them all!"

## PSALM                               *Psalm 19:8, 10, 12—13, 14 (9a)*

**R. The precepts of the Lord give joy to the heart.**

The law of the Lord is perfect, **/** refreshing the soul; **/** the decree of the Lord is trustworthy, **/** giving wisdom to the simple. **R.**

The fear of the LORD is pure, **/** enduring forever; **/** the ordinances of the LORD are true, **/** all of them just. **R.**

Though your servant is careful of them, **/** very diligent in keeping them, **/** yet who can detect failings?/Cleanse me from my unknown faults! **R.**

From wanton sin especially, restrain your servant; **/** let it not rule over me. **/** Then shall I be blameless and innocent **/** of serious sin. **R.**

## SECOND READING                                        *James 5:1—6*

Come now, you rich, weep and wail over your impending miseries. Your wealth has rotted away, your clothes have become moth—eaten, your gold and silver have corroded, and that corrosion will be a testimony against you; it will devour your flesh like a fire. You have stored up treasure for the last days. Behold, the wages you withheld from the workers who harvested your fields are crying aloud; and the cries of the harvesters have reached the ears of the Lord of hosts. You have lived on earth in luxury and pleasure; you have fattened your hearts for the day of slaughter. You have condemned; you have murdered the righteous one; he offers you no resistance.

**ALLELUIA** *see John 17:17b, 17a*

R. Alleluia, alleluia. Your word, O Lord, is truth; consecrate us in the truth. R.

**GOSPEL** *Mark 9:38—43, 45, 47—48*

At that time, John said to Jesus, "Teacher, we saw someone driving out demons in your name, and we tried to prevent him because he does not follow us." Jesus replied, "Do not prevent him. There is no one who performs a mighty deed in my name who can at the same time speak ill of me. For whoever is not against us is for us. Anyone who gives you a cup of water to drink because you belong to Christ, amen, I say to you, will surely not lose his reward.

"Whoever causes one of these little ones who believe in me to sin, it would be better for him if a great millstone were put around his neck and he were thrown into the sea. If your hand causes you to sin, cut it off. It is better for you to enter into life maimed than with two hands to go into Gehenna, into the unquenchable fire. And if your foot causes you to sin, cut if off. It is better for you to enter into life crippled than with two feet to be thrown into Gehenna. And if your eye causes you to sin, pluck it out. Better for you to enter into the kingdom of God with one eye than with two eyes to be thrown into Gehenna, where 'their worm does not die, and the fire is not quenched.'"

**PRAYER OVER THE OFFERINGS**

Grant us, O merciful God, that this our offering may find acceptance with you and that through it the wellspring of all blessing may be laid open before us. Through Christ our Lord.

**COMUNION ANTIPHON** *Cf. Ps 118: 49 – 50*

Remember your word to your servant, O Lord, by which you have given me hope. This is my comfort when I am brought low.

**OR** *1 Jn 3: 16*

By this we came to know the love of God: that Christ laid down his life for us; so we ought to lay down our lives for one another.

**PRAYER AFTER COMMUNION**

May this heavenly mystery, O Lord, restore us in mind and body, that we may be coheirs in glory with Christ, to whose suffering we are united whenever we proclaim his Death. Who lives and reigns for ever and ever.

## LESSONS LEARNT FROM THE READINGS / HOMILY

1 _____ 2 _____
3 _____ 4 _____
5 _____ 6 _____

## ACTION POINTS FOR THE WEEK

1 _____ 2 _____
3 _____ 4 _____
5 _____ 6 _____

## PRAYER POINTS FOR THE WEEK

1 _____ 2 _____
3 _____ 4 _____
5 _____ 6 _____

## THIS WEEK, I AM GRATEFUL FOR

1 _____ 2 _____
3 _____ 4 _____
5 _____ 6 _____

## *15*        *OCTOBER*

### 03 OCTOBER 2021, 27TH SUNDAY IN ORDINARY TIME

**ENTRANCE ANTIPHON**                    **Cf. Est 4: 17**

Within your will, O Lord, all things are established, and there is none that can resist your will. For you have made all things, the heaven and the earth, and all that is held within the circle of heaven; you are the Lord of all.

**COLLECT**

Almighty ever-living God, who in the abundance of your kindness surpass the merits and the desires of those who entreat you, pour out your mercy upon us to pardon what conscience dreads and to give what prayer does not dare to ask. Through our Lord Jesus Christ, your Son, who lives and reigns with you in the unity of the Holy Spirit, one God, for ever and ever.

**FIRST READING**                                              *Genesis 2:18—24*

The LORD God said: "It is not good for the man to be alone. I will make a suitable partner for him." So the LORD God formed out of the ground various wild animals and various birds of the air, and he brought them to the man to see what he would call them; whatever the man called each of them would be its name. The man gave names to all the cattle, all the birds of the air, and all wild animals; but none proved to be the suitable partner for the man.

So the LORD God cast a deep sleep on the man, and while he was asleep, he took out one of his ribs and closed up its place with flesh. The LORD God then built up into a woman the rib that he had taken from the man. When he brought her to the man, the man said:

"This one, at last, is bone of my bones and flesh of my flesh; this one shall be called 'woman,' for out of 'her man' this one has been taken." That is why a man leaves his father and mother and clings to his wife, and the two of them become one flesh.

**PSALM**                                    *Psalm 128:1—2, 3, 4—5, 6 (see 5)*
**R. May the Lord bless us all the days of our lives.**
Blessed are you who fear the LORD, **/** who walk in his ways! **/** For you shall eat the fruit of your handiwork; **/** blessed shall you be, and favored.
**R.**
Your wife shall be like a fruitful vine **/** in the recesses of your home; **/** your children like olive plants **/** around your table. **R.**
Behold, thus is the man blessed **/** who fears the LORD. **/** The LORD bless you from Zion: **/** may you see the prosperity of Jerusalem **/** all the days of your life. **R.**
May you see your children's children. **/** Peace be upon Israel! **R.**

**SECOND READING**                                           *Hebrews 2:9—11*

Brothers and sisters: He "for a little while" was made "lower than the angels," that by the grace of God he might taste death for everyone.

For it was fitting that he, for whom and through whom all things exist, in bringing many children to glory, should make the leader to their salvation perfect through suffering. He who consecrates and those who are being consecrated all have one origin. Therefore, he is not ashamed to call them "brothers."

**ALLELUIA**                                                   *1 John 4:12*

**R. Alleluia, alleluia.** If we love one another, God remains in us and his love is brought to perfection in us. **R.**

**GOSPEL EITHER:**                                                *Mark 10:2—16*

The Pharisees approached Jesus and asked, "Is it lawful for a husband to divorce his wife?" They were testing him. He said to them in reply, "What did Moses command you?" They replied, "Moses permitted a husband to write a bill of divorce and dismiss her." But Jesus told them, "Because of the hardness of your hearts he wrote you this commandment. But from the beginning of creation, *God made them male and female. For this reason a man shall leave his father and mother and be joined to his wife, and the two shall become one flesh.* So they are no longer two but one flesh. Therefore what God has joined together, no human being must separate." In the house the disciples again questioned Jesus about this. He said to them, "Whoever divorces his wife and marries another commits adultery against her; and if she divorces her husband and marries another, she commits adultery."

And people were bringing children to him that he might touch them, but the disciples rebuked them. When Jesus saw this he became indignant and said to them, "Let the children come to me; do not prevent them, for the kingdom of God belongs to such as these. Amen, I say to you, whoever does not accept the kingdom of God like a child will not enter it." Then he embraced them and blessed them, placing his hands on them.

**OR:**                                                         *Mark 10:2—12*

The Pharisees approached Jesus and asked, "Is it lawful for a husband to divorce his wife?" They were testing him. He said to them in reply, "What did Moses command you?" They replied, "Moses permitted a husband to write a bill of divorce and dismiss her."

But Jesus told them, "Because of the hardness of your hearts he wrote you this commandment. But from the beginning of creation, God made them male and female. For this reason a man shall leave his father and mother and be joined to his wife, and the two shall become one flesh. So they are no longer two but one flesh. Therefore what God has joined together, no human being must separate."

In the house the disciples again questioned Jesus about this. He said to them, "Whoever divorces his wife and marries another commits adultery against her; and if she divorces her husband and marries another, she commits adultery."

## PRAYER OVER THE OFFERINGS
Accept, O Lord, we pray, the sacrifices instituted by your commands and, through the sacred mysteries, which we celebrate with dutiful service, graciously complete the sanctifying work by which you are pleased to redeem us. Through Christ our Lord.

## COMMUNION ANTIPHON                                    Lam 3: 25
The Lord is good to those who hope in him, to the soul that seeks him.

## OR                                                   Cf. 1Cor 10: 17
Though many, we are one bread, one body, for we all partake of the one Bread and one Chalice.

## PRAYER AFTER COMMUNION
Grant us, almighty God, that we may be refreshed and nourished by the Sacrament which we have received, so as to be transformed into what we consume. Through Christ our Lord.

## LESSONS LEARNT FROM THE READINGS / HOMILY
1 _____ 2 _____
3 _____ 4 _____
5 _____ 6 _____

## ACTION POINTS FOR THE WEEK
1 _____ 2 _____
3 _____ 4 _____
5 _____ 6 _____

## PRAYER POINTS FOR THE WEEK
1 _____ 2 _____
3 _____ 4 _____
5 _____ 6 _____

## THIS WEEK, I AM GRATEFUL FOR
1 _____ 2 _____
3 _____ 4 _____
5 _____ 6 _____

# 10 OCTOBER 2021, 28TH SUNDAY IN ORDINARY TIME

**ENTRANCE ANTIPHON** Ps 129: 3 – 4

If you, O Lord, should mark iniquities, Lord, who could stand? But with you is found forgiveness, O God of Israel.

**COLLECT**

May your grace, O Lord, we pray, at all times go before us and follow after and make us always determined to carry out good works. Through our Lord Jesus Christ, your Son, who lives and reigns with you in the unity of the Holy Spirit, one God, for ever and ever.

**FIRST READING** *Wisdom 7:7—11*

I prayed, and prudence was given me; I pleaded, and the spirit of wisdom came to me. I preferred her to scepter and throne, and deemed riches nothing in comparison with her, nor did I liken any priceless gem to her; because all gold, in view of her, is a little sand, and before her, silver is to be accounted mire. Beyond health and comeliness I loved her, and I chose to have her rather than the light, because the splendor of her never yields to sleep. Yet all good things together came to me in her company, and countless riches at her hands.

**RPSALM** *Psalm 90:12—13, 14—15, 16—17 (14)*

**R. Fill us with your love, O Lord, and we will sing for joy!**

Teach us to number our days aright, **/** that we may gain wisdom of heart. **/** Return, O LORD! How long? **/** Have pity on your servants! **R.**

Fill us at daybreak with your kindness, **/** that we may shout for joy and gladness all our days. **/** Make us glad, for the days when you afflicted us, **/** for the years when we saw evil. **R.**

Let your work be seen by your servants **/** and your glory by their children; **/** and may the gracious care of the Lord our God be ours; **/** prosper the work of our hands for us! **/** Prosper the work of our hands! **R.**

**SECOND READING** *Hebrews 4:12—13*

Brothers and sisters: Indeed the word of God is living and effective, sharper than any two–edged sword, penetrating even between soul and spirit, joints and marrow, and able to discern reflections and thoughts of the heart. No creature is concealed from him, but everything is naked and exposed to the eyes of him to whom we must render an account.

**ALLELUIA** *Matthew 5:3*

**R. Alleluia, alleluia.** Blessed are the poor in spirit, for theirs is the kingdom of heaven. **R.**

**GOSPEL EITHER:** *Mark 10:17—30*

As Jesus was setting out on a journey, a man ran up, knelt down before him, and asked him, "Good teacher, what must I do to inherit eternal life?" Jesus answered him, "Why do you call me good? No one is good but God alone. You know the commandments:

*You shall not kill; you shall not commit adultery; you shall not steal; you shall not bear false witness; you shall not defraud; honor your father and your mother."*

He replied and said to him, "Teacher, all of these I have observed from my youth." Jesus, looking at him, loved him and said to him, "You are lacking in one thing. Go, sell what you have, and give to the poor and you will have treasure in heaven; then come, follow me." At that statement his face fell, and he went away sad, for he had many possessions.

Jesus looked around and said to his disciples, "How hard it is for those who have wealth to enter the kingdom of God!" The disciples were amazed at his words. So Jesus again said to them in reply, "Children, how hard it is to enter the kingdom of God! It is easier for a camel to pass through the eye of a needle than for one who is rich to enter the kingdom of God." They were exceedingly astonished and said among themselves, "Then who can be saved?" Jesus looked at them and said, "For human beings it is impossible, but not for God. All things are possible for God." Peter began to say to him, "We have given up everything and followed you." Jesus said, "Amen, I say to you, there is no one who has given up house or brothers or sisters or mother or father or children or lands for my sake and for the sake of the gospel who will not receive a hundred times more now in this present age: houses and brothers and sisters and mothers and children and lands, with persecutions, and eternal life in the age to come."

**OR:** *Mark 10:17—27*

As Jesus was setting out on a journey, a man ran up, knelt down before him, and asked him, "Good teacher, what must I do to inherit eternal life?" Jesus answered him, "Why do you call me good? No one is good but God alone. You know the commandments:

*You shall not kill; you shall not commit adultery; you shall not steal; you shall not bear false witness; you shall not defraud; honor your father and your mother."*

He replied and said to him, "Teacher, all of these I have observed from my youth." Jesus, looking at him, loved him and said to him, "You are lacking in one thing. Go, sell what you have, and give to the poor and you will have treasure in heaven; then come, follow me." At that statement his face fell, and he went away sad, for he had many possessions.

Jesus looked around and said to his disciples, "How hard it is for those who have wealth to enter the kingdom of God!" The disciples were amazed at his words. So Jesus again said to them in reply, "Children, how hard it is to enter the kingdom of God! It is easier for a camel to pass through the eye of a needle than for one who is rich to enter the kingdom of God." They were exceedingly astonished and said among themselves, "Then who can be saved?" Jesus looked at them and said, "For human beings it is impossible, but not for God. All things are possible for God."

**PRAYER OVER THE OFFERINGS**
Accept, O Lord, the prayers of your faithful with the sacrificial offerings, that, through these acts of devotedness, we may pass over to the glory of heaven. Through Christ our Lord.

**COMMUNION ANTIPHON**                    Cf. Ps 33: 11
The rich suffer want and go hungry, but those who seek the Lord lack no blessing.

**OR**                                          1Jn 3: 2
When the Lord appears, we shall be like him, for we shall see him as he is.

**PRAYER AFTER COMMUNION**
We entreat your majesty most humbly, O Lord, that, as you feed us with the nourishment which comes from the most holy Body and Blood of your Son, so you may make us sharers of his divine nature. Who lives and reigns for ever and ever.

**LESSONS LEARNT FROM THE READINGS / HOMILY**

| 1 | 2 |
|---|---|
| 3 | 4 |
| 5 | 6 |

## ACTION POINTS FOR THE WEEK

1 _____  2 _____

3 _____  4 _____

5 _____  6 _____

## PRAYER POINTS FOR THE WEEK

1 _____  2 _____

3 _____  4 _____

5 _____  6 _____

## THIS WEEK, I AM GRATEFUL FOR

1 _____  2 _____

3 _____  4 _____

5 _____  6 _____

## 17 OCTOBER 2021, 29TH SUNDAY IN ORDINARY TIME

**ENTRANCE ANTIPHON**                                **Cf. Ps 16: 6, 8**

To you I call; for you will surely heed me, O God; turn your ear to me; hear my words. Guard me as the apple of your eye; in the shadow of your wings protect me.

**COLLECT**

Almighty ever-living God, grant that we may always conform our will to yours and serve your majesty in sincerity of heart. Through our Lord Jesus Christ, your Son, who lives and reigns with you in the unity of the Holy Spirit, one God, for ever and ever.

**FIRST READING**                                *Isaiah 53:10—11*

The LORD was pleased to crush him in infirmity.

If he gives his life as an offering for sin, he shall see his descendants in a long life, and the will of the LORD shall be accomplished through him.

Because of his affliction he shall see the light in fullness of days; through his suffering, my servant shall justify many, and their guilt he shall bear.

**PSALM**                                *Psalm 33:4—5, 18—19, 20, 22 (22)*

**R. Lord, let your mercy be on us, as we place our trust in you.**

Upright is the word of the LORD, **/** and all his works are trustworthy. **/** He loves justice and right; **/** of the kindness of the LORD the earth is full. **R.**
See, the eyes of the LORD are upon those who fear him, **/** upon those who hope for his kindness; **/** to deliver them from death **/** and preserve them in spite of famine. **R.**
Our soul waits for the LORD, **/** who is our help and our shield. **/** May your kindness, O LORD, be upon us **/** who have put our hope in you. **R.**

**SECOND READING** *Hebrews 4:14—16*

Brothers and sisters: Since we have a great high priest who has passed through the heavens, Jesus, the Son of God, let us hold fast to our confession. For we do not have a high priest who is unable to sympathize with our weaknesses, but one who has similarly been tested in every way, yet without sin. So let us confidently approach the throne of grace to receive mercy and to find grace for timely help.

**ALLELUIA** *Mark 10:45*

**R. Alleluia, alleluia.** The Son of Man came to serve and to give his life as a ransom for many. **R.**

**GOSPEL EITHER:** *Mark 10:35—45*

James and John, the sons of Zebedee, came to Jesus and said to him, "Teacher, we want you to do for us whatever we ask of you." He replied, "What do you wish me to do for you?" They answered him, "Grant that in your glory we may sit one at your right and the other at your left." Jesus said to them, "You do not know what you are asking. Can you drink the cup that I drink or be baptized with the baptism with which I am baptized?" They said to him, "We can." Jesus said to them, "The cup that I drink, you will drink, and with the baptism with which I am baptized, you will be baptized; but to sit at my right or at my left is not mine to give but is for those for whom it has been prepared." When the ten heard this, they became indignant at James and John. Jesus summoned them and said to them, "You know that those who are recognized as rulers over the Gentiles lord it over them, and their great ones make their authority over them felt. But it shall not be so among you. Rather, whoever wishes to be great among you will be your servant; whoever wishes to be first among you will be the slave of all. For the Son of Man did not come to be served but to serve and to give his life as a ransom for many."

**OR:**                                                                   *MARK 10:42—45*

Jesus summoned the Twelve and said to them, "You know that those who are recognized as rulers over the Gentiles lord it over them, and their great ones make their authority over them felt. But it shall not be so among you. Rather, whoever wishes to be great among you will be your servant; whoever wishes to be first among you will be the slave of all. For the Son of Man did not come to be served but to serve and to give his life as a ransom for many."

**PRAYER OVER THE OFFERINGS**

Grant us, Lord, we pray, a sincere respect for your gifts, that, through the purifying action of your grace, we may be cleansed by the very mysteries we serve. Through Christ our Lord.

**COMMUNION ANTIPHON**                                     Cf. Ps 32: 18 – 19

Behold, the eyes of the Lord are on those who fear him, who hope in his merciful love, to rescue their souls from death,to keep them alive in famine.

**OR**                                      Mk 10: 45

The Son of Man has come to give his life as a ransom for many.

**PRAYER AFTER COMMUNION**

Grant, O Lord, we pray, that, benefiting from participation in heavenly things, we may be helped by what you give in this present age and prepared for the gifts that are eternal. Through Christ our Lord.


**LESSONS LEARNT FROM THE READINGS / HOMILY**

| 1 | 2 |
|---|---|
| 3 | 4 |
| 5 | 6 |


**ACTION POINTS FOR THE WEEK**

| 1 | 2 |
|---|---|
| 3 | 4 |
| 5 | 6 |


**PRAYER POINTS FOR THE WEEK**

| 1 | 2 |
|---|---|
| 3 | 4 |
| 5 | 6 |

## THIS WEEK, I AM GRATEFUL FOR

| 1 | 2 |
|---|---|
| 3 | 4 |
| 5 | 6 |

## 24 OCTOBER 2021, 30TH SUNDAY IN ORDINARY TIME

**ENTRANCE ANTIPHON**                                    **Cf. Ps 104: 3 – 4**

Let the hearts that seek the Lord rejoice; turn to the Lord and his strength; constantly seek his face.

**COLLECT**

Almighty ever-living God, increase our faith, hope and charity, and make us love what you command, so that we may merit what you promise. Through our Lord Jesus Christ, your Son, who lives and reigns with you in the unity of the Holy Spirit, one God, for ever and ever.

**FIRST READING**                                        *Jeremiah 31:7—9*

Thus says the LORD: Shout with joy for Jacob, exult at the head of the nations; proclaim your praise and say: The LORD has delivered his people, the remnant of Israel. Behold, I will bring them back from the land of the north; I will gather them from the ends of the world, with the blind and the lame in their midst, the mothers and those with child; they shall return as an immense throng. They departed in tears, but I will console them and guide them; I will lead them to brooks of water, on a level road, so that none shall stumble. For I am a father to Israel, Ephraim is my first—born.

**PSALM**                                        *Psalm 126:1—2, 2—3, 4—5, 6 (3)*

**R. The Lord has done great things for us; we are filled with joy.**

When the LORD brought back the captives of Zion, / we were like men dreaming. / Then our mouth was filled with laughter, / and our tongue with rejoicing. **R.**

Then they said among the nations, / "The LORD has done great things for them." / The LORD has done great things for us; / we are glad indeed. **R.**

Restore our fortunes, O LORD, / like the torrents in the southern desert. / Those that sow in tears / shall reap rejoicing. **R.**

Although they go forth weeping, / carrying the seed to be sown, / they shall come back rejoicing, / carrying their sheaves. **R.**

## SECOND READING                                               *Hebrews 5:1—6*

Brothers and sisters: Every high priest is taken from among men and made their representative before God, to offer gifts and sacrifices for sins. He is able to deal patiently with the ignorant and erring, for he himself is beset by weakness and so, for this reason, must make sin offerings for himself as well as for the people. No one takes this honor upon himself but only when called by God, just as Aaron was. In the same way, it was not Christ who glorified himself in becoming high priest, but rather the one who said to him:

You are my son: this day I have begotten you; just as he says in another place: You are a priest forever according to the order of Melchizedek.

## ALLELUIA                                                   *see 2 Timothy 1:10*

R. Alleluia, alleluia. Our Savior Jesus Christ destroyed death and brought life to light through the Gospel. **R.**

## GOSPEL                                                        *Mark 10:46—52*

As Jesus was leaving Jericho with his disciples and a sizable crowd, Bartimaeus, a blind man, the son of Timaeus, sat by the roadside begging. On hearing that it was Jesus of Nazareth, he began to cry out and say, "Jesus, son of David, have pity on me." And many rebuked him, telling him to be silent. But he kept calling out all the more, "Son of David, have pity on me." Jesus stopped and said, "Call him." So they called the blind man, saying to him, "Take courage; get up, Jesus is calling you." He threw aside his cloak, sprang up, and came to Jesus. Jesus said to him in reply, "What do you want me to do for you?" The blind man replied to him, "Master, I want to see." Jesus told him, "Go your way; your faith has saved you." Immediately he received his sight and followed him on the way.

## PRAYER OVER THE OFFERINGS

Look, we pray, O Lord, on the offerings we make to your majesty, that whatever is done by us in your service may be directed above all to your glory. Through Christ our Lord.

## COMMUNION ANTIPHON                                           **Cf. Ps 19: 6**

We will ring out our joy at your saving help and exult in the name of our God.

**OR**                                                                        **Eph 5: 2**

Christ loved us and gave himself up for us, as a fragrant offering to God.

**COMMUNION ANTIPHON**

May your Sacraments, O Lord, we pray, perfect in us what lies within them, that what we now celebrate in signs we may one day possess in truth. Through Christ our Lord.

**LESSONS LEARNT FROM THE READINGS / HOMILY**

1 _____ 2 _____
3 _____ 4 _____
5 _____ 6 _____

**ACTION POINTS FOR THE WEEK**

1 _____ 2 _____
3 _____ 4 _____
5 _____ 6 _____

**PRAYER POINTS FOR THE WEEK**

1 _____ 2 _____
3 _____ 4 _____
5 _____ 6 _____

**THIS WEEK, I AM GRATEFUL FOR**

1 _____ 2 _____
3 _____ 4 _____
5 _____ 6 _____

## 31 OCTOBER 2021, 31ST SUNDAY IN ORDINARY TIME

**ENTRANCE ANTIPHON**                                            **Cf. Ps 37: 22 – 23**

Forsake me not, O Lord, my God; be not far from me! Make haste and come to my help, O Lord, my strong salvation!

**COLLECT**

Almighty and merciful God, by whose gift your faithful offer you right and praiseworthy service, grant, we pray, that we may hasten without stumbling to receive the things you have promised. Through our Lord

Jesus Christ, your Son, who lives and reigns with you in the unity of the Holy Spirit, one God, for ever and ever.

## FIRST READING                                    *Deuteronomy 6:2—6*

Moses spoke to the people, saying: "Fear the LORD, your God, and keep, throughout the days of your lives, all his statutes and commandments which I enjoin on you, and thus have long life. Hear then, Israel, and be careful to observe them, that you may grow and prosper the more, in keeping with the promise of the LORD, the God of your fathers, to give you a land flowing with milk and honey.

"Hear, O Israel! The LORD is our God, the LORD alone! Therefore, you shall love the LORD, your God, with all your heart, and with all your soul, and with all your strength. Take to heart these words which I enjoin on you today."

## PSALM                                    *Psalm 18:2—3, 3—4, 47, 51 (2)*

**R. I love you, Lord, my strength.**

I love you, O LORD, my strength, **/** O LORD, my rock, my fortress, my deliverer. **R.**

My God, my rock of refuge, **/** my shield, the horn of my salvation, my stronghold! **/** Praised be the LORD, I exclaim, **/** and I am safe from my enemies. **R.**

The LORD lives! And blessed be my rock! **/** Extolled be God my savior, **/** you who gave great victories to your king **/** and showed kindness to your anointed. **R.**

## SECOND READING                                    *Hebrews 7:23—28*

Brothers and sisters: The levitical priests were many because they were prevented by death from remaining in office, but Jesus, because he remains forever, has a priesthood that does not pass away. Therefore, he is always able to save those who approach God through him, since he lives forever to make intercession for them.

It was fitting that we should have such a high priest: holy, innocent, undefiled, separated from sinners, higher than the heavens. He has no need, as did the high priests, to offer sacrifice day after day, first for his own sins and then for those of the people; he did that once for all when he offered himself. For the law appoints men subject to weakness to be high priests, but the word of the oath, which was taken after the law, appoints a son, who has been made perfect forever.

**ALLELUIA** *John 14:23*

R. Alleluia, alleluia. Whoever loves me will keep my word, says the Lord; and my Father will love him and we will come to him. **R.**

**GOSPEL** *Mark 12:28b—34*

One of the scribes came to Jesus and asked him, "Which is the first of all the commandments?" Jesus replied, "The first is this: Hear, O Israel! The Lord our God is Lord alone! You shall love the Lord your God with all your heart, with all your soul, with all your mind, and with all your strength. The second is this: You shall love your neighbor as yourself. There is no other commandment greater than these." The scribe said to him, "Well said, teacher. You are right in saying, 'He is One and there is no other than he.' And 'to love him with all your heart, with all your understanding, with all your strength, and to love your neighbor as yourself' is worth more than all burnt offerings and sacrifices." And when Jesus saw that he answered with understanding, he said to him, "You are not far from the kingdom of God." And no one dared to ask him any more questions.

**PRAYER OVER THE OFFERINGS**

May these sacrificial offerings, O Lord, become for you a pure oblation, and for us a holy outpouring of your mercy. Through Christ our Lord.

**COMMUNION ANTIPHON** *Cf. Ps 15: 11*

You will show me the path of life, the fullness of joy in your presence, O Lord.

**OR** *Jn 6: 58*

Just as the living Father sent me and I have life because of the Father, so whoever feeds on me shall have life because of me, says the Lord.

**PRAYER AFTER COMMUNION**

May the working of your power, O Lord, increase in us, we pray, so that, renewed by these heavenly Sacraments, we may be prepared by your gift for receiving what they promise. Through Christ our Lord.

**LESSONS LEARNT FROM THE READINGS / HOMILY**

1 _____ 2 _____

3 _____ 4 _____

| 5 | 6 |

## ACTION POINTS FOR THE WEEK

| 1 | 2 |
| 3 | 4 |
| 5 | 6 |

## PRAYER POINTS FOR THE WEEK

| 1 | 2 |
| 3 | 4 |
| 5 | 6 |

## THIS WEEK, I AM GRATEFUL FOR

| 1 | 2 |
| 3 | 4 |
| 5 | 6 |

## 16 *NOVEMBER*

## 01 NOVEMBER 2021, ALL SAINTS – SOLEMNITY

**ENTRANCE ANTIPHON**

Let us all rejoice in the Lord, as we celebrate the feast day in honour of all the Saints, at whose festival the Angels rejoice and praise the Son of God.

**COLLECT**

Almighty ever-living God, by whose gift we venerate in one celebration the merits of all the Saints, bestow on us, we pray, through the prayers of so many intercessors, an abundance of the reconciliation with you for which we earnestly long. Through our Lord Jesus Christ, your Son, who lives and reigns with you in the unity of the Holy Spirit, one God, for ever and ever.

**FIRST READING**                    *Revelation 7:2—4, 9—14*

I, John, saw another angel come up from the East, holding the seal of the living God. He cried out in a loud voice to the four angels who were given power to damage the land and the sea, "Do not damage the land or the sea or the trees until we put the seal on the foreheads of the servants of our God." I heard the number of those who had been marked with the seal, one hundred and forty–four thousand marked from every tribe of the children if Israel.

After this I had a vision of a great multitude, which no one could count, from every nation, race, people, and tongue. They stood before the throne and before the Lamb, wearing white robes and holding palm branches in their hands. They cried out in a loud voice:

"Salvation comes from our God, who is seated on the throne, and from the Lamb."

All the angels stood around the throne and around the elders and the four living creatures. They prostrated themselves before the throne, worshiped God, and exclaimed:

"Amen. Blessing and glory, wisdom and thanksgiving, honor, power, and might be to our God forever and ever. Amen."

Then one of the elders spoke up and said to me, "Who are these wearing white robes, and where did they come from?" I said to him, "My lord, you are the one who knows." He said to me, "These are the ones who have survived the time of great distress; they have washed their robes and made them white in the blood of the Lamb."

## PSALM                            *Psalm 24:1bc—2, 3—4ab, 5—6 (see 6)*
**R. Lord, this is the people that longs to see your face.**
The LORD's are the earth and its fullness; **/** the world and those who dwell in it. **/** For he founded it upon the seas **/** and established it upon the rivers. **R.**
Who can ascend the mountain of the LORD? **/** or who may stand in his holy place? **/** One whose hands are sinless, whose heart is clean, **/** who desires not what is vain. **R.**
He shall receive a blessing from the LORD, **/** a reward from God his savior. **/** Such is the race that seeks for him, **/** that seeks the face of the God of Jacob. **R.**

## SECOND READING                            *1 John 3:1—3*
Beloved: See what love the Father has bestowed on us that we may be called the children of God. Yet so we are. The reason the world does not know us is that it did not know him. Beloved, we are God's children now; what we shall be has not yet been revealed. We do know that when it is revealed we shall be like him, for we shall see him as he is. Everyone who has this hope based on him makes himself pure, as he is pure.

## ALLELUIA
**John 10:27**

**R. Alleluia, alleluia.** Come to me, all you who labor and are burdened, and I will give you rest, says the Lord. **R.**

## GOSPEL
**Matthew 5:1—12a**

When Jesus saw the crowds, he went up the mountain, and after he had sat down, his disciples came to him. He began to teach them, saying:

"Blessed are the poor in spirit, for theirs is the Kingdom of heaven. Blessed are they who mourn, for they will be comforted. Blessed are the meek, for they will inherit the land. Blessed are they who hunger and thirst for righteousness, for they will be satisfied. Blessed are the merciful, for they will be shown mercy. Blessed are the clean of heart, for they will see God. Blessed are the peacemakers, for they will be called children of God. Blessed are they who are persecuted for the sake of righteousness, for theirs is the Kingdom of heaven. Blessed are you when they insult you and persecute you and utter every kind of evil against you falsely because of me. Rejoice and be glad, for your reward will be great in heaven."

## PRAYER OVER THE OFFERINGS

May these offerings we bring in honour of all the Saints be pleasing to you, O Lord, and grant that, just as we believe the Saints to be already assured of immortality, so we may experience their concern for our salvation. Through Christ our Lord.

## COMMUNION ANTIPHON
**Mt 5: 8 – 10**

Blessed are the clean of heart, for they shall see God. Blessed are the peacemakers, for they shall be called children of God. Blessed are they who are persecuted for the sake of righteousness, for theirs is the kingdom of heaven.

## PRAYER AFTER COMMUNION

As we adore you, O God, who alone are holy and wonderful in all your Saints, we implore your grace, so that, coming to perfect holiness in the fullness of your love, we may pass from this pilgrim table to the banquet of our heavenly homeland. Through Christ our Lord.

## LESSONS LEARNT FROM THE READINGS / HOMILY

| 1 | 2 |
|---|---|
| 3 | 4 |

| 5 | 6 |
|---|---|

## ACTION POINTS FOR THE WEEK

| 1 | 2 |
|---|---|
| 3 | 4 |
| 5 | 6 |

## PRAYER POINTS FOR THE WEEK

| 1 | 2 |
|---|---|
| 3 | 4 |
| 5 | 6 |

## THIS WEEK, I AM GRATEFUL FOR

| 1 | 2 |
|---|---|
| 3 | 4 |
| 5 | 6 |

# 07 NOVEMBER 2021, 32ND SUNDAY IN ORDINARY TIME

**ENTRANCE ANTIPHON**                                   **Cf. Ps 87: 3**

Let my prayer come into your presence. Incline your ear to my cry for help, O Lord.

**COLLECT**

Almighty and merciful God, graciously keep from us all adversity, so that, unhindered in mind and body alike, we may pursue in freedom of heart the things that are yours. Through our Lord Jesus Christ, your Son, who lives and reigns with you in the unity of the Holy Spirit, one God, for ever and ever.

**FIRST READING**                                   *1 Kings 17:10—16*

In those days, Elijah the prophet went to Zarephath. As he arrived at the entrance of the city, a widow was gathering sticks there; he called out to her, "Please bring me a small cupful of water to drink." She left to get it, and he called out after her, "Please bring along a bit of bread." She answered, "As the LORD, your God, lives, I have nothing baked; there is only a handful of flour in my jar and a little oil in my jug. Just now I was collecting a couple of sticks, to go in and prepare something for myself and my son; when we have eaten it, we shall die." Elijah said to her, "Do not be afraid. Go and do as you propose. But first make me a little cake and bring it to me. Then you can prepare something for yourself and your son. For the LORD, the God of Israel, says, 'The jar of flour shall not go empty, nor the jug of oil run dry, until the day when the LORD sends rain upon the earth.'" She left and did as Elijah had said. She was able to eat for a year, and he and her son as well; the jar of flour did not go empty, nor the jug of oil run dry, as the LORD had foretold through Elijah.

**PSALM** *Psalm 146:7, 8—9, 9—10 (1b)*
**R. Praise the Lord, my soul! or R. Alleluia.**
The LORD keeps faith forever, **/** secures justice for the oppressed, **/** gives food to the hungry. **/** The LORD sets captives free. **R.**
The LORD gives sight to the blind; **/** the LORD raises up those who were bowed down. **/** The LORD loves the just; **/** the LORD protects strangers. **R.**
The fatherless and the widow he sustains, **/** but the way of the wicked he thwarts. **/** The LORD shall reign forever; **/** your God, O Zion, through all generations. Alleluia. **R.**

**SECOND READING** *Hebrews 9:24—28*
Christ did not enter into a sanctuary made by hands, a copy of the true one, but heaven itself, that he might now appear before God on our behalf. Not that he might offer himself repeatedly, as the high priest enters each year into the sanctuary with blood that is not his own; if that were so, he would have had to suffer repeatedly from the foundation of the world. But now once for all he has appeared at the end of the ages to take away sin by his sacrifice. Just as it is appointed that human beings die once, and after this the judgment, so also Christ, offered once to take away the sins of many, will appear a second time, not to take away sin but to bring salvation to those who eagerly await him.

**ALLELUIA** *Matthew 5:3*
**R. Alleluia, alleluia.** Blessed are the poor in spirit, for theirs is the kingdom of heaven. **R.**

**GOSPEL EITHER:** *Mark 12:38—44*
In the course of his teaching Jesus said to the crowds, "Beware of the scribes, who like to go around in long robes and accept greetings in the marketplaces, seats of honor in synagogues, and places of honor at

banquets. They devour the houses of widows and, as a pretext recite lengthy prayers. They will receive a very severe condemnation."

He sat down opposite the treasury and observed how the crowd put money into the treasury. Many rich people put in large sums. A poor widow also came and put in two small coins worth a few cents. Calling his disciples to himself, he said to them, "Amen, I say to you, this poor widow put in more than all the other contributors to the treasury. For they have all contributed from their surplus wealth, but she, from her poverty, has contributed all she had, her whole livelihood."

**OR:**                                                                      *Mark 12:41—44*
Jesus sat down opposite the treasury and observed how the crowd put money into the treasury. Many rich people put in large sums. A poor widow also came and put in two small coins worth a few cents. Calling his disciples to himself, he said to them, "Amen, I say to you, this poor widow put in more than all the other contributors to the treasury. For they have all contributed from their surplus wealth, but she, from her poverty, has contributed all she had, her whole livelihood."

**PRAYER OVER THE OFFERINGS**
Look with favour, we pray, O Lord, upon the sacrificial gifts offered here, that, celebrating in mystery the Passion of your Son, we may honour it with loving devotion. Through Christ our Lord.

**COMMUNION ANTIPHON**      **Cf. Ps 22: 1 – 2**
The Lord is my shepherd; there is nothing I shall want. Fresh and green are the pastures where he gives me repose, near restful waters he leads me.

**OR**                                            **Cf. Lk 24: 35**
The disciples recognized the Lord Jesus in the breaking of bread.

**PRAYER AFTER COMMUNION**
Nourished by this sacred gift, O Lord, we give you thanks and beseech your mercy, that, by the pouring forth of your Spirit, the grace of integrity may endure in those your heavenly power has entered. Through Christ our Lord.

**LESSONS LEARNT FROM THE READINGS / HOMILY**
1                                                      2

| 3 | 4 |
|---|---|
| 5 | 6 |

## ACTION POINTS FOR THE WEEK

| 1 | 2 |
|---|---|
| 3 | 4 |
| 5 | 6 |

## PRAYER POINTS FOR THE WEEK

| 1 | 2 |
|---|---|
| 3 | 4 |
| 5 | 6 |

## THIS WEEK, I AM GRATEFUL FOR

| 1 | 2 |
|---|---|
| 3 | 4 |
| 5 | 6 |

# 14 NOVEMBER 2021, 33RD SUNDAY IN ORDINARY TIME

**ENTRANCE ANTIPHON**                    **Jer 29: 11, 12, 14**

The Lord said: I think thoughts of peace and not of affliction. You will call upon me, and I will answer you, and I will lead back your captives from every place.

**COLLECT**

Grant us, we pray, O Lord our God, the constant gladness of being devoted to you, for it is full and lasting happiness to serve with constancy the author of all that is good. Through our Lord Jesus Christ, your Son, who lives and reigns with you in the unity of the Holy Spirit, one God, for ever and ever.

**FIRST READING**                         *Daniel 12:1—3*

In those days, I, Daniel, heard this word of the Lord: "At that time there shall arise Michael, the great prince, guardian of your people; it shall be a time unsurpassed in distress since nations began until that time. At that time your people shall escape, everyone who is found written in the book.

"Many of those who sleep in the dust of the earth shall awake; some shall live forever, others shall be an everlasting horror and disgrace.

"But the wise shall shine brightly like the splendor of the firmament, and those who lead the many to justice shall be like the stars forever."

## PSALM                                    Psalm 16:5, 8, 9—10, 11 (1)
**R. You are my inheritance, O Lord!**
O LORD, my allotted portion and my cup, / you it is who hold fast my lot. / I set the LORD ever before me; / with him at my right hand I shall not be disturbed. **R.**
Therefore my heart is glad and my soul rejoices, / my body, too, abides in confidence; / because you will not abandon my soul to the netherworld, / nor will you suffer your faithful one to undergo corruption. **R.**
You will show me the path to life, / fullness of joys in your presence, / the delights at your right hand forever. **R.**

## SECOND READING                              Hebrews 10:11—14, 18
Brothers and sisters: Every priest stands daily at his ministry, offering frequently those same sacrifices that can never take away sins. But this one offered one sacrifice for sins, and took his seat forever at the right hand of God; now he waits until his enemies are made his footstool. For by one offering he has made perfect forever those who are being consecrated.

Where there is forgiveness of these, there is no longer offering for sin.

## ALLELUIA                                              Luke 21:36
**R. Alleluia, alleluia.** Be vigilant at all times and pray that you have the strength to stand before the Son of Man. **R.**

## GOSPEL                                              Mark 13:24—32
Jesus said to his disciples: "In those days after that tribulation the sun will be darkened, and the moon will not give its light, and the stars will be falling from the sky, and the powers in the heavens will be shaken.

"And then they will see the 'Son of Man coming in the clouds' with great power and glory, and then he will send out the angels and gather his elect from the four winds, from the end of the earth to the end of the sky.

"Learn a lesson from the fig tree. When its branch becomes tender and sprouts leaves, you know that summer is near. In the same way, when you see these things happening, know that he is near, at the gates. Amen, I say to you, this generation will not pass away until all these things have taken place. Heaven and earth will pass away, but my words will not pass away.

"But of that day or hour, no one knows, neither the angels in heaven, nor the Son, but only the Father."

## PRAYER OVER THE OFFERINGS
Grant, O Lord, we pray, that what we offer in the sight of your majesty may obtain for us the grace of being devoted to you and gain us the prize of everlasting happiness. Through Christ our Lord.

## COMMUNION ANTIPHON                                      Ps 72: 28
To be near God is my happiness, to place my hope in God the Lord.

## OR                                                      Mk 11: 23 – 24
Amen, I say to you, whatever you ask in prayer, believe that you will receive, and it shall be given to you, says the Lord.

## PRAYER AFTER COMMUNION
We have partaken of the gifts of this sacred mystery, humbly imploring, O Lord, that what your Son commanded us to do in memory of him may bring us growth in charity. Through Christ our Lord.

## LESSONS LEARNT FROM THE READINGS / HOMILY
1 _____ 2 _____
3 _____ 4 _____
5 _____ 6 _____

### ACTION POINTS FOR THE WEEK
1 _____ 2 _____
3 _____ 4 _____
5 _____ 6 _____

### PRAYER POINTS FOR THE WEEK
1 _____ 2 _____
3 _____ 4 _____
5 _____ 6 _____

## THIS WEEK, I AM GRATEFUL FOR

1 _____ 2 _____
3 _____ 4 _____
5 _____ 6 _____

# 21 NOVEMBER 2021, SOLEMNITY OF CHRIST THE KING

**ENTRANCE ANTIPHON**          Rv 5: 12, 1: 6

How worthy is the Lamb who was slain, to receive power and divinity, and wisdom and strength and honour. To him belong glory and power for ever and ever.

**COLLECT**

Almighty ever-living God, whose will is to restore all things in your beloved Son, the King of the universe, grant, we pray, that the whole creation, set free from slavery, may render your majesty service and ceaselessly proclaim your praise.Through our Lord Jesus Christ, your Son, who lives and reigns with you in the unity of the Holy Spirit, one God, for ever and ever.

**FIRST READING**          *Daniel 7:13—14*

As the visions during the night continued, I saw one like a Son of man coming, on the clouds of heaven; when he reached the Ancient One and was presented before him, the one like a Son of man received dominion, glory, and kingship; all peoples, nations, and languages serve him. His dominion is an everlasting dominion that shall not be taken away, his kingship shall not be destroyed.

**RESPONSORIAL PSALM**          *Psalm 93:1, 1—2, 5 (1a)*

**R. The Lord is king; he is robed in majesty.**

The LORD is king, in splendor robed; robed / is the LORD and girt about with strength. **R.**

And he has made the world firm, / not to be moved. / Your throne stands firm from of old; / from everlasting you are, O LORD. **R.**

Your decrees are worthy of trust indeed; / holiness befits your house, / O LORD, for length of days. **R.**

## SECOND READING

Jesus Christ is the faithful witness, the firstborn of the dead and ruler of the kings of the earth. To him who loves us and has freed us from our sins by his blood, who has made us into a kingdom, priests for his God and Father, to him be glory and power forever and ever. Amen.

Behold, he is coming amid the clouds, and every eye will see him, even those who pierced him. All the peoples of the earth will lament him. Yes. Amen.

"I am the Alpha and the Omega," says the Lord God, "the one who is and who was and who is to come, the almighty."

## ALLELUIA *Mark 11:9, 10*

**R. Alleluia, alleluia.** Blessed is he who comes in the name of the Lord! Blessed is the kingdom of our father David that is to come! **R.**

## GOSPEL *John 18:33b—37*

Pilate said to Jesus, "Are you the King of the Jews?" Jesus answered, "Do you say this on your own or have others told you about me?" Pilate answered, "I am not a Jew, am I? Your own nation and the chief priests handed you over to me. What have you done?" Jesus answered, "My kingdom does not belong to this world. If my kingdom did belong to this world, my attendants would be fighting to keep me from being handed over to the Jews. But as it is, my kingdom is not here." So Pilate said to him, "Then you are a king?" Jesus answered, "You say I am a king. For this I was born and for this I came into the world, to testify to the truth. Everyone who belongs to the truth listens to my voice."

## PRAYER OVER THE OFFERINGS

As we offer you, O Lord, the sacrifice by which the human race is reconciled to you, we humbly pray, that your Son himself may bestow on all nations the gifts of unity and peace. Through Christ our Lord.

## COMMUNION ANTIPHON *Ps 28: 10 – 11*

The Lord sits as King for ever. The Lord will bless his people with peace.

## PRAYER AFTER COMMUNION

Having received the food of immortality, we ask, O Lord, that, glorying in obedience to the commands of Christ, the King of the universe, we may live with him eternally in his heavenly kingdom. Who lives and reigns for ever and ever.

**LESSONS LEARNT FROM THE READINGS / HOMILY**

1 _____ 2 _____

3 _____ 4 _____

5 _____ 6 _____

**ACTION POINTS FOR THE WEEK**

1 _____ 2 _____

3 _____ 4 _____

5 _____ 6 _____

**PRAYER POINTS FOR THE WEEK**

1 _____ 2 _____

3 _____ 4 _____

5 _____ 6 _____

**THIS WEEK, I AM GRATEFUL FOR**

1 _____ 2 _____

3 _____ 4 _____

5 _____ 6 _____

# 28 NOVEMBER 2021, 1ST SUNDAY OF ADVENT

**ENTRANCE ANTIPHON**                    Cf. Ps 24: 1 – 3

To you, I lift up my soul, O my God. In you, I have trusted; let me not be put to shame. Nor let my enemies exult over me; and let none who hope in you be put to shame.

**COLLECT**

Grant your faithful, we pray, almighty God, the resolve to run forth to meet your Christ with righteous deeds at his coming, so that, gathered at his right hand, they may be worthy to possess the heavenly kingdom. Through our Lord Jesus Christ, your Son, who lives and reigns with you in the unity of the Holy Spirit, one God, for ever and ever.

**FIRST READING**                    *Jeremiah 33:14—16*

The days are coming, says the LORD, when I will fulfill the promise I made to the house of Israel and Judah. In those days, in that time, I will raise up for David a just shoot; he shall do what is right and just in the land. In those days Judah shall be safe and Jerusalem shall dwell secure; this is what they shall call her: "The LORD our justice."

**PSALM**                                        *Psalm 25:4—5, 8—9, 10, 14 (1b)*
**R. To you, O Lord, I lift my soul.**
Your ways, O LORD, make known to me; **/** teach me your paths, **/** guide me in your truth and teach me, **/** for you are God my savior, and for you I wait all the day. **R.**
Good and upright is the Lord; **/** thus he shows sinners the way. **/** He guides the humble to justice, **/** and teaches the humble his way. **R.**
All the paths of the LORD are kindness and constancy **/** toward those who keep his covenant and his decrees. **/** The friendship of the LORD is with those who fear him, **/** and his covenant, for their instruction. **R.**

**SECOND READING**                              *1 Thessalonians 3:12—4:2*
Brothers and sisters: May the Lord make you increase and abound in love for one another and for all, just as we have for you, so as to strengthen your hearts, to be blameless in holiness before our God and Father at the coming of our Lord Jesus with all his holy ones. Amen.

Finally, brothers and sisters, we earnestly ask and exhort you in the Lord Jesus that, as you received from us how you should conduct yourselves to please God —and as you are conducting yourselves— you do so even more. For you know what instructions we gave you through the Lord Jesus.

**ALLELUIA**                                              *John 10:27*
**R. Alleluia, alleluia.** Show us, Lord, your love; and grant us your salvation. **R.**

**GOSPEL**                                              *Luke 21:25—28, 34—36*
Jesus said to his disciples: "There will be signs in the sun, the moon, and the stars, and on earth nations will be in dismay, perplexed by the roaring of the sea and the waves. People will die of fright in anticipation of what is coming upon the world, for the powers of the heavens will be shaken. And then they will see the Son of Man coming in a cloud with power and great glory. But when these signs begin to happen, stand erect and raise your heads because your redemption is at hand.

"Beware that your hearts do not become drowsy from carousing and drunkenness and the anxieties of daily life, and that day catch you by surprise like a trap. For that day will assault everyone who lives on the face of the earth. Be vigilant at all times and pray that you have the strength to escape the tribulations that are imminent and to stand before the Son of Man."

## PRAYER OVER THE OFFERINGS
Accept, we pray, O Lord, these offerings we make, gathered from among your gifts to us, and may what you grant us to celebrate devoutly here below gain for us the prize of eternal redemption. Through Christ our Lord.

## COMMUNION ANTIPHON                                            Ps 84: 13
 The Lord will bestow his bounty, and our earth shall yield its increase.

## PRAYER AFTER COMMUNION
May these mysteries, O Lord, in which we have participated, profit us, we pray, for even now, as we walk amid passing things, you teach us by them to love the things of heaven and hold fast to what endures. Through Christ our Lord.

## LESSONS LEARNT FROM THE READINGS / HOMILY

| | |
|---|---|
| 1 | 2 |
| 3 | 4 |
| 5 | 6 |

### ACTION POINTS FOR THE WEEK

| | |
|---|---|
| 1 | 2 |
| 3 | 4 |
| 5 | 6 |

### PRAYER POINTS FOR THE WEEK

| | |
|---|---|
| 1 | 2 |
| 3 | 4 |
| 5 | 6 |

### THIS WEEK, I AM GRATEFUL FOR

| | |
|---|---|
| 1 | 2 |
| 3 | 4 |
| 5 | 6 |

## 05 DECEMBER 2021. 2ND SUNDAY OF ADVENT

**ENTRANCE ANTIPHON** **Cf. Is 30: 19, 30**

O people of Sion, behold, the Lord will come to save the nations, and the Lord will make the glory of his voice heard in the joy of your heart.

**COLLECT**

Almighty and merciful God, may no earthly undertaking hinder those who set out in haste to meet your Son, but may our learning of heavenly wisdom gain us admittance to his company. Who lives and reigns with you in the unity of the Holy Spirit, one God, for ever and ever.

**FIRST READING** *Baruch 5:1—9*

Jerusalem, take off your robe of mourning and misery; put on the splendor of glory from God forever: wrapped in the cloak of justice from God, bear on your head the mitre that displays the glory of the eternal name. For God will show all the earth your splendor: you will be named by God forever the peace of justice, the glory of God's worship.

Up, Jerusalem! stand upon the heights; look to the east and see your children gathered from the east and the west at the word of the Holy One, rejoicing that they are remembered by God. Led away on foot by their enemies they left you: but God will bring them back to you borne aloft in glory as on royal thrones. For God has commanded that every lofty mountain be made low, and that the age—old depths and gorges be filled to level ground, that Israel may advance secure in the glory of God. The forests and every fragrant kind of tree have overshadowed Israel at God's command; for God is leading Israel in joy by the light of his glory, with his mercy and justice for company.

**PSALM** *Psalm 126:1—2, 2—3, 4—5, 6 (3)*

**R. The Lord has done great things for us; we are filled with joy.**

When the LORD brought back the captives of Zion, / we were like men dreaming. / Then our mouth was filled with laughter, / and our tongue with rejoicing. **R.**

Then they said among the nations, / "The LORD has done great things for them." / The LORD has done great things for us; / we are glad indeed. **R.**

Restore our fortunes, O LORD, / like the torrents in the southern desert. / Those who sow in tears / shall reap rejoicing. **R.**

Although they go forth weeping, **/** carrying the seed to be sown, **/** they shall come back rejoicing, **/** carrying their sheaves. **R.**

## SECOND READING                                    *Philippians 1:4—6, 8—11*

Brothers and sisters: I pray always with joy in my every prayer for all of you, because of your partnership for the gospel from the first day until now. I am confident of this, that the one who began a good work in you will continue to complete it until the day of Christ Jesus. God is my witness, how I long for all of you with the affection of Christ Jesus. And this is my prayer: that your love may increase ever more and more in knowledge and every kind of perception, to discern what is of value, so that you may be pure and blameless for the day of Christ, filled with the fruit of righteousness that comes through Jesus Christ for the glory and praise of God.

## ALLELUIA                                                          *Luke 3:4, 6*

**R. Alleluia, alleluia.** Prepare the way of the Lord, make straight his paths: All flesh shall see the salvation of God. **R.**

## GOSPEL                                                           *Luke 3:1—6*

In the fifteenth year of the reign of Tiberius Caesar, when Pontius Pilate was governor of Judea, and Herod was tetrarch of Galilee, and his brother Philip tetrarch of the region of Ituraea and Trachonitis, and Lysanias was tetrarch of Abilene, during the high priesthood of Annas and Caiaphas, the word of God came to John the son of Zechariah in the desert. John went throughout the whole region of the Jordan, proclaiming a baptism of repentance for the forgiveness of sins, as it is written in the book of the words of the prophet Isaiah:

*A voice of one crying out in the desert: "Prepare the way of the Lord, make straight his paths. Every valley shall be filled and every mountain and hill shall be made low. The winding roads shall be made straight, and the rough ways made smooth, and all flesh shall see the salvation of God."*

## PRAYER OVER THE OFFERINGS

Be pleased, O Lord, with our humble prayers and offerings, and, since we have no merits to plead our cause, come, we pray, to our rescue with the protection of your mercy. Through Christ our Lord.

**COMMUNION ANTIPHON**                                   Bar 5: 5; 4: 36

Jerusalem, arise and stand upon the heights, and behold the joy which comes to you from God.

**PRAYER AFTER COMMUNION**

Replenished by the food of spiritual nourishment, we humbly beseech you, O Lord, that, through our partaking in this mystery, you may teach us to judge wisely the things of earth and hold firm to the things of heaven. Through Christ our Lord.

## LESSONS LEARNT FROM THE READINGS / HOMILY

1 _____ 2 _____

3 _____ 4 _____

5 _____ 6 _____

## ACTION POINTS FOR THE WEEK

1 _____ 2 _____

3 _____ 4 _____

5 _____ 6 _____

## PRAYER POINTS FOR THE WEEK

1 _____ 2 _____

3 _____ 4 _____

5 _____ 6 _____

## THIS WEEK, I AM GRATEFUL FOR

1 _____ 2 _____

3 _____ 4 _____

5 _____ 6 _____

## 08 DECEMBER 2021, SOLEMNITY OF THE IMMACULATE CONCEPTION OF THE BLESSED VIRGIN MARY

**ENTRANCE ANTIPHON**                                    Is 61: 10

I rejoice heartily in the Lord, in my God is the joy of my soul; for he has clothed me with a robe of salvation, and wrapped me in a mantle of justice, like a bride adorned with her jewels.

## COLLECT

O God, who by the Immaculate Conception of the Blessed Virgin prepared a worthy dwelling for your Son, grant, we pray, that, as you preserved her from every stain by virtue of the Death of your Son, which you foresaw, so, through her intercession, we, too, may be cleansed and admitted to your presence. Through our Lord Jesus Christ, your Son, who lives and reigns with you in the unity of the Holy Spirit, one God, for ever and ever.

## FIRST READING                                      *Genesis 3:9—15, 20*

After the man, Adam, had eaten of the tree, the LORD God called to the man and asked him, "Where are you?" He answered, "I heard you in the garden; but I was afraid, because I was naked, so I hid myself." Then he asked, "Who told you that you were naked? You have eaten, then, from the tree of which I had forbidden you to eat!" The man replied, "The woman whom you put here with me— she gave me fruit from the tree, and so I ate it." The LORD God then asked the woman, "Why did you do such a thing?" The woman answered, "The serpent tricked me into it, so I ate it."

Then the LORD God said to the serpent: "Because you have done this, you shall be banned from all the animals and from all the wild creatures; on your belly shall you crawl, and dirt shall you eat all the days of your life. I will put enmity between you and the woman, and between your offspring and hers; he will strike at your head, while you strike at his heel."

The man called his wife Eve, because she became the mother of all the living.

## PSALM                               *Psalm 98:1, 2—3ab, 3cd—4 (1a)*

**R. Sing to the Lord a new song, for he has done marvelous deeds.**

Sing to the LORD a new song, / for he has done wondrous deeds; / his right hand has won victory for him, / his holy arm. **R.**

The LORD has made his salvation known: / in the sight of the nations he has revealed his justice. / He has remembered his kindness and his faithfulness / toward the house of Israel. **R.** All the ends of the earth have seen / the salvation by our God. / Sing joyfully to the LORD, all you lands; / break into song; sing praise. **R.**

**SECOND READING**                                    *Ephesians 1:3—6, 11—12*

Brothers and sisters: Blessed be the God and Father of our Lord Jesus Christ, who has blessed us in Christ with every spiritual blessing in the heavens, as he chose us in him, before the foundation of the world, to be holy and without blemish before him. In love he destined us for adoption to himself through Jesus Christ, in accord with the favor of his will, for the praise of the glory of his grace that he granted us in the beloved.

In him we were also chosen, destined in accord with the purpose of the One who accomplishes all things according to the intention of his will, so that we might exist for the praise of his glory, we who first hoped in Christ.

**ALLELUIA**                                           *see Luke 1:28*

**R. Alleluia, alleluia.** Hail, Mary, full of grace, the Lord is with you; blessed are you among women. **R.**


**GOSPEL**                                              *Luke 1:26—38*

The angel Gabriel was sent from God to a town of Galilee called Nazareth, to a virgin betrothed to a man named Joseph, of the house of David, and the virgin's name was Mary. And coming to her, he said, "Hail, full of grace! The Lord is with you." But she was greatly troubled at what was said and pondered what sort of greeting this might be. Then the angel said to her, "Do not be afraid, Mary, for you have found favor with God. Behold, you will conceive in your womb and bear a son, and you shall name him Jesus. He will be great and will be called Son of the Most High, and the Lord God will give him the throne of David his father, and he will rule over the house of Jacob forever, and of his Kingdom there will be no end." But Mary said to the angel, "How can this be, since I have no relations with a man?" And the angel said to her in reply, "The Holy Spirit will come upon you, and the power of the Most High will overshadow you. Therefore the child to be born will be called holy, the Son of God. And behold, Elizabeth, your relative, has also conceived a son in her old age, and this is the sixth month for her who was called barren; for nothing will be impossible for God." Mary said, "Behold, I am the handmaid of the Lord. May it be done to me according to your word." Then the angel departed from her.

**PRAYER OVER THE OFFERINGS**

Graciously accept the saving sacrifice which we offer you, O Lord, on the Solemnity of the Immaculate Conception of the Blessed Virgin Mary, and grant that, as we profess her, on account of your prevenient grace, to be untouched by any stain of sin, so, through her intercession, we may be delivered from all our faults. Through Christ our Lord.

## COMMUNION ANTIPHON

Glorious things are spoken of you, O Mary, for from you arose the sun of justice, Christ our God.

## PRAYER AFTER COMMUNION

May the Sacrament we have received, O Lord our God, heal in us the wounds of that fault from which in a singular way you preserved Blessed Mary in her Immaculate Conception. Through Christ our Lord.

## LESSONS LEARNT FROM THE READINGS / HOMILY

1 _____   2 _____

3 _____   4 _____

5 _____   6 _____

## ACTION POINTS FOR THE WEEK

1 _____   2 _____

3 _____   4 _____

5 _____   6 _____

## PRAYER POINTS FOR THE WEEK

1 _____   2 _____

3 _____   4 _____

5 _____   6 _____

## THIS WEEK, I AM GRATEFUL FOR

1 _____   2 _____

3 _____   4 _____

5 _____   6 _____

## 12 DECEMBER 2021, 3RD SUNDAY OF ADVENT

**ENTRANCE ANTIPHON**                    Phil 4: 4 – 5

Rejoice in the Lord always; again I say, rejoice. Indeed, the Lord is near.

## COLLECT

O God, who see how your people faithfully await the feast of the Lord's Nativity, enable us, we pray, to attain the joys of so great a salvation and to celebrate them always with solemn worship and glad rejoicing. Through our Lord Jesus Christ, your Son, who lives and reigns with you in the unity of the Holy Spirit, one God, for ever and ever.

## FIRST READING                                                    *Zephaniah 3:14—18a*

Shout for joy, O daughter Zion! Sing joyfully, O Israel! Be glad and exult with all your heart, O daughter Jerusalem! The LORD has removed the judgment against you, he has turned away your enemies; the King of Israel, the LORD, is in your midst, you have no further misfortune to fear. On that day, it shall be said to Jerusalem: Fear not, O Zion, be not discouraged! The LORD, your God, is in your midst, a mighty savior; he will rejoice over you with gladness, and renew you in his love, he will sing joyfully because of you, as one sings at festivals.

## CANTICLE                                                    *Isaiah 12:2—3, 4, 5—6*

**R. Cry out with joy and gladness: for among you is the great and Holy One of Israel.**

God indeed is my savior; **/** I am confident and unafraid. **/** My strength and my courage is the LORD, **/** and he has been my savior. **/** With joy you will draw water **/** at the fountain of salvation. **R.**

Give thanks to the LORD, acclaim his name; **/** among the nations make known his deeds, **/** proclaim how exalted is his name. **R.**

Sing praise to the LORD for his glorious achievement; **/** let this be known throughout all the earth. **/** Shout with exultation, O city of Zion, **/** for great in your midst **/** is the Holy One of Israel! **R.**

## SECOND READING                                                    *Philippians 4:4—7*

Brothers and sisters: Rejoice in the Lord always. I shall say it again: rejoice! Your kindness should be known to all. The Lord is near. Have no anxiety at all, but in everything, by prayer and petition, with thanksgiving, make your requests known to God. Then the peace of God that surpasses all understanding will guard your hearts and minds in Christ Jesus.

## ALLELUIA                                                    *Isaiah 61:1 (cited in luke 4:18)*

**R. Alleluia, alleluia.** The Spirit of the Lord is upon me, because he has anointed me to bring glad tidings to the poor. **R.**

## GOSPEL

The crowds asked John the Baptist, "What should we do?" He said to them in reply, "Whoever has two cloaks should share with the person who has none. And whoever has food should do likewise." Even tax collectors came to be baptized and they said to him, "Teacher, what should we do?" He answered them, "Stop collecting more than what is prescribed." Soldiers also asked him, "And what is it that we should do?" He told them, "Do not practice extortion, do not falsely accuse anyone, and be satisfied with your wages."

Now the people were filled with expectation, and all were asking in their hearts whether John might be the Christ. John answered them all, saying, "I am baptizing you with water, but one mightier than I is coming. I am not worthy to loosen the thongs of his sandals. He will baptize you with the Holy Spirit and fire. His winnowing fan is in his hand to clear his threshing floor and to gather the wheat into his barn, but the chaff he will burn with unquenchable fire." Exhorting them in many other ways, he preached good news to the people.

## PRAYER OVER THE OFFERINGS

May the sacrifice of our worship, Lord, we pray, be offered to you unceasingly, to complete what was begun in sacred mystery and powerfully accomplish for us your saving work. Through Christ our Lord.

## COMMUNION ANTIPHON  Cf. Is 35: 4

Say to the faint of heart: Be strong and do not fear. Behold, our God will come, and he will save us.

## PRAYER AFTER COMMUNION

We implore your mercy, Lord, that this divine sustenance may cleanse us of our faults and prepare us for the coming feasts. Through Christ our Lord.

## LESSONS LEARNT FROM THE READINGS / HOMILY

| 1 | 2 |
|---|---|
| 3 | 4 |
| 5 | 6 |

## ACTION POINTS FOR THE WEEK

| 1 | 2 |
|---|---|

# 19 DECEMBER 2021, 4TH SUNDAY OF ADVENT

**ENTRANCE ANTIPHON**                    Cf. Is 45: 8

Drop down dew from above, you heavens, and let the clouds rain down the Just One; let the earth be opened and bring forth a Saviour.

**COLLECT**

Pour forth, we beseech you, O Lord, your grace into our hearts, that we, to whom the Incarnation of Christ your Son was made known by the message of an Angel, may by his Passion and Cross be brought to the glory of his Resurrection. Who lives and reigns with you in the unity of the Holy Spirit, one God, for ever and ever.

**FIRST READING**                    *Micah 5:1—4a*

Thus says the LORD: You, Bethlehem–Ephrathah too small to be among the clans of Judah, from you shall come forth for me one who is to be ruler in Israel; whose origin is from of old, from ancient times. Therefore the Lord will give them up, until the time when she who is to give birth has borne, and the rest of his kindred shall return to the children of Israel. He shall stand firm and shepherd his flock by the strength of the LORD, in the majestic name of the LORD, his God; and they shall remain, for now his greatness shall reach to the ends of the earth; he shall be peace.

**PSALM**                    *Psalm 80:2—3, 15—16, 18—19 (4)*

R. Lord, make us turn to you; let us see your face and we shall be saved.

O shepherd of Israel, hearken, **/** from your throne upon the cherubim, shine forth. **/** Rouse your power, **/** and come to save us. **R.**

Once again, O LORD of hosts, **/** look down from heaven, and see; **/** take care of this vine, **/** and protect what your right hand has planted, **/** the son of man whom you yourself made strong. **R.**

May your help be with the man of your right hand, **/** with the son of man whom you yourself made strong. **/** Then we will no more withdraw from you; **/** give us new life, and we will call upon your name. **R.**

## SECOND READING                                                  *Hebrews 10:5—10*

Brothers and sisters: When Christ came into the world, he said:

"Sacrifice and offering you did not desire, but a body you prepared for me; in holocausts and sin offerings you took no delight. Then I said, 'As is written of me in the scroll, behold, I come to do your will, O God.'"

First he says, "Sacrifices and offerings, holocausts and sin offerings, you neither desired nor delighted in." These are offered according to the law. Then he says, "Behold, I come to do your will." He takes away the first to establish the second. By this "will," we have been consecrated through the offering of the body of Jesus Christ once for all.

## ALLELUIA                                                                   *Luke 1:38*

**R. Alleluia, alleluia.** Behold, I am the handmaid of the Lord. May it be done to me according to your word. **R.**

## GOSPEL                                                                    *Luke 1:39—45*

Mary set out and traveled to the hill country in haste to a town of Judah, where she entered the house of Zechariah and greeted Elizabeth. When Elizabeth heard Mary's greeting, the infant leaped in her womb, and Elizabeth, filled with the Holy Spirit, cried out in a loud voice and said, *"Blessed are you among women, and blessed is the fruit of your womb. And how does this happen to me, that the mother of my Lord should come to me? For at the moment the sound of your greeting reached my ears, the infant in my womb leaped for joy. Blessed are you who believed that what was spoken to you by the Lord would be fulfilled."*

## PRAYER OVER THE OFFERINGS

May the Holy Spirit, O Lord, sanctify these gifts laid upon your altar, just as he filled with his power the womb of the Blessed Virgin Mary. Through Christ our Lord.

**COMMUNION ANTIPHON**                                    Is 7: 14

Behold, a Virgin shall conceive and bear a son; and his name will be called Emmanuel.

**PRAYER AFTER COMMUNION**

Having received this pledge of eternal redemption, we pray, almighty God, that, as the feast day of our salvation draws ever nearer, so we may press forward all the more eagerly to the worthy celebration of the mystery of your Son's Nativity. Who lives and reigns for ever and ever.

**LESSONS LEARNT FROM THE READINGS / HOMILY**

| 1 | 2 |
|---|---|
| 3 | 4 |
| 5 | 6 |

**ACTION POINTS FOR THE WEEK**

| 1 | 2 |
|---|---|
| 3 | 4 |
| 5 | 6 |

**PRAYER POINTS FOR THE WEEK**

| 1 | 2 |
|---|---|
| 3 | 4 |
| 5 | 6 |

**THIS WEEK, I AM GRATEFUL FOR**

| 1 | 2 |
|---|---|
| 3 | 4 |
| 5 | 6 |

## 25 DECEMBER 2021, CHRISTMAS DAY – VIGIL MASS

**ENTRANCE ANTIPHON**                                 Cf. Ex 16: 6 – 7

Today you will know that the Lord will come, and he will save us, and in the morning you will see his glory.

**COLLECT**

O God, who gladden us year by year as we wait in hope for our redemption, grant that, just as we joyfully welcome your Only Begotten

Son as our Redeemer, we may also merit to face him confidently when he comes again as our Judge. Who lives and reigns with you in the unity of the Holy Spirit, one God, for ever and ever.

## FIRST READING                                           *Isaiah 62:1—5*

For Zion's sake I will not be silent, for Jerusalem's sake I will not be quiet, until her vindication shines forth like the dawn and her victory like a burning torch.

Nations shall behold your vindication, and all the kings your glory; you shall be called by a new name pronounced by the mouth of the LORD. You shall be a glorious crown in the hand of the LORD, a royal diadem held by your God. No more shall people call you "Forsaken," or your land "Desolate," but you shall be called "My Delight," and your land "Espoused." For the LORD delights in you and makes your land his spouse. As a young man marries a virgin, your Builder shall marry you; and as a bridegroom rejoices in his bride so shall your God rejoice in you.

## PSALM                              *Psalm 89:4—5, 16—17, 27, 29 (2a)*

**R. Forever I will sing the goodness of the Lord.**

I have made a covenant with my chosen one, / I have sworn to David my servant: / forever will I confirm your posterity / and establish your throne for all generations. **R.**

Blessed the people who know the joyful shout; / in the light of your countenance, O LORD, they walk. / At your name they rejoice all the day, / and through your justice they are exalted. **R.**

He shall say of me, "You are my father, / my God, the rock, my savior." / Forever I will maintain my kindness toward him, / and my covenant with him stands firm. **R.**

## SECOND READING                                   *Acts 13:16—17, 22—25*

When Paul reached Antioch in Pisidia and entered the synagogue, he stood up, motioned with his hand, and said, "Fellow Israelites and you others who are God—fearing, listen. The God of this people Israel chose our ancestors and exalted the people during their sojourn in the land of Egypt. With uplifted arm he led them out of it. Then he removed Saul and raised up David as king; of him he testified, 'I have found David, son of Jesse, a man after my own heart; he will carry out my every wish.' From this man's descendants God, according to his promise, has brought to

Israel a savior, Jesus. John heralded his coming by proclaiming a baptism of repentance to all the people of Israel; and as John was completing his course, he would say, 'What do you suppose that I am? I am not he. Behold, one is coming after me; I am not worthy to unfasten the sandals of his feet.'"

## ALLELUIA                                                    *John 10:27*

R. **Alleluia, alleluia.** Tomorrow the wickedness of the earth will be destroyed: the Savior of the world will reign over us. **R.**

## GOSPEL EITHER:                                        *Matthew 1:1—25*

The book of the genealogy of Jesus Christ, the son of David, the son of Abraham.

Abraham became the father of Isaac, Isaac the father of Jacob, Jacob the father of Judah and his brothers. Judah became the father of Perez and Zerah, whose mother was Tamar. Perez became the father of Hezron, Hezron the father of Ram, Ram the father of Amminadab. Amminadab became the father of Nahshon, Nahshon the father of Salmon, Salmon the father of Boaz, whose mother was Rahab. Boaz became the father of Obed, whose mother was Ruth. Obed became the father of Jesse, Jesse the father of David the king.

David became the father of Solomon, whose mother had been the wife of Uriah. Solomon became the father of Rehoboam, Rehoboam the father of Abijah, Abijah the father of Asaph. Asaph became the father of Jehoshaphat, Jehoshaphat the father of Joram, Joram the father of Uzziah. Uzziah became the father of Jotham, Jotham the father of Ahaz, Ahaz the father of Hezekiah. Hezekiah became the father of Manasseh, Manasseh the father of Amos, Amos the father of Josiah. Josiah became the father of Jechoniah and his Brothers at the time of the Babylonian exile.

After the Babylonian exile, Jechoniah became the father of Shealtiel, Shealtiel the father of Zerubbabel, Zerubbabel the father of Abiud. Abiud became the father of Eliakim, Eliakim the father of Azor, Azor the father of Zadok. Zadok became the father of Achim, Achim the father of Eliud, Eliud the father of Eleazar. Eleazar became the father of Matthan, Matthan the father of Jacob, Jacob the father of Joseph, the husband of Mary. Of her was born Jesus who is called the Christ.

Thus the total number of generations from Abraham to David is fourteen generations; from David to the Babylonian exile, fourteen generations; from the Babylonian exile to the Christ, fourteen generations.

Now this is how the birth of Jesus Christ came about. When his mother Mary was betrothed to Joseph, but before they lived together, she was found with child through the Holy Spirit. Joseph her husband, since he was a righteous man, yet unwilling to expose her to shame, decided to divorce her quietly. Such was his intention when, behold, the angel of the Lord appeared to him in a dream and said, "Joseph, son of David, do not be afraid to take Mary your wife into your home. For it is through the Holy Spirit that this child has been conceived in her. She will bear a son and you are to name him Jesus, because he will save his people from their sins." All this took place to fulfill what the Lord had said through the prophet:

*Behold, the virgin shall conceive and bear a son, and they shall name him Emmanuel,* which means "God is with us." When Joseph awoke, he did as the angel of the Lord had commanded him and took his wife into his home. He had no relations with her until she bore a son, and he named him Jesus.

**OR:**                                    *Matthew 1:18—25*

This is how the birth of Jesus Christ came about. When his mother Mary was betrothed to Joseph, but before they lived together, she was found with child through the Holy Spirit. Joseph her husband, since he was a righteous man, yet unwilling to expose her to shame, decided to divorce her quietly. Such was his intention when, behold, the angel of the Lord appeared to him in a dream and said, "Joseph, son of David, do not be afraid to take Mary your wife into your home. For it is through the Holy Spirit that this child has been conceived in her. She will bear a son and you are to name him Jesus, because he will save his people from their sins." All this took place to fulfill what the Lord had said through the prophet: *Behold, the virgin shall conceive and bear a son, and they shall name him Emmanuel,* which means "God is with us." When Joseph awoke, he did as the angel of the Lord had commanded him and took his wife into his home. He had no relations with her until she bore a son, and he named him Jesus.

**PRAYER OVER THE OFFERINGS**

As we look forward, O Lord, to the coming festivities, may we serve you all the more eagerly for knowing that in them you make manifest the beginnings of our redemption. Through Christ our Lord.

**COMMUNION ANTIPHON Cf. Is 40: 6**

The glory of the Lord will be revealed, and all flesh will see the salvation of our God.

**PRAYER AFTER COMMUNION**

Grant, O Lord, we pray, that we may draw new vigour from celebrating the Nativity of your Only Begotten Son, by whose heavenly mystery we receive both food and drink. Who lives and reigns for ever and ever.

# CHRISTMAS DAY – MIDNIGHT MASS

**ENTRANCE ANTIPHON**                    **Ps 2: 7**

The Lord said to me: You are my Son. It is I who have begotten you this day.

**OR**

Let us all rejoice in the Lord, for our Saviour has been born in the world. Today true peace has come down to us from heaven.

**COLLECT**

O God, who have made this most sacred night radiant with the splendour of the true light, grant, we pray, that we, who have known the mysteries of his light on earth, may also delight in his gladness in heaven. Who lives and reigns with you in the unity of the Holy Spirit, one God, for ever and ever.

**FIRST READING**                    *Isaiah 9:1—6*

The people who walked in darkness have seen a great light; upon those who dwelt in the land of gloom a light has shone. You have brought them abundant joy and great rejoicing, as they rejoice before you as at the harvest, as people make merry when dividing spoils. For the yoke that burdened them, the pole on their shoulder, and the rod of their taskmaster you have smashed, as on the day of Midian. For every boot that tramped in battle, every cloak rolled in blood, will be burned as fuel for flames. For a child is born to us, a son is given us; upon his shoulder dominion rests. They name him Wonder–Counselor, God–Hero, Father–Forever, Prince of Peace. His dominion is vast and forever peaceful, from David's throne, and over his kingdom, which he confirms and sustains by judgment and justice, both now and forever. The zeal of the LORD of hosts will do this!

**PSALM:** *Psalm 96:1—2, 2—3, 11—12, 13 (Luke 2:11)*

**R. Today is born our Savior, Christ the Lord.**

Sing to the LORD a new song; / sing to the LORD, all you lands. / Sing to the LORD; bless his name. **R**

Announce his salvation, day after day. / Tell his glory among the nations; / among all peoples, his wondrous deeds. **R.**

Let the heavens be glad and the earth rejoice; / let the sea and what fills it resound; / let the plains be joyful and all that is in them! / Then shall all the trees of the forest exult. **R.**

They shall exult before the LORD, for he comes; / for he comes to rule the earth. / He shall rule the world with justice / and the peoples with his constancy. **R.**

**SECOND READING** *Titus 2:11—14*

Beloved: The grace of God has appeared, saving all and training us to reject godless ways and worldly desires and to live temperately, justly, and devoutly in this age, as we await the blessed hope, the appearance of the glory of our great God and savior Jesus Christ, who gave himself for us to deliver us from all lawlessness and to cleanse for himself a people as his own, eager to do what is good.

**ALLELUIA** *John 10:27*

**R. Alleluia, alleluia.** I proclaim to you good news of great joy: today a Savior is born for us, Christ the Lord. **R.**

**GOSPEL** *Luke 2:1—14*

In those days a decree went out from Caesar Augustus that the whole world should be enrolled. This was the first enrollment, when Quirinius was governor of Syria. So all went to be enrolled, each to his own town. And Joseph too went up from Galilee from the town of Nazareth to Judea, to the city of David that is called Bethlehem, because he was of the house and family of David, to be enrolled with Mary, his betrothed, who was with child.

While they were there, the time came for her to have her child, and she gave birth to her firstborn son. She wrapped him in swaddling clothes and laid him in a manger, because there was no room for them in the inn.

Now there were shepherds in that region living in the fields and keeping the night watch over their flock. The angel of the Lord appeared to them and the glory of the Lord shone around them, and they were struck with great fear. The angel said to them, "Do not be afraid; for behold, I proclaim to you good news of great joy that will be for all the people. For today in the city of David a savior has been born for you who is Christ and Lord. And this will be a sign for you: you will find an infant wrapped in swaddling clothes and lying in a manger." And suddenly there was a multitude of the heavenly host with the angel, praising God and saying: "Glory to God in the highest and on earth peace to those on whom his favor rests."

**PRAYER OVER THE OFFERINGS**
May the oblation of this day's feast be pleasing to you, O Lord, we pray, that through this most holy exchange we may be found in the likeness of Christ, in whom our nature is united to you. Who lives and reigns for ever and ever.

**COMMUNION ANTIPHON**      Jn 1: 14
The Word became flesh, and we have seen his glory.

**PRAYER AFTER COMMUNION**
Grant us, we pray, O Lord our God, that we, who are gladdened by participation in the feast of our Redeemer's Nativity, may through an honourable way of life become worthy of union with him. Who lives and reigns for ever and ever.

# CHRISTMAS DAY – MASS AT DAWN

**ENTRANCE ANTIPHON**      Cf. Is 9: 1, 5; Lk 1: 33
Today a light will shine upon us, for the Lord is born for us; and he will be called Wondrous God, Prince of peace, Father of future ages: and his reign will be without end.

**COLLECT**
Grant, we pray, almighty God, that, as we are bathed in the new radiance of your incarnate Word, the light of faith, which illumines our minds, may also shine through in our deeds. Through our Lord Jesus Christ, your Son, who lives and reigns with you in the unity of the Holy Spirit, one God, for ever and ever.

**FIRST READING**      *Isaiah 62:11—12*
See, the LORD proclaims to the ends of the earth: say to daughter Zion,

your savior comes! Here is his reward with him, his recompense before him. They shall be called the holy people, the redeemed of the LORD, and you shall be called "Frequented," a city that is not forsaken.

## RESPONSORIAL PSALM                                       *Psalm 97:1, 6, 11—12*
**R. A light will shine on us this day: the Lord is born for us.**
The LORD is king; let the earth rejoice; **/** let the many isles be glad. **/** The heavens proclaim his justice, **/** and all peoples see his glory. **R.**
Light dawns for the just; **/** and gladness, for the upright of heart. **/** Be glad in the LORD, you just, **/** and give thanks to his holy name. **R.**

## SECOND READING                                                    *Titus 3:4—7*
Beloved: When the kindness and generous love of God our savior appeared, not because of any righteous deeds we had done but because of his mercy, he saved us through the bath of rebirth and renewal by the Holy Spirit, whom he richly poured out on us through Jesus Christ our savior, so that we might be justified by his grace and become heirs in hope of eternal life.

## ALLELUIA                              *Luke 2:14*
**R. Alleluia, alleluia.** Glory to God in the highest, and on earth peace to those on whom his favor rests. **R.**

## GOSPEL                                                              *Luke 2:15—20*
When the angels went away from them to heaven, the shepherds said to one another, "Let us go, then, to Bethlehem to see this thing that has taken place, which the Lord has made known to us." So they went in haste and found Mary and Joseph, and the infant lying in the manger. When they saw this, they made known the message that had been told them about this child. All who heard it were amazed by what had been told them by the shepherds. And Mary kept all these things, reflecting on them in her heart. Then the shepherds returned, glorifying and praising God for all they had heard and seen, just as it had been told to them.

## PRAYER OVER THE OFFERINGS
May our offerings be worthy, we pray, O Lord, of the mysteries of the Nativity this day, that, just as Christ was born a man and also shone forth as God, so these earthly gifts may confer on us what is divine. Through Christ our Lord.

**COMMUNION ANTIPHON** Cf. Zec 9: 9

Rejoice, O Daughter Sion; lift up praise, Daughter Jerusalem: Behold, your King will come, the Holy One and Saviour of the world.

**PRAYER AFTER COMMUNION**

Grant us, Lord, as we honour with joyful devotion the Nativity of your Son, that we may come to know with fullness of faith the hidden depths of this mystery and to love them ever more and more. Through Christ our Lord.

## CHRISTMAS DAY – MASS OF THE DAY

**ENTRANCE ANTIPHON** Cf. Is 9: 6

A child is born for us, and a son is given to us; his sceptre of power rests upon his shoulder, and his name will be called Messenger of great counsel.

**COLLECT**

O God, who wonderfully created the dignity of human nature and still more wonderfully restored it, grant, we pray, that we may share in the divinity of Christ, who humbled himself to share in our humanity. Who lives and reigns with you in the unity of the Holy Spirit, one God, for ever and ever.

**FIRST READING** *Isaiah 52:7—10*

How beautiful upon the mountains are the feet of him who brings glad tidings, announcing peace, bearing good news, announcing salvation, and saying to Zion, "Your God is King!"

Hark! Your sentinels raise a cry, together they shout for joy, for they see directly, before their eyes, the LORD restoring Zion. Break out together in song, O ruins of Jerusalem! For the LORD comforts his people, he redeems Jerusalem. The LORD has bared his holy arm in the sight of all the nations; all the ends of the earth will behold the salvation of our God.

**PSALM** *Psalm 98:1, 2—3, 3—4, 5—6 (3c)*

**R. All the ends of the earth have seen the saving power of God.**

Sing to the LORD a new song, **/** for he has done wondrous deeds; **/** his right hand has won victory for him, **/** his holy arm. **R.**

The LORD has made his salvation known: **/** in the sight of the nations he has revealed his justice. **/** He has remembered his kindness and his faithfulness **/** toward the house of Israel. **R.**

All the ends of the earth have seen **/** the salvation by our God. **/** Sing joyfully to the LORD, all you lands; **/** break into song; sing praise. **R.**

Sing praise to the LORD with the harp, **/** with the harp and melodious song. **/** With trumpets and the sound of the horn **/** sing joyfully before the King, the LORD.**R**

## SECOND READING                                    *Hebrews 1:1—6*

Brothers and sisters: In times past, God spoke in partial and various ways to our ancestors through the prophets; in these last days, he has spoken to us through the Son, whom he made heir of all things and through whom he created the universe, who is the refulgence of his glory, the very imprint of his being, and who sustains all things by his mighty word. When he had accomplished purification from sins, he took his seat at the right hand of the Majesty on high, as far superior to the angels as the name he has inherited is more excellent than theirs.

For to which of the angels did God ever say: "You are my son; this day I have begotten you"? Or again: "I will be a father to him, and he shall be a son to me"? And again, when he leads the firstborn into the world, he says: "Let all the angels of God worship him."

## ALLELUIA                              *John 10:27*

R. Alleluia, alleluia. A holy day has dawned upon us. Come, you nations, and adore the Lord. For today a great light has come upon the earth. **R.**

## GOSPEL EITHER:                              *John 1:1—18*

In the beginning was the Word, and the Word was with God, and the Word was God. He was in the beginning with God. All things came to be through him, and without him nothing came to be. What came to be through him was life, and this life was the light of the human race; the light shines in the darkness, and the darkness has not overcome it.

A man named John was sent from God. He came for testimony, to testify to the light, so that all might believe through him. He was not the light, but came to testify to the light. The true light, which enlightens everyone, was coming into the world.

He was in the world, and the world came to be through him, but the world did not know him. He came to what was his own, but his own people did not accept him.

But to those who did accept him he gave power to become

children of God, to those who believe in his name, who were born not by natural generation nor by human choice nor by a man's decision but of God.

And the Word became flesh and made his dwelling among us, and we saw his glory, the glory as of the Father's only Son, full of grace and truth.

John testified to him and cried out, saying, "This was he of whom I said, 'The one who is coming after me ranks ahead of me because he existed before me.'" From his fullness we have all received, grace in place of grace, because while the law was given through Moses, grace and truth came through Jesus Christ. No one has ever seen God. The only Son, God, who is at the Father's side, has revealed him.

## OR: GOSPEL                                    *John 1:1—5, 9—14*

In the beginning was the Word, and the Word was with God, and the Word was God. He was in the beginning with God. All things came to be through him, and without him nothing came to be. What came to be through him was life, and this life was the light of the human race; the light shines in the darkness, and the darkness has not overcome it.

The true light, which enlightens everyone, was coming into the world.

He was in the world, and the world came to be through him, but the world did not know him. He came to what was his own, but his own people did not accept him.

But to those who did accept him he gave power to become children of God, to those who believe in his name, who were born not by natural generation nor by human choice nor by a man's decision but of God.

And the Word became flesh and made his dwelling among us, and we saw his glory, the glory as of the Father's only Son, full of grace and truth.

## PRAYER OVER THE OFFERINGS

Make acceptable, O Lord, our oblation on this solemn day, when you manifested the reconciliation that makes us wholly pleasing in your sight and inaugurated for us the fullness of divine worship. Through Christ our Lord.

**COMMUNION ANTIPHON**                                    **Cf. Ps 97: 3**

All the ends of the earth have seen the salvation of our God.

**PRAYER AFTER COMMUNION**

Grant, O merciful God, that, just as the Saviour of the world, born this day, is the author of divine generation for us, so he may be the giver even of immortality. Who lives and reigns for ever and ever.

**LESSONS LEARNT FROM THE READINGS / HOMILY**

| 1 | 2 |
|---|---|
| 3 | 4 |
| 5 | 6 |

**ACTION POINTS FOR THE WEEK**

| 1 | 2 |
|---|---|
| 3 | 4 |
| 5 | 6 |

**PRAYER POINTS FOR THE WEEK**

| 1 | 2 |
|---|---|
| 3 | 4 |
| 5 | 6 |

**THIS WEEK, I AM GRATEFUL FOR**

| 1 | 2 |
|---|---|
| 3 | 4 |
| 5 | 6 |

## 26 DECEMBER 2021, FEAST OF THE HOLY FAMILY

**ENTRANCE ANTIPHON**                                    **Lk 2: 16**

The shepherds went in haste, and found Mary and Joseph and the Infant lying in a manger.

**COLLECT**

O God, who were pleased to give us the shining example of the Holy Family, graciously grant that we may imitate them in practising the virtues of family life and in the bonds of charity, and so, in the joy of your house, delight one day in eternal rewards. Through our Lord Jesus Christ, your

Son, who lives and reigns with you in the unity of the Holy Spirit, one God, for ever and ever.

**FIRST READING EITHER:** *Sirach 3:2 – 6, 12 – 14*

God sets a father in honor over his children; a mother's authority he confirms over her sons. Whoever honors his father atones for sins, and preserves himself from them. When he prays, he is heard; he stores up riches who reveres his mother. Whoever honors his father is gladdened by children, and, when he prays, is heard. Whoever reveres his father will live a long life; he who obeys his father brings comfort to his mother.

My son, take care of your father when he is old; grieve him not as long as he lives. Even if his mind fail, be considerate of him; revile him not all the days of his life; kindness to a father will not be forgotten, firmly planted against the debt of your sins—a house raised in justice to you.

**OR:** *1 Samuel 1:20—22, 24—28*

In those days Hannah conceived, and at the end of her term bore a son whom she called Samuel, since she had asked the LORD for him. The next time her husband Elkanah was going up with the rest of his household to offer the customary sacrifice to the LORD and to fulfill his vows, Hannah did not go, explaining to her husband, "Once the child is weaned, I will take him to appear before the LORD and to remain there forever; I will offer him as a perpetual nazirite."

Once Samuel was weaned, Hannah brought him up with her, along with a three–year–old bull, an ephah of flour, and a skin of wine, and presented him at the temple of the LORD in Shiloh. After the boy's father had sacrificed the young bull, Hannah, his mother, approached Eli and said: "Pardon, my lord! As you live, my lord, I am the woman who stood near you here, praying to the LORD. I prayed for this child, and the LORD granted my request. Now I, in turn, give him to the LORD; as long as he lives, he shall be dedicated to the LORD." Hannah left Samuel there.

**PSALM EITHER:** *Psalm 128:1-2, 3, 4-5.*

**R. Blessed are those who fear the Lord and walk in his ways.**

Blessed is everyone who fears the LORD, / who walks in his ways! / For you shall eat the fruit of your handiwork; / blessed shall you be, and favored. **R.**

Your wife shall be like a fruitful vine / in the recesses of your home; / your children like olive plants / around your table. **R.**

Behold, thus is the man blessed / who fears the LORD. / The LORD bless you from Zion: / may you see the prosperity of Jerusalem / all the days of your life. **R.**

**OR**                                            *Psalm 84:2—3, 5—6, 9—10 (see 5a)*
**R. Blessed are they who dwell in your house, O Lord.**

How lovely is your dwelling place, O LORD of hosts! / My soul yearns and pines for the courts of the LORD. / My heart and my flesh cry out for the living God. **R.**

Happy they who dwell in your house! / Continually they praise you. / Happy the men whose strength you are! / Their hearts are set upon the pilgrimage. **R.**

O LORD of hosts, hear our prayer; / hearken, O God of Jacob! / O God, behold our shield, / and look upon the face of your anointed. **R.**

**SECOND READING EITHER:**                        *Colossians 3:12-21*

Brothers and sisters: Put on, as God's chosen ones, holy and beloved, heartfelt compassion, kindness, humility, gentleness, and patience, bearing with one another and forgiving one another, if one has a grievance against another; as the Lord has forgiven you, so must you also do. And over all these put on love, that is, the bond of perfection. And let the peace of Christ control your hearts, the peace into which you were also called in one body. And be thankful. Let the word of Christ dwell in you richly, as in all wisdom you teach and admonish one another, singing psalms, hymns, and spiritual songs with gratitude in your hearts to God. And whatever you do, in word or in deed, do everything in the name of the Lord Jesus, giving thanks to God the Father through him.

Wives, be subordinate to your husbands, as is proper in the Lord. Husbands, love your wives, and avoid any bitterness toward them. Children, obey your parents in everything, for this is pleasing to the Lord. Fathers, do not provoke your children, so they may not become discouraged.

**SECOND READING**                               *1 John 3:1—2, 21—24*

Beloved: See what love the Father has bestowed on us that we may be called the children of God. And so we are. The reason the world does not know us is that it did not know him. Beloved, we are God's children now;

what we shall be has not yet been revealed. We do know that when it is revealed we shall be like him, for we shall see him as he is.

Beloved, if our hearts do not condemn us, we have confidence in God and receive from him whatever we ask, because we keep his commandments and do what pleases him. And his commandment is this: we should believe in the name of his Son, Jesus Christ, and love one another just as he commanded us. Those who keep his commandments remain in him, and he in them, and the way we know that he remains in us is from the Spirit he gave us.

## ALLELUIA                                                              *see Acts 16:14b*
R. **Alleluia, alleluia.** Open our hearts, O Lord, to listen to the words of your Son. **R.**

## GOSPEL                                                                 *Luke 2:41—52*
Each year Jesus' parents went to Jerusalem for the feast of Passover, and when he was twelve years old, they went up according to festival custom. After they had completed its days, as they were returning, the boy Jesus remained behind in Jerusalem, but his parents did not know it. Thinking that he was in the caravan, they journeyed for a day and looked for him among their relatives and acquaintances, but not finding him, they returned to Jerusalem to look for him. After three days they found him in the temple, sitting in the midst of the teachers, listening to them and asking them questions, and all who heard him were astounded at his understanding and his answers. When his parents saw him, they were astonished, and his mother said to him, "Son, why have you done this to us? Your father and I have been looking for you with great anxiety." And he said to them, "Why were you looking for me? Did you not know that I must be in my Father's house?" But they did not understand what he said to them. He went down with them and came to Nazareth, and was obedient to them; and his mother kept all these things in her heart. And Jesus advanced in wisdom and age and favor before God and man.

## PRAYER OVER THE OFFERINGS
We offer you, Lord, the sacrifice of conciliation, humbly asking that, through the intercession of the Virgin Mother of God and Saint Joseph, you may establish our families firmly in your grace and your peace. Through Christ our Lord.

**COMMUNION ANTIPHON**                           **Bar 3: 38**

Our God has appeared on the earth, and lived among us.

**PRAYER AFTER COMMUNION**

Bring those you refresh with this heavenly Sacrament, most merciful Father, to imitate constantly the example of the Holy Family, so that, after the trials of this world, we may share their company for ever. Through Christ our Lord.

**LESSONS LEARNT FROM THE READINGS / HOMILY**

1 _____ 2 _____
3 _____ 4 _____
5 _____ 6 _____

**ACTION POINTS FOR THE WEEK**

1 _____ 2 _____
3 _____ 4 _____
5 _____ 6 _____

**PRAYER POINTS FOR THE WEEK**

1 _____ 2 _____
3 _____ 4 _____
5 _____ 6 _____

**THIS WEEK, I AM GRATEFUL FOR**

1 _____ 2 _____
3 _____ 4 _____
5 _____ 6 _____

# ABOUT THE AUTHOR

This publication is the handiwork of the Catholic Liturgical World Team, which comprises of 15 members, some of who are laity, priests and religious persons. This team is a body specialized in the publication of litugy related works, including: **Catholic Missal, Liturgy of the Hour, Mass Reflections**, etc.

Made in the USA
Middletown, DE
05 October 2020